Praise for *Medical Medium*

'Anthony William is the Edgar Cayce of our time, reading the body with outstanding precision and insight. Anthony identifies the underlying causes of diseases that often baffle the most astute conventional and alternative healthcare practitioners. Anthony's practical and profound medical advice makes him one of the most powerfully effective healers of the 21st century.'

—— Ann Louise Gittleman, *New York Times* bestselling author of 30 books on health and healing and creator of the highly popular Fat Flush detox and diet plan

'Within the first three minutes of speaking with me, Anthony precisely identified my medical issue! This healer really knows what he's talking about. Anthony's abilities as the Medical Medium are unique and fascinating, and his book makes complex diseases that confuse even many doctors easy to understand and address. Highly recommended.'

— Dr Alejandro Junger, *New York Times* bestselling author of *Clean* and *Clean Eats* and founder of the immensely popular Clean Program

'Anthony William's God-given gift for healing is nothing short of miraculous. This landmark book sharing Anthony's immense knowledge of how to prevent and combat disease will impact the medical community for decades. Don't wait until this information trickles its way into the mainstream in 5 to 15 years. Buy this book and start getting healthier right now.'

— David James Elliot, *Scorpion*, *Trumbo*, *Mad Men* and *CSI:NY*; star for ten years of CBS's *JAG*

'Anthony is a seer and a wellness sage. His gift is remarkable. With his guidance I've been able to pinpoint and address a health issue that's been plaguing me for years.'

— Kris Carr, *New York Times* bestselling author of four health books, including *Crazy Sexy Diet* and *Crazy Sexy Kitchen*

'Anthony is not only a warm, compassionate healer, he is also authentic and accurate, with God-given skills. He has been a total blessing in my life.'

— Naomi Campbell, model, actress, activist

'A mesmerizing read, this book provides an entirely fresh perspective on stubborn, seemingly undiagnosable health issues that is mind-blowing. My family and friends have been the recipients of Anthony's inspired gift of healing, and we've benefited more than I can express with rejuvenated physical and mental health.'

— Scott Bakula, star of *NCIS: New Orleans, Quantum Leap* and *Star Trek: Enterprise*

'Whenever Anthony William recommends a natural way of improving your health, it works. I've seen this with my daughter and the improvement was impressive. His approach of using natural ingredients is a more effective way of healing.'

— Martin D. Shafiroff, Managing Director of Barclays Capital; rated #1 Broker in America by WealthManagement.com and #1 Wealth Advisor by *Barron's*

'Any quantum physicist will tell you there are things at play in the universe we can't yet understand. I truly believe Anthony has a handle on them. He has an amazing gift for intuitively tapping into the most effective methods for healing. And his story in this book is fascinating in the best way possible – he makes you see the world and your health in a new light.'

— Caroline Leavitt, *New York Times* bestselling author of ten books, including *Is This Tomorrow*

'As a Hollywood businesswoman, I know value. Some of Anthony's clients spent over $1 million seeking help for their "mystery illness" until they finally discovered him. With this book, you can access Anthony's secrets for less than the cost of a single doctor's visit. The keys to your health that this book provides aren't merely a great value; they're priceless.'

— Nanci Chambers, co-star of *JAG*; Hollywood producer and entrepreneur

'I rely on Anthony William for my and my family's health. Even when doctors are stumped, Anthony always knows what the problem is and the pathway for healing. In this clear, friendly and compassionate book, Anthony provides the solutions to many of the deeply confounding health challenges of our time.'

— Chelsea Field, co-star of *The Last Boy Scout* and *Andre*

MEDICAL MEDIUM

MEDICAL MEDIUM

Secrets Behind Chronic and Mystery
Illness and How to Finally Heal

ANTHONY WILLIAM

HAY HOUSE

Carlsbad, California • New York City • London • Sydney
Johannesburg • Vancouver • Hong Kong • New Delhi

First published and distributed in the United Kingdom by:
Hay House UK Ltd, Astley House, 33 Notting Hill Gate, London W11 3JQ
Tel: +44 (0)20 3675 2450; Fax: +44 (0)20 3675 2451; www.hayhouse.co.uk

Published and distributed in the United States of America by:
Hay House Inc., PO Box 5100, Carlsbad, CA 92018-5100
Tel: (1) 760 431 7695 or (800) 654 5126
Fax: (1) 760 431 6948 or (800) 650 5115; www.hayhouse.com

Published and distributed in Australia by:
Hay House Australia Ltd, 18/36 Ralph St, Alexandria NSW 2015
Tel: (61) 2 9669 4299; Fax: (61) 2 9669 4144; www.hayhouse.com.au

Published and distributed in the Republic of South Africa by:
Hay House SA (Pty) Ltd, PO Box 990, Witkoppen 2068
info@hayhouse.co.za; www.hayhouse.co.za

Published and distributed in India by:
Hay House Publishers India, Muskaan Complex, Plot No.3, B-2,
Vasant Kunj, New Delhi 110 070
Tel: (91) 11 4176 1620; Fax: (91) 11 4176 1630; www.hayhouse.co.in

Distributed in Canada by:
Raincoast Books, 2440 Viking Way, Richmond, B.C. V6V 1N2
Tel: (1) 604 448 7100; Fax: (1) 604 270 7161; www.raincoast.com

Text © 2015 by Anthony William

Indexer: Jay Kreider
Cover design: David Somoroff; Interior design: Riann Bender

The moral rights of the author have been asserted.

A catalogue record for this book is available from the British Library.

ISBN: 978-1-78180-536-7

Printed and bound in Great Britain by CPI Group (UK) Ltd, Croydon, CR0 4YY

For Indigo, Ruby, and Great Blue

CONTENTS

FOREWORD

How do you know what you know?

Most of the things you know, you've learned—from your caregivers, from your friends, at school, in books, and in the streets. These are the things you know that you know.

But inside of you there are other types of knowing. There is, for example, the knowing that you are, that you exist. That you are you. This knowing you are born with.

There is another type of knowing that is hard to talk about, because most people take it for granted. This is the knowing that your body has of how to function. Without you being a cardiologist, your heart knows how to pump blood. Without you being a gastroenterologist, your gut knows how to digest food and absorb it.

Then there is the knowing that comes as a feeling, such as your gut instinct or intuition. This knowing is highly intelligent and kind of magic. It lets you know things without ever having seen or heard of them—and it may save your life. This is the kind of knowledge that people advise you to trust. But where does it come from? And how does it let you know about things? Who decides when this knowing will communicate with you?

As a man of science, I have been taught to the point of indoctrination that I must only trust what I can observe, measure, test, and reproduce. But as a man with a heart, I cannot measure the love I feel for my wife and kids—yet it is more real than any cell I ever studied under a microscope, and so much more important.

From time immemorial there have been accounts of people who have extraordinary abilities—different kinds of knowing with almost miraculous qualities. Savants who know things that computers have difficulty coming up with. Prodigies in every area of the human realm, such as music, art, and sports, to name just a few.

Lately I have become aware of some individuals who communicate with those who have crossed over to the other side. These crossover mediums are sweeping the country with their fascinating messages that people swear could only come from their deceased loved ones. One of my all-time favorite books is Brian Weiss's *Many Lives, Many Masters*. Dr. Weiss hypnotizes patients, who then regress to past lives and even to spaces in between lives where spiritual masters relay extraordinary messages. These sessions have a profound healing effect on the people who experience them.

And then there are the healers. Men and women—some of them famous—with the ability to make the blind see, the crippled walk, and the sick fully recover. These healers are the ones I am most fascinated with. Maybe a little because of envy. I would love to be given the gift of healing fully with my touch. I would go on a healing spree, starting at the children's hospitals.

Whenever I hear about anyone with a special healing-related ability, I immediately want to meet them, make them part of my network, experience their gift for myself, refer patients to them, and hopefully learn the ability myself. That is how I got in touch with Anthony William.

A few years ago, I was having abdominal pains daily and went for a sonogram in which we saw a tumor in my liver. A follow-up MRI confirmed it, as well as swollen inguinal lymph nodes. I became alarmed and scheduled a biopsy of one of the lymph nodes, and while waiting for the procedure day, I was given Anthony's number. I got an appointment fast, and within the first minute of our consultation, he told me about my liver—and went so far as to correctly predict the biopsy results. More importantly, he prescribed a regimen of supplements and foods that immediately resolved my abdominal pains, which were completely unrelated to my liver tumor (a benign old cyst previously undiscovered).

Since then, I have consulted with Anthony about my wife and kids and always received advice that worked. I have also sent many of my curious and open-minded patients to him and have gotten wonderful feedback from each and every one of them. Where his knowing comes from is for you to interpret. It is my belief that it comes from the same frequency as intuition, just at a stronger volume. In fact, Anthony himself describes it as a voice that speaks into his ear.

When Anthony told me he had written a book, I was jumping with excitement. Finally I could hear from someone with an uncanny healing ability about how this works, about his personal history and experience. And when I read the book I was blown away. It is well-written, sincere, interesting, humble, fascinating. I could not put it down, and I am so happy for you, because you are about to have that same experience. A journey into the mind and soul of a true healer, this is better than space travel.

I hope you enjoy this book as much as I did.

With much love,
Alejandro Junger, M.D.
New York Times best-selling author of *Clean,*
Clean Eats, and *Clean Gut*

INTRODUCTION

Do you feel confused by the contradictory health information out there and just want one clear guide?

Are you frightened by the rise of diseases such as cancer and seeking tools for prevention?

Do you want to lose weight? To look and feel younger? Have more energy? To help a loved one who's ailing? To safeguard your family's well-being?

Have you tried everything, gone everywhere, and your health still isn't where you want to be? Do you want reassurance that you haven't imagined or caused your suffering?

Do you want to feel like yourself again? To regain mental clarity and balance? To gain spiritual support and tap into your soul's potential?

Do you want to rise up and meet the challenges of the 21st century?

Then this book is for you. You will not find these answers anywhere else.

This book is unlike anything you've read. You won't find citation after citation, references to study after study, because this is fresh, ahead-of-its-time information that comes from the heavens. In places where I mention numbers and other details that sound like statistics—for example, how many people suffer from a given condition—the facts actually come from Spirit, a source I'll explain more in Chapter 1, "Origins of the Medical Medium." In those very few instances where Spirit referred me to earthly sources for particular details, you'll see endnotes. Science has discovered some of what I write about here, and has yet to discover much of it. Everything I share in these pages comes from a higher authority, the essence of compassion, that wants everyone to heal and live up to their potential.

This book unveils many of Spirit's most precious medical secrets. It's the answer for anyone who's suffering from a chronic condition or a mystery illness that doctors haven't been able to resolve.

It's not just a book for people who are sick, though. It's a book for every person on the planet.

Health trends and fads come and go. When one is popular, it's hugely persuasive for people's consciousness. Then the new attraction comes along, the old one fades, and we're too distracted by the shiny new packaging to realize it contains the same misconceptions all over again. With each decade that goes by, we forget about the medical mistakes of the previous period, and history repeats itself.

Unlike other books in the health industry that repackage the same old theories with catchy new names, the pages that follow contain healing guidance that Spirit is revealing for the first time.

THE QUICKENING

Spirit calls our current era the *Quickening*. Never before has civilization changed at such a fast pace.

Technology has revolutionized virtually everything about our lives. We live in a period of breathtaking wonder and opportunity.

It's also an era of danger. By the time we mentally process something that's just happened, it's already old news. We're in such a rush that we always feel the need to be a step ahead. Along with up-to-the-minute information at our fingertips come greater demands, responsibilities—and health pitfalls. Lightning-fast advances sometimes come at the price of unconsidered vulnerabilities.

These changes affect all of humankind—and womankind especially bears the brunt. It's women who face the greatest expectations in our current day, women whose bodies so often get pushed to the brink. And chronic illness has become such a widespread issue, both for women and for men.

If we don't interrupt the constant flow of misinformation, if we don't recognize what our foremothers and forefathers have gone through and redirect our course, then the generations to come will have to endure unnecessary suffering. To keep up with the changing times—to survive—we must learn to adapt. The only way to do that is to protect our health.

The popular approach right now in books about chronic illness is to advise readers to eliminate inflammatory foods from their diets—and that's as far as it goes. The information out there doesn't explain what actually causes autoimmune disorders or chronic conditions, or how to rid yourself of the root problems. That is why people stay sick.

But there are genuine explanations for the conditions that leave doctors stumped, and there are powerful methods to deal with the challenges we face in the modern era.

This book is the guide to truly freeing yourself. I've written it so you can truly heal—and keep yourself from getting sucked into the trends and fads and mistakes and half-truths and errors and distractions and deceptions about health and wellness. I've written it so we can help today's children grow into healthy adults.

I'm in no way anti-science. I don't question that we're made of atoms, or that the earth is billions of years old, or the value of the scientific method. What I know, and the secrets this book contains, *will* eventually be recognized by the scientific community.

If you or a loved one is sick, though, do you feel you have 20 or 30 or 50 years to wait for answers? Can you bear to watch your daughter or son grow up to face the same health issues that you have, and the same limits of medicine?

That's why it's time this book reached the public—so *you* can read it now.

HOW TO USE THIS BOOK

You may be reading this book for any number of reasons. Perhaps a doctor has handed you a diagnosis, and you want to know what's really behind the label. Maybe you have symptoms you don't know how to name, and you're searching for answers. Maybe you're a health-care professional, or the loved one of someone who's sick, and you want to know the best way to provide care. Or you may have a general interest in optimal health and well-being, and you want to learn how to tap into your best self and your purpose in life.

This book has something for everyone, regardless of what food program, diet, or nutritional belief system you may practice. It's for anyone who wants access to the most advanced knowledge about healing available.

Here's how it works: In Part I, "Where It All Begins," I explain who I am and what I'm all about. You'll learn about my connection with Spirit and my life's work of helping people recover from the mystery factors keeping them sick, come back to life, and prevent further health issues. I also discuss *mystery illness,* and why it's much more pervasive than anyone realizes.

Validation and knowledge are two of the most powerful tools for recovery, so the chapters in the middle two sections are devoted to explaining the real stories behind dozens of ailments.

Part II, "The Hidden Epidemic," is all about the Epstein-Barr virus, an overlooked pathogen that's secretly behind debilitating conditions such as fibromyalgia, chronic fatigue syndrome, multiple sclerosis, rheumatoid arthritis, thyroid disorders, and more. Epstein-Barr's various strains and stages are plaguing people, especially women, in so many different ways—it's the mystery illness of mystery illnesses.

Part III, "Secrets Behind Other Mystery Illnesses," moves on to other health conditions that are widely misunderstood and includes descriptions of their surprising and varied causes. None of this information can wait another moment to reach the hands of the public.

At the end of each chapter in both Parts II and III, you'll also find targeted healing suggestions, including recommended foods and supplements for specific illnesses. Consult with your doctor or health-care practitioner about supplement dosages.

Then turn to Part IV, "How to Finally Heal," where I disclose the true secrets to vibrant health. These are the big pieces of the puzzle missing from the health world today. Part IV is about recovery, prevention, and self-realization—so whether your focus is shedding illness, going from good health to great, or tapping into your true self, you'll find resources here. These resources include tips for optimal digestion, a healing cleanse, hidden ingredients that can hinder your health, insights into the most healing foods on the planet, options for detoxification, and instructions for spiritual techniques like healing the soul through unique meditations and calling upon angels for support.

Throughout the book, you'll find case histories that tell my clients' stories of getting back on their feet—sometimes literally—after health and spiritual struggles. While I've changed all names and identifying details, the heart of each client's experience remains. I hope that each case history offers you comfort that you're not alone, as well as hope for your own bright future.

The word *quicken* doesn't just mean "become faster." It also means "spring to life." Historically, it referred to the first signs of movement a fetus showed in the womb.

Which is to say, this time of the Quickening isn't just about life speeding up. It's also about rebirth.

A new world is emerging. If we're to keep up—and not fall prey to the dangers that accompany rapid change—we must adapt.

Every word of this book is devoted to helping you with that process.

I'm about getting people better. I've helped tens of thousands of people fully recover from what ailed them, stave off further illness, and live vibrant lives, and I want to share this success with the wider world.

You'll see me use the term "medical communities" often throughout the book. By this I mean the conventional and alternative medical communities, as well as the newer fields of integrative and functional medicine. I don't take sides with any of them; I also don't point fingers. The information here is neutral, independent. It's about practitioners and healers getting ahold of this knowledge, learning how to help more people. It is about *you* getting ahold of this knowledge and learning how to heal yourself. It is about the truth.

Aren't we all looking for truth? Truth about our world, the universe? Truth about ourselves? About life? About why we are here? About our purpose?

When we're sick, we question ourselves. We feel cut off from life, from what we were put on earth to do. We doubt basic truths, like the body's ability to heal, because we haven't yet connected to what's really behind our illnesses. We go from doctor to doctor, medical community to medical community, looking for an answer. We lose faith in life itself.

When we become well, though, doubt melts away. We have energy to devote to our true purpose. We watch ourselves transform, and we believe in the good in life again. We connect to laws of the universe, like that of renewal.

The truth about the world, ourselves, life, purpose—it all comes down to healing.

And the truth about healing is now in your hands.

PART I

WHERE IT ALL BEGINS

CHAPTER 1

Origins of the Medical Medium

In this book, I reveal truths you won't learn anywhere else. You won't hear them from your doctor, read them in other books, or find them on the web.

These are secrets that have not yet surfaced, and that I'm bringing to light for the first time.

I'm not a physician. I have no medical training. Yet I can tell you things about your health that no one else can. I can give you clarity on chronic and mystery illnesses that doctors often misdiagnose, treat incorrectly, or tag with certain labels even when they don't truly understand what causes the symptoms.

Since I was a young child, I've been helping individuals heal with the insights I'm about to share. Now, it's time for you to learn these secrets.

It's how Spirit has told me it's meant to be.

AN UNEXPECTED GUEST

My story begins when I'm four years old.

As I'm waking up one Sunday morning, I hear an elderly man speaking.

His voice is just outside my right ear. It's very clear.

He says, "I am the Spirit of the Most High. There is no spirit above me but God."

I'm confused and alarmed. Is someone else in my room? I open my eyes and look around, but don't see anybody. *Maybe someone's talking or playing a radio outside,* I think.

I get up and walk to the window. There are no people—it's too early in the morning. I have no idea what's going on, and I'm not sure I want to.

I run downstairs to be with my parents and feel safe. I don't say anything about the voice. But as the day goes on, a feeling builds up—that I'm being watched.

In the evening I settle into my chair at the dinner table. With me are my parents, my grandparents, and some other family members.

As we're eating, I suddenly see a strange man standing behind my grandmother. He has gray hair and a gray beard, and is wearing a brown robe. I assume he's a family friend who's come to join our meal. Instead of sitting down with us, though, he keeps standing behind my grandmother . . . and looking only at me.

When none of my family reacts to his presence, I slowly realize that I'm the only one who sees him. I look away to see if he'll disappear. When I look back, he's still there staring at me. His mouth doesn't move, but I can hear his voice by my right ear. It's the same voice I heard when waking up. This time he says, in a calming tone, "I am here for you."

I stop eating.

"What's wrong?" my mom asks. "You're not hungry?"

I don't answer, just keep looking at the man, who lifts his right arm and waves for me to come over to my grandmother.

Feeling an undeniable instinct to follow his instruction, I climb out of my chair and walk to Grandma.

He takes my hand and puts it on my grandmother's chest while she's eating.

Grandma backs away with a start. "What are you doing?" she asks.

The gray man looks at me. "Say 'lung cancer.'"

I'm at a loss. I don't even know what *lung cancer* means.

I try to say it, but it comes out as a mumble.

"Do it again," he tells me. "Lung."

"Lung," I say.

"Cancer."

"Cancer," I say.

My entire family is staring at me now.

I'm still focused on the gray man.

"Now say, 'Grandma has lung cancer.'"

"Grandma has lung cancer," I say.

I hear a fork clatter on the table.

The gray man pulls my hand from Grandma and gently places it at my side. Then he turns and starts climbing steps that weren't there before.

He looks back at me and says, "You will hear from me all the time, but you may never see me again. Not to worry." He continues climbing until he steps through the ceiling of my house—and now *does* disappear.

My grandmother stares at me. "Did you say what I thought you said?"

There's a panic at the table. What just happened doesn't make sense for a number of reasons—starting with the fact that, as far as we know, Grandma is fine. She hasn't noticed any problems or seen any doctors.

The next morning I wake up . . . and hear the voice again: "I am the Spirit of the Most High. There is no spirit above me but God."

Just like the previous morning, I look around but don't see anyone.

From that day on the same thing happens every morning, without fail.

Meanwhile, my grandmother is shaken by what I said to her. Even though she feels fine, she makes an appointment for a general checkup.

A few weeks later she visits her doctor—and a chest X-ray reveals that she has lung cancer.

THE VOICE

As the mysterious visitor continues to greet me every morning, I start to pay attention to what he sounds like.

His crystal-clear voice is somewhere between baritone and tenor—a bit on the low side, but not *very* low. It has depth and resonance. Even though he's near my right ear, his speech has the stereo effect of surround sound.

It's hard to gauge his age. Sometimes he sounds like an exceptionally strong, healthy 80-year-old, matching the gray man I saw at dinner. At other times he sounds thousands of years old.

You might say he has a soothing voice. Yet I can't get used to his presence.

Other mediums sometimes hear inner voices, but mine isn't internal. It's a voice directly outside my right ear, as if someone were standing next to me. I can't will it to go away.

I can physically block it. When I put my hand in front of my ear, I can make the voice sound very faint. As soon as I move my hand away, he's at full volume again.

I ask him to stop talking to me. At first I'm polite about it. Then I'm not.

It doesn't matter what I say, though. He talks whenever he wants to.

SPIRIT OF THE MOST HIGH

I start calling the voice by name, Spirit of the Most High. Sometimes I call him *Spirit* for short, or *Most High*.

By age eight I hear Spirit continually throughout the day. He tells me about the physical health of anyone I encounter.

No matter where I am or what I'm doing, I'm told about the aches, pains, and illnesses of whomever's nearby, and also what the person needs to do to become better. The relentlessness of this ongoing and intimate information is extremely stressful.

I ask Spirit to stop telling me these things I don't want to know.

He tells me that he's trying to teach me as much as possible, and that we can't spare a moment. When I tell him it's too demanding, he ignores me.

I learn that I *can* engage in some conversation with him, though. When I'm old enough to pose some fundamental questions, I ask, "Who are you? *What* are you? Where did you come from? And why are you here?"

Spirit replies, "First I will tell you what I am not.

"I am not an angel. And I am not a person. I was never a human being. I am not a 'spirit guide,' either.

"I am a *word.*"

I blink fast, trying to take this in. All I can think to ask is, "Which word?"

Spirit replies, "Compassion."

I'm not sure how to respond. But I don't need to. Spirit keeps talking. "I am literally the living essence of the word *compassion.* I sit at the fingertip of God."

"Spirit, I don't understand. Are *you* God?"

"No," the voice replies. "At the fingertip of God sits a word, and that word is compassion. I am that word. A living word. The closest word to God."

I shake my head. "How can you be just a word?"

"A word is an energy source. Certain words hold great power. God pours light into words such as I and instills us with the breath of life. I am *more* than a word."

"Is there anyone else like you?" I ask.

"Yes: Faith. Hope. Joy. Peace. And more. They are all living words, but I sit above all of them, because I am the closest to God."

"Do these words speak to people, too?"

"Not as I do to you. These words are not heard by the ear. They live in each person's heart and soul. As do I. Words such as joy and peace do not stand alone in the heart. They require compassion to be complete."

"Why can't peace be enough by itself?" I ask. Many times since Spirit entered my life, I've wished for peace and quiet.

"Compassion is the understanding of suffering," Spirit replies. "There is no peace, joy, or hope until those who suffer are understood. Compassion is the soul of these words; without it, they are empty. Compassion fills them with truth, honor, and purpose.

"*I* am compassion. And no other sits above me but God."

Trying to make sense of this, I ask, "Then what is God?"

"God is a word. God is *love,* which is above all other words. God is also *more* than a word. Because God loves all. God is the most powerful source of existence.

"People can love. But people do not love all others unconditionally. God does."

It's too much for me to process. I end the conversation with one personal question: "Do you talk to anyone else?" *Because if you do,* I'm thinking, *I'm going to seek them out so I don't have to feel so alone.*

"The angels and other beings look to me for guidance. I provide all who care to listen with the lessons and wisdom of God," Spirit says. "But on earth, I speak directly only to you."

ME AND MY SHADOW

As you might imagine, this is a lot to absorb at age eight.

There are other mediums who've had shocking things happen at a young age. None of their experiences quite match mine.

Being able to hear a spirit voice clearly at all times, and freely engage in conversation with it, is extraordinary even among mediums. Even more unusual is for that voice to speak outside my ear, so that it's an independent source separate from my thoughts. It's essentially having someone follow me around everywhere—someone who keeps telling me things I really don't want to hear about the health of everyone around me.

The upside is, I receive health information that's incredibly accurate—much more so than any other medium alive. Plus I'm regularly informed about my *own* health, which is a great rarity. Even the most famous mediums in history normally couldn't read their own conditions.

I'm also given insights into health that are decades ahead of what's known by medical communities.

A major downside is that I have no privacy. When I'm eight years old, I spend a week building a dam in a stream by my house. Spirit tells me it's a bad idea, that it will flood the neighbor's lawn.

"It'll be fine," I say.

Then a downpour comes, the stream rises—and it floods the neighbor's lawn. As the man from the house yells at me, I hear in my ear, "I told you. You didn't listen to me." Of course, that just makes the situation worse.

Spirit is constantly watching my every move, and telling me what I should and shouldn't do. It makes having any kind of normal childhood nearly impossible. That same year I build the dam, I know in great detail about the physical and emotional health of my best friend, the little girl I have a crush on, and even my teacher—who's struggling through an awful relationship with her boyfriend. I can read every bit of it, and it's agonizing.

Not one to offer empty comfort, Spirit tells me to expect worse. "Your biggest challenges are yet to come."

"What do you mean?" I ask.

"Only one or two people per century are given this gift," he says. "It is not a typical intuitive or psychic ability. It is something that most fail to survive. You will find it almost unbearable not to be able to live like a normal person, never mind a normal teenager.

"Eventually you will see almost nothing but the suffering of others. You will somehow have to find a way of becoming comfortable with that. Otherwise, the chances are you will end your life."

READING BODIES

Spirit becomes both my best friend and my albatross. I appreciate that he's training me for a job the higher powers have chosen for me. Still, the stress he puts me under is extraordinary.

One day he tells me to go to a large, beautiful cemetery near my home. "I want you to stand over that grave," he says, "and figure out how the person died."

That's quite a request to make of an eight-year-old.

At this point, though, I've been so bombarded with the health information of both friends and strangers that I try to view this as just one more case.

And with Spirit's help, I'm able to do what he asks.

This adds another dimension to the gift: not only does Spirit verbally inform me of what's wrong with someone's health, he also helps me visualize physical scans of the person's body.

I spend years in different cemeteries performing this exercise with hundreds of corpses. I become so good at it that I can almost instantly sense if someone's died of heart attack, stroke, cancer, liver disease, car accident, suicide, or murder.

Along with this, Spirit teaches me to look very deeply into the bodies of the living. He promises that once this training is concluded, I'll be able to scan and read *anyone* with extreme accuracy.

Whenever I get tired or want to do something more fun, Spirit tells me, "Someday you'll be performing scans on people that will mean the difference between life and death. You will be able to tell if a person's lungs are about to collapse, or an artery is about to clot and shut down someone's heart."

Once, I reply, "Who cares? Why does it matter? Why should *I* care?"

"You *must* care," Spirit responds. "What all of us do here on earth matters. The good works you perform matter to your soul. You must take this responsibility seriously."

SELF-HEALING

At age nine, while other boys are riding bikes and playing baseball, I'm constantly witnessing disease in the people around me and listening to Spirit tell me what's needed for them to get better. I'm learning what adults do wrong for their health and exactly what actions they should take to heal . . . but seldom do.

At this point I'm so filled with health-related knowledge and training that it's hard not to start applying it.

One opportunity arises when I get sick myself. Eating out with my family one evening, I ignore Spirit's usual dietary recommendations and eat a dish that gives me food poisoning. For two weeks, I lie in bed unable to keep anything down. My parents take me to the doctor's office and even the ER one night when it gets really bad, but the fever and the pain in my gut don't stop.

Finally Spirit cuts through my delirium and tells me it's *E. coli*. He gives me a direct order to go to my great-grandfather's house and pick a box of heirloom pears from his tree. Spirit says I'm to eat nothing but these ripe pears, and I'll heal.

I do as he says and recover rapidly.

FIRE HIM, GOD

At age ten, I try to go over Spirit's head and deal directly with his boss.

I figure I can't tell God what I want through prayer because Spirit will hear me.

So I climb some of the highest trees I can find to get as close to God as possible and carve messages in their trunks.

One of the first messages is, "God, I love Spirit, but it's time we cut out the middle man."

This is followed by some frank questions:

"God, why do people have to be sick?"

"God, why can't *you* fix everybody?"

"God, why do *I* have to help people?"

While these seem to me very reasonable things to ask, I receive no answers.

So I find some even more dangerously tall trees, and I climb to the highest branches in hopes that my recklessness will get God's attention. This time I carve requests for direct action:

"God, please give me back silence."

"God, I don't want to hear Spirit anymore. Make him go away."

As I carve in the words, "God, let me be free," I lose my foothold and almost slip off the branch. *Not* that *kind of free!* I think. I inch my way back down to safety, defeated.

None of these messages makes any difference. Spirit just keeps talking to me.

If he's aware of my attempts to subvert his authority, he's gracious enough not to mention it. There's more important work at hand.

FIRST CLIENTS

At age 11, I want to do something productive and fun that'll take my mind off the voice by my ear, so I get a job carrying clubs at a golf course.

My gift is not so easily abandoned, though. While caddying, I can't help telling golfers about their conditions. I often know about their stiff joints, bad knees, sore hips, hurt ankles, tendonitis, and more before they do.

So I say, "Your swing's a little off, but that's not surprising considering your carpal tunnel situation," or "You'd do better if you dealt with your inflamed left hip."

They look at me with amazement and ask, "How did you know that?" Then they request advice on how to get better, and I tell them what to eat, what changes to make to their behavior, therapies to try, and so on.

After caddying for several years, I crave a change. I decide that if I'm going to recommend food and supplements for healing, I might as well work in a place that sells them. So I get a job as stock boy in a local supermarket.

My clients come by whenever they like, and I take time out of replenishing shelves to help them. The owner of the supermarket doesn't mind that my work for him is periodically interrupted, because I'm bringing in new customers.

Besides, he's a client, too.

It's a little odd to conduct health consultations in a supermarket aisle. It's also difficult, because supplements are barely available yet and the variety of food is limited. Spirit keeps explaining that in a couple of decades, stores will supply many more options for people's health. In the meantime, he helps me get creative with healing plans—and I love being able to walk a client to exactly what she needs to buy to get better.

WITH GREAT POWER COMES GREAT GUILT

At age 14, I sometimes sit in a bus or a train, pick up on some health issue with the guy in front of me, and tap him on the shoulder to tell him about it. At times the response is gratitude. Other times the reaction is to accuse me of invading his privacy, stealing his medical records, or worse. That's a lot of distrust and hostility to deal with—especially for a boy going through puberty.

As I grow older, I learn to be careful about who I try to help unasked. If I see someone regularly, I still feel impelled to share what I know. So I develop the habit of first reading her emotional state to determine whether she's approachable. That cuts down on the number of uncomfortable situations.

If someone is a stranger, I'll usually keep whatever I'm seeing to myself. This becomes a burden, though. When I'm a teen, I start feeling even more accountable for my actions. So if someone is in danger of kidney disease, or has cancer, and I do nothing, part of me feels it's my fault if the person ends up seriously ill or dead. When this is multiplied hundreds of times a day, the sense of guilt and responsibility becomes overwhelming.

ESCAPE ATTEMPTS

As my teenage years continue, life becomes more difficult. For instance, most people watch television to relax and escape. But when I watch, I get a health reading on everyone on the screen. I automatically scan the condition of every person I see who needs help, whether they know they have a condition or not. When that happens over and over, TV is draining, not fun.

It's even worse when I go to a movie theater. I'm uncontrollably reading the health of every person in my row, the row in front of me, the row in back of me, and so on.

And that's not the end of it. I read the health of the people *in the movie*. I'm able to determine the condition of each actor during the time the film was shot, as well as the health of the actor in the present moment. Imagine what it's like to be on a movie date and get bombarded by medical information about the people around you and up on the big screen.

Considering the last thing most teens want is to feel different from everyone else, this period is especially rocky. My feelings of alienation and being overwhelmed by responsibility lead to some rebellious teen impulses. I pursue various ways to escape my "gift."

I start spending a lot of time in the woods. I find nature soothing, and especially appreciate the absence of other people. With the help of Spirit, I learn to identify different species of birds during the day. At night he teaches me the names of stars—both what scientists call them and the names God has given them. It's not fully an escape, though, because Spirit also teaches me how to recognize herbs and foods growing around me—red clover, plantain, dandelion, burdock root, wild rose hips and petals, wild apples, wild berries—and how to use them for healing.

I also develop an interest in repairing cars. I like fixing up mechanical objects because they don't require me to become emotionally involved. Even if I fail to repair a junker Chevy with a bad engine, I never feel remotely as awful as I do when I can't help people because they're in too advanced a stage of disease to be healed.

But this hobby doesn't go as planned, either. People start noticing what I'm doing and coming over: "Wow, that's amazing! Can you fix *my* car?" I don't have it in me to say no—especially since Spirit is doing the hardest part, which is figuring out what's wrong.

One day when I'm 15, my mother and I stop at a station to get gasoline. I walk into the garage and find a bunch of mechanics staring at a car as if they're trying to solve a puzzle.

"What's going on?" I ask.

One of the men says, "We've worked on this car for weeks. It should run perfectly. But we can't get it to start."

Spirit immediately tells me the solution. "Open up the wire harness in the back of the firewall," I pass along to the mechanics. "Buried in dozens of other wires you'll find a white one that's broken. Put that wire together and the car will run fine."

"That's ridiculous!" says another of the men.

"What's the harm in checking?" asks the first one. So they go in—and sure enough, there's a white wire broken in half.

They look at me with their jaws hanging open.

"Are you the owner of this car?" asks the skeptical mechanic. "Or are you a friend of his?"

"No," I reply. "I just have a knack for these things."

In a minute they fix the wire and try the car again. It starts up perfectly.

One of the mechanics starts dancing around. Another calls it "a miracle."

Word gets around, and soon a bunch of garages in my town, and also several neighboring towns, use me as the go-to guy for troubleshooting seemingly unfixable vehicles. When I show up to assist on a job, the mechanics who called me—much older guys with years of experience—are always incredulous. "What's this 15-year-old doing here?" they all ask. When I get the job done, though, they change their minds.

So instead of escaping responsibility, I gain more. On top of healing people, I become a car doctor.

The last straw is when I realize how emotional people are about their cars. A lot of times, they're even more invested in their cars' well-being than in their own health. At that point cars stop being fun for me.

I try some other rebellious activities. For example, I join a rock band, because loud music helps drown out Spirit's voice. Spirit does not appreciate this. He patiently waits until I'm finished making a racket, then resumes his commentary on the health of those around me.

Nothing really works to make my gift go away. It becomes increasingly clear that I'm stuck with Spirit and my ability—and can't escape the path that's been laid out for me.

STARTING TO COMMIT

By the time I'm a young man, thanks to my training with Spirit, I've indirectly read and scanned thousands of people and helped hundreds along the way.

One day I think, *Okay, this is the hand I've been dealt. I have a special purpose. I just have to accept it—for now.*

I also think, *This can't possibly go on forever. At some point I'll have fulfilled my responsibilities and will be set free to live a normal life.* Spirit has never said any such thing to me, yet I need to believe it to keep going.

In my early 20s, I begin doing in earnest what Spirit has repeatedly told me is my destiny. I open my door to sick people who come for help, discover the true root causes of their illnesses, and tell them what they need to do to become healthy.

And despite my griping about the various stresses I've endured, it's fulfilling work. It feels good to help people.

In fact, sometimes what I can do is so empowering that I let the feeling of being all-knowing go to my head.

A good example is the time my neighbor approaches me about his wife, who can't walk or use her legs. She's been to dozens of doctors, and none of them have helped. My neighbor tells her, "Look, Anthony seems to know a lot about this stuff. Let's take a chance."

Under my care, within a year she's able to walk again.

I'm in my garden pulling up some onions when my neighbor comes around. "I just want to thank you again, Anthony," he says. "We went all over the country to meet top experts, and they couldn't do a thing. It doesn't make any sense—somehow you knew exactly what was wrong and what she needed. I don't know how it's possible. You're not even a doctor."

I look at him with onions in my hand and say, "It's because I'm always right. I can fix any problem because there's nothing I'm wrong about. Just remember that—I'm always right and will always be right."

Then I turn around, walk a few feet, and step on a rake that slaps me in the face so hard it knocks me out.

As I lie on the ground, my concerned neighbor rushes to my side and stands over me. In my dazed state I think he's my constant companion. "Spirit?" I ask.

Spirit of the Most High replies, *"I'm* always right. *You're* always wrong. Remember that. I'm always *right.* You're always *wrong."*

Whenever I get cocky, I think of that moment. It's a reminder that while some of the things I do as a healer with the help of Spirit might be considered miraculous, I'm still a regular guy who can make lots of poor decisions when flying solo.

THE TURNING POINT

When I'm a young adult, Spirit assumes I've passed the crisis point that led others with my gift over the centuries to end their lives. He assumes I've accepted that using my abilities to heal people is what I'll do for the rest of my life.

Which goes to show that even Spirit of the Most High can't predict everything when it comes to free will.

One day in late fall, I'm at a retreat by the water with no one but my girlfriend—who'll eventually become my wife—and my dog, August (short for Augustine).

I've had August for a year and am very close to her. She replaced my family dog, who was with me for 15 years. Just like that dog, August is essential to my sanity.

We're sitting by a large, deep bay. The water is icy cold, and the current is strong.

It's our last day. With great reluctance, we start getting ready to leave the peaceful isolation of this place.

Suddenly, with no warning, my dog jumps into the bay. I sense she picked up on my feelings. This is her way of saying, "We don't have to go. Let's stay here and keep playing."

Unfortunately, both the cold and the current take hold of her. She immediately starts slipping from us.

We stand on the shore, screaming at August to come back. I throw stones into the water to try to lead my dog back to me. This is our special signal—whenever I splash stones in the shallows, she returns to shore. But today, the current pulls her farther and farther away.

August goes 50 feet out. I see her struggling to get back and losing the battle. Then the cold freezes her so thoroughly that she stops paddling . . . and goes straight down.

I toss off my jacket, boots, and pants, and jump into the freezing water.

I've swum 15 feet out when Spirit of the Most High says, "If you keep going, you are not going to make it."

"It doesn't matter!" I yell. "I'm not abandoning August. I have to save my dog."

I swim another 15 feet—and then the merciless cold takes over. My body goes numb.

Spirit says, "You've done it now. You cannot turn back, and you cannot go forward. This is it."

"Really? You rob me of a normal, peaceful life, I dedicate my whole being to your work of healing, and this is all I get from you? You say, 'This is it,' and leave us to die?"

All the angst and anger I've suppressed since I was four years old comes pouring out. I let Spirit have it about my years of pent-up frustration over this continual torture I've always had to accept as a "gift": being set apart from everyone else, knowing too much about everyone at way too early an age, and being told what I had to do with my life instead of given even the slightest choice.

I tell Spirit, "I put up with a lot—sacrificing my childhood, experiencing everybody's pain and suffering, taking responsibility for healing thousands of strangers, and draining myself physically and mentally every day. And now you're telling me I can't even protect my own family?

"No, dammit!" I shout as the freezing waves threaten to engulf me. "If this is how you want me to end, Spirit, so be it. I'm getting my dog back, or I'm going down with her."

A very long second passes. Numb and exhausted, I realize that I may have finally pushed things too far. A few more moments without help, and I'll be following my dog August into the depths below.

I turn my head toward the shore to get one last glimpse of the girl I planned to spend the rest of my life with.

Spirit says, "You need to swim out twenty more feet."

In shock, I shout, "How?"

To my great surprise, I feel renewed strength. I resume swimming. In my mind, I continue to yell at Spirit that I deserve to survive this *with* my dog. Otherwise we should both die.

Spirit says, "I will get you to your dog. In return, you must commit to me. We go through this life the way we're supposed to. You accept that it is by the holy power of God you are destined to do this work for the rest of your life."

"Okay!" I shout. "Deal. Let me find August, and I'll work for you with no complaints ever again."

I swim the additional 20 feet. Spirit says, "Hold your breath and go eight feet down, then open your eyes."

As I hold my breath, a surge of power courses through my body. All of a sudden I can feel my legs again.

I swim what feels like eight feet down, open my eyes—and see an angel.

I've never encountered an angel before. I'm seeing what looks like a woman who has no trouble breathing underwater, with a glorious source of light behind her, light radiating from her eyes, and huge, beautiful wings of light growing out of her back. There's no question she's a divine being.

And in her arms is August, surrounded by a beautiful, peaceful light. For a moment, it feels like time stands still. My vision is surprisingly clear underwater, and I have no fear or trouble holding my breath.

I grab my dog by her collar. Then *something* pushes me upward with her.

We both reach the surface of the water.

The bay is still icy cold, and the current is still trying to violently pull us away from land and life. The wind is blowing strong.

When I open my eyes again, I see Spirit for a moment standing right above the water. It's the only time I've seen Spirit since the first day he appeared to me at age four.

"We don't have much time," he says. "The angel is leaving."

Just as I register once again that all could have been lost, another surge of power charges through my body. As I start swimming back through the frigid waters—holding onto August, who seems lifeless—it feels almost as if I'm being pulled across the 50 feet to safety.

My dog and I soon make it back to shore—and to my girlfriend, who is crying with relief.

As I drag myself and my dog up to the rocky sand, I cry in agony—not because I'm feeling the initial stages of hypothermia, but because I'm afraid my dog is gone. All I can think is, *Let her still be alive.*

She opens her eyes, gasps for air, and comes to life. The sun appears from behind the clouds, and a streak of light races across the water and shines on my dog August. I look at the light and say, "Spirit, thank you."

And I realize: this is the first time since Spirit entered my life that I've ever thanked him for anything. The battles I've waged with Spirit of the Most High since I was four years old have to end. It's time for me to acknowledge the cards I've been dealt.

Even before this point, people in need have been coming to me in droves.

With this pledge, I wholly dedicate myself to helping them, without qualification and for the rest of my life.

I don't have to pretend the abilities I've been granted are a problem-free blessing. Yet I stop complaining and finally accept who I am.

That's when I truly assume my role as the Medical Medium.

THE PROCESS

Once I commit to my calling, I develop a routine for fulfilling it as efficiently as possible.

I don't need to be in the same room with a person to perform a reading, so I arrange to speak with clients by phone. This allows me to help anyone in the world, regardless of location, and it minimizes the transition time between clients. I've helped tens of thousands of clients this way.

When I perform a scan, Spirit creates a very bright white light that lets me see into the client. While that's critical for obtaining what I need as the Medical Medium, the intensity of the light creates a kind of "snow blindness" that impairs my vision in the real world, and it accumulates as the day goes on. When I'm finished working, it takes 30 to 60 minutes for my sight to return to normal.

(As a side note, I bring my assistant with me whenever I go somewhere that will have a lot of people and voices, because I'll usually lose a substantial portion of my sight due to "automatic" readings. For example, whenever I have to fly somewhere, I end up inadvertently reading everyone on my plane. By the time we land I'm completely blind, so I need my assistant to lead me around until the effect wears off.)

A deep and comprehensive reading of a client's condition takes only about three minutes. However, I have to spend 10 to 30 minutes explaining what I've discovered and my advice for healing, especially for new clients.

Sometimes I need to spend time bolstering or "reconstructing" a client. That's because I deal with more than just people's physical illnesses.

SOUL, HEART, AND SPIRIT

When I perform a reading, I go beyond a person's physical health. I also examine the client's soul, heart, and spirit. These are three entirely different components of one's being that always get grouped together.

The first component is the *soul*. This is the consciousness of a person, or what some call "the ghost in the machine."

Your soul resides in your brain, where your soul stores your *memories* and *experiences*. When you pass from this mortal realm, your soul carries those memories as it moves onward. Even if someone has a brain injury or brain disease that keeps him or her from remembering certain things, the soul will bring all the memories with it when that person passes on.

Your soul also stores your hope and your faith, both of which help keep you on the right path.

Ideally, you should have a fully intact soul. Over the course of life's hardships, though, a soul can become fractured and even lose pieces of itself. This is caused by traumatic events, such as the death of a loved one, betrayal by a loved one, or betrayal of oneself.

When I scan a client, fractures in her or his soul resemble cracks in a cathedral window. I can tell where the fractures are, because that's where the light comes streaming through.

As for a soul with missing pieces, it's like a house at night that's meant to have all of its lights on . . . except some of its rooms are stuck in the dark.

This soul damage can result in a loss of energy, or even loss of life force. That's why it's important to be aware of it. Sometimes a client's problem isn't physical—rather, it's an affliction of the soul.

A person with soul damage is vulnerable. If you ever hear a friend say, "I'm not ready for another relationship, I'm still hurting from my breakup," she's acknowledging that she has soul damage, and that her soul needs time to heal before she risks putting herself out there again.

Along the same lines, if you ever observe someone hungrily pursuing spiritual learning in any form—religion, spiritual gurus, self-help books, meditation retreats—it may be because that person's soul has been damaged, and she or he is instinctively searching for ways to make it healthy and complete again. That's a critical job for each of us—when your time here ends, your soul should be sufficiently intact to survive its journey beyond the stars, where God will receive it.

The second component of one's being is the physical *heart*. This is where your *love, compassion,* and *joy* reside. Having a healthy soul doesn't necessarily make you a whole person. You can have an unblemished soul and a broken, injured heart.

Your heart serves as the compass for your actions, guiding you to do the right thing when your soul becomes lost.

Also, your heart is a kind of safety net that can compensate for soul damage. When your soul suffers fractures and losses, a strong heart will get you through until your soul has managed to heal.

Your heart keeps a record of your good intentions, too. This means you can have a battered soul and a warm, loving heart. In fact, it's common for someone's heart to grow larger as a result of the roller-coaster ride her or his soul has gone through. Great losses can lead to deeper understanding . . . and greater love and compassion.

The third key component I look at when I scan a client is that person's *spirit*—which in this context refers to someone's *will* and *physical strength*. Your spirit is not your soul. They are two separate parts of you. It's your spirit that enables you to climb, run, and fight. Even if your soul's been battered and your heart is faint, your spirit can keep you physically going while you look for opportunities to heal. For example, sometimes I'll tell a very ill client to start walking, go out to watch birds, and look at sunsets. That helps the client regain her or his spirit, and that can be the start to rebuilding the heart and soul.

Every human being is different, with individual experiences, feelings, and soul states. To be a compassionate healer, you have to adapt to each unique condition and personality to alleviate that person's pain and suffering. Spirit tells me this compassion is the most important element in healing.

THE ONE AND ONLY MEDICAL MEDIUM

While there are obvious disadvantages to having a voice continually talking into my ear, there are also huge advantages.

Because Spirit is distinct and separate from me, it doesn't matter if on a given day I'm feeling upset or ill or bored. Spirit is unaffected by my emotions and will consistently provide an accurate reading of each client's health.

I'm not an intuitive who needs to get into a certain headspace or has good days and bad days performing my job. Some clients ask me, "Should I take off my jewelry to allow you to get you a better read?" It doesn't matter if they're wrapped in tinfoil; I'm going to be able to get the answers they need and find out what's wrong.

Another way I'm different from most mediums is that I have no problem getting information about the health of my family and friends, or about my own health. Again, because Spirit is separate from me, all I have to do is ask, and he tells me what I want to know.

This is one of the things that makes me unique.

One day a skeptical reporter demands I diagnose her on the spot: "I want you to tell me where it hurts. Does it hurt in my toe? My leg?

My stomach? Does it hurt in my arm? My butt? Do I even hurt at all? Let's see what your voice says."

Spirit immediately tells me, "She *does* hurt. She hurts on the left side of her head. Chronic migraines torment her." I reach over, touch the left side of her head, and say, "Spirit tells me you hurt here." She starts crying.

That's the caliber of instant accuracy Spirit provides.

If I get a call at 2 A.M. from a client whose daughter is about to go into emergency surgery and the client wants to know if it's the right choice, I have to be able to tell the doctor in one minute if that little girl merely has a bad case of food poisoning, or if her appendix is about to explode.

I have to be able to tell whether someone's recovering or is bleeding internally, if a child's fever is due to the flu or meningitis, if someone is suffering from heat sickness or is about to have a stroke. Spirit delivers this information every time.

Padre Pio and Edgar Cayce, those famous mystical healers of the 20th century, were the only two mediums in recent history who accessed the level of compassion that Spirit demands of me. Their work as compassionate healers was in some ways similar to mine. However, our strengths and gifts are unique to each of us.

No other medium does what I do. No one else alive has a spirit voice providing profound on-target health information with crystal clarity.

I've devoted my life to this work. It's who I am. And it's the gift I will use to provide you with the medical information in the chapters that follow.

CHAPTER 2

The Truth about Mystery Illness

If you feel that you've been searching for health answers for far too long, you're not alone.

On average, a client comes to me after ten years of doctor shopping, having visited 20 different practitioners. Sometimes it's more like 50 to 100 doctors in that timeframe. One woman I spoke with had gone to almost *400* doctors in seven years.

These people may have gotten labels for their conditions—lupus, for example, or fibromyalgia, Lyme disease, multiple sclerosis (MS), chronic fatigue syndrome, migraines, thyroid disorder, rheumatoid arthritis, colitis, irritable bowel syndrome, celiac disease, insomnia, depression, and many others—yet they couldn't get better.

Or maybe doctors couldn't find tags for the symptoms these people had and doled out that old, misbegotten chestnut of a diagnosis, "It's all in your head."

What these clients were really dealing with was mystery illness.

A mystery illness isn't just an unidentified disease, and it's not just the news story about eight kids in the Midwest who are hospitalized for sudden, unexplained symptoms. I've certainly had clients come to me for answers in those situations, yet it's a fraction of what I see day in and day out, a tiny subset of the much larger category of mystery illness.

Limiting the definition of mystery illness to rare, acute diseases is not helpful. It tricks the public. It makes people think that the medical cases that stump doctors are minimal and affect only a minute portion of the population.

Truth is, millions of people suffer from mystery illness. A mystery illness is any ailment that leaves anyone perplexed for any reason. It can be a mystery because there isn't a name for a given set of symptoms—and so it's written off as a sign of mental imbalance. A mystery illness can also be an established, chronic condition for which there's no effective treatment of the root cause (because medical communities don't yet understand it), or a condition that's frequently misdiagnosed.

We're talking not just about the conditions I listed above, but also type 2 diabetes, hypoglycemia, TMJ, *Candida,* menopause complications, ADHD, PTSD, Bell's palsy, shingles, leaky gut syndrome, and more. These are merely labels, with no meaning behind them besides confusion and suffering. That makes them mystery illnesses.

And what about autoimmune disease—the mistaken theory that the body, in certain circumstances, attacks itself? Not true. (More on that in later chapters.) It's another label that diverts from the truth that medical science has not yet figured out why people are in chronic pain. Autoimmune disease is mystery illness.

If you visit a physician and complain of elbow pain, then hear that you have rheumatoid arthritis (RA), that's just a tag—not an answer. You may receive prescriptions for medications and physical therapy, yet no explanation of *why* you have it, or how you can heal from it. The doctor may say that RA is the body attacking itself—that is, the immune system mistaking parts of your body for invaders and trying to destroy them.

That's misguided. *The body doesn't attack itself.*

The truth? RA is just a name for one particular mystery illness. The tag *joint hurting disease* would be more accurate—it reveals as much as medical research has so far uncovered about the disorder.

There's a real explanation for RA, though. The answer is in this book.

Mystery illness is at an all-time high. With each new decade to come, the number of people suffering from autoimmune disorders and other chronic mystery illnesses will double or triple. It's time to expand the definition of mystery illness, to wake up to the fact that millions of people need answers.

In the chapters that follow, I'll reveal the true nature of dozens of these ailments, and I'll tell you what steps you need to take to heal or protect yourself.

The mystery will be revealed.

HEALING MERRY-GO-ROUND

When people present their mystery symptoms to doctor after doctor with no progress, I call that the *healing merry-go-round*. As hard as you try to get off the ride, you just keep going in circles.

In most professions, the job is black-and-white. That's not to say that people such as plumbers, mechanics, accountants, and lawyers have easy occupations. They don't. Yet they operate within sets of rules. The accountant who can't get her columns to balance will eventually figure out the mistake in the ledger and post a correcting journal entry. The plumber who comes to fix a malfunctioning dishwasher will, even if the source of the problem is confusing at first, eventually figure out that a certain part needs to be replaced—or if that doesn't work, he'll install a new appliance.

Even some aspects of medicine are clear-cut. When someone gets into a skiing accident, for example, there's no mystery about what caused the broken leg—and no mystery about how to fix it. With something like a bone fracture—where cause, effect, and treatment are well-defined—it's like a ferry ride: there's an end to the trip, and it's somewhere different from where you started. Perhaps there's fog along the way that complicates the journey—a patient's fractures are splintered, or she gets a pen cap stuck in her cast—but there's an established Point A and Point B, and medical personnel are trained to carry the patient from one place to the other.

Medical science is incredibly advanced at physical body repair. It's developed lifesaving technology that allows patients to make radical recoveries from car accidents, broken bones, heart transplants, and so much more. Where would we be without the dedicated people who perform routine procedures and revolutionary surgeries every day?

In the 20th century, medical science made great breakthroughs in virology, too . . . but it all got swept under the carpet. Because there was no funding to take these discoveries to the next level, these amazing doctors were left in the lurch as their findings about certain viruses went largely ignored.

With mystery illness, the causes of symptoms often aren't evident. There's no clear trigger, no clear explanation of someone's suffering. Doctors' training doesn't map out Point A and Point B. There's no rule book for them to follow. A skeptical physician may not even see a clear indication that someone *is* suffering—and so launch the patient on a continual search for validation that her or his condition is even real.

So many people with chronic illnesses aren't getting better. Sometimes it doesn't feel so much like a *merry*-go-round as a *glum*-go-round.

It's time for that to change.

I'm here to tell you that the fact that there's no rule book for mystery illness doesn't have to be a bad thing. Take the legal profession, for example. Countless people become lawyers because they're drawn to justice. They enroll in law school, get jobs . . . and then the realization hits that the justice they can bring to their clients is limited. It's all within the confines of human-devised, and sometimes unjust, laws. Having rule books isn't always a good thing.

Because there's no rule book for mystery illness, there are also no limits to recovery—if you plug in to the secrets I reveal in the pages to come. Healing is one of the greatest freedoms God offers us. Healing is the law of the universe, the light, or whatever you choose to call the higher source—not the law of humans—and so it grants true justice. Untethered by statute, healing from mystery illness can exceed imagination.

ADDICTED TO ANSWERS

The medical establishment is a bit of an addict—one that gets its fix from being the authority on health. So what can happen when neither alternative nor conventional doctors have the answers? Denial.

This denial may come in the form of mislabeling a condition instead of saying, "I don't know." It may come in the form of prescribing drugs or diets that hinder instead of heal. Or sometimes a physician may express that denial as dismissal—and refer a patient to a psychiatrist to "help" the patient with symptoms the physician insists are psychosomatic.

As with any addiction, the first step is for medical communities to admit they have a problem.

Whether conventional or alternative, traditional or nontraditional, if medical communities don't admit that the epidemic of women flattened by fatigue and muscle pain is real and that no one knows the true root cause, how are researchers ever going to find adequate funding to uncover the real cause of fibromyalgia? The same goes for every other mystery illness.

If you're ill, do you feel like you have decades to suffer before solutions surface in medical communities?

Many mothers come to me explaining that 20 years earlier, they came down with mystery symptoms and were diagnosed with thyroid disorder, migraines, hormone imbalances, or MS. Now they're watching their daughters go through the same exact thing. When they first got their diagnoses, these women say to me, they never would have thought that after two decades, medicine wouldn't have cures for their conditions, or even adequate explanations. They couldn't have guessed that medical advances regarding chronic conditions would have moved at such a glacial pace. They couldn't have imagined they'd have to watch their daughters suffer just as they did.

It shouldn't take ages to discover the true reason for a person's aches and pains or to discern a reliable treatment for those underlying issues. Patients shouldn't feel like they are fumbling in the dark for answers.

It's time for medical communities to be honest and open, to accept that the medical model needs to adapt and move forward, to make the same leaps and bounds regarding chronic illness that it's made in other areas, such as life-saving surgeries. If we're to avoid several more decades of nonsense names for disorders, then it's time for medicine to admit that diagnostic tests are sometimes inadequate or fallible, that doctors' training sometimes leaves them operating on guesswork alone.

It's time for the medical establishment to seek out the answers we'll explore in this book.

TYPES OF MYSTERY ILLNESS

Mystery illness falls into three categories.

The first type is *unnamed illness*. A person may go from doctor to doctor describing her or his symptoms, withstand test after test, and hear that nothing is wrong. The blood work, MRIs, ultrasounds, and other imaging and exams don't raise any red flags. Often the only explanation the patient receives for the aches and pains is that it's all in the patient's head—that she or he is a hypochondriac, anxious, depressed, overworked, or bored. This can be crazy-making to someone suffering from a legitimate disorder. And if a doctor does believe the patient's pain is real yet can't explain its cause, she or he may call it *idiopathic*—which is just a fancy word for "unknown."

Ineffective treatment is the second category of mystery illness. In this scenario, the medical establishment does have a name for a given set of symptoms, but no viable avenue for recovery. The prescribed treatment makes no difference in the patient's health, or it worsens the condition, or the patient is told that she or he is simply stuck with feeling this way for life. At best, a patient will receive medications that manage the symptoms—such as those of MS—but don't make the condition itself any better.

With the third type of mystery illness, *misdiagnosis,* the patient also receives a name for what ails her—except it's wrong. Sometimes diagnostic trends are responsible. For example, hormones have taken the blame for any number of women's ailments that have nothing to do with menopause, perimenopause, or even just hormonal imbalance. Practitioners want to help their patients, though, so if they hear of others giving certain labels to certain sets of symptoms, they may follow the movement. In fact, alternative doctors have recently gone down the hormone path, taking their cue from the past decades' hormone movement in conventional medicine. This is an example of how trends can cross over and blur the lines between alternative and conventional.

On the journey to find answers, people might find themselves in all three of these categories at one point or another. At the first doctor, a patient may hear that her or his symptoms are psychosomatic and that she or he should take up a hobby as a new focus and mood booster. The next practitioner may validate that there is a true problem, slap a name like lupus on it, then offer an ineffective course of treatment. Still not feeling well, the patient may turn to a third health professional, only to get a new diagnosis—this time incorrect—along with "remedies" that take her or him in the opposite direction from healing.

FADS AREN'T THE FUTURE

Fads in medicine don't become popular because they work.

Maybe a particular car or phone or clothing brand becomes trendy because of its quality and usefulness, or because it's fun, but diagnoses and treatments don't gather steam because of their healing benefits. The theory or thought process or catchphrase behind a medical trend has far more power over someone's consciousness than the results or benefits.

Health trends are a bait-and-switch. They attract people with the allure of vibrant well-being, meanwhile offering only time-wasting techniques and leading people to question their own commitment and capabilities. If they could just have stayed longer with that workout regimen, they tell themselves—or that protein powder routine or that diet that eliminated fruit—they could have achieved the results that were promised.

To understand how medical trends work, imagine a restaurant that always serves a special turkey dinner the week of Thanksgiving. The dinner has gotten so much hype over the years that the buzz trumps the meal itself. No one notices that the restaurant has never actually served turkey—the kitchen has secretly been cooking goose instead. If the meat tastes different from what one diner expected, he won't say anything and will just figure his own perception is off. It's a classic bait-and-switch, just like many medical trends.

Health trends are like the emperor with no clothes. They try to distract from what they lack with false confidence and denial. That's because health trends can have a life force all their own. If a belief system finds some followers who market it heavily and catchily, then as the decades pass, it can become a grizzly bear of power over common sense. This fad process is behind the mistaken belief that a no-carb diet will solve *Candida* issues, the incorrect conviction that Hashimoto's disease is a condition in which the body's own immune system attacks the thyroid, and the misguided attempts to treat Lyme disease with antibiotics.

Some trends aren't all bad. Let's look at what's going on with hypothyroidism. So many women are walking around with this condition, suffering, whether diagnostic tests have spotted it or not. A recent trend among sensitive integrative medical doctors is to recognize these women's symptoms as real, to validate that these women are neither hypochondriacs nor bored housewives. Such doctors will usually say, "It's not showing up on tests, but I think your thyroid is off," and then treat the disease with a combination of medication and diet.

This is progress for women who have felt continually disregarded. At the same time, hypothyroidism is still in its mystery phase—because the doctors still haven't pointed to the underlying cause of the thyroid disease. The patients' hypothyroidism isn't going away, regardless of the medication they're taking. Many patients don't know that the thyroid medicine does nothing for the thyroid itself, nor was it originally prescribed for the thyroid. It doesn't eliminate the hypothyroidism. The thyroid stays underactive; the medication only helps curb the symptoms.

The same goes for any number of conditions. Take the ones I listed at the beginning of this chapter: fibromyalgia, lupus, Lyme disease, MS, chronic fatigue syndrome, migraines, colitis, rheumatoid arthritis, irritable bowel syndrome, celiac disease, insomnia, depression . . . It may seem like medical communities are addressing these illnesses because they have names, or because compelling theories surface about them, or because popular treatments are available. Yet it's important to understand that medicine is still in the Dark Ages when it comes to aches and pains and mystery disorders. You also have to know that misdiagnoses are rampant. There's still a lot of confusion in the medical world about what's causing what.

Which is all to say: trends aren't answers.

IT'S NOT IN YOUR HEAD

It's an all-too-common phenomenon, particularly for women: an actual, valid illness meets with skepticism, disregard, or misinformation from the establishment that's meant to have the answers. Doctors can't help that they don't know the causes of these debilitating mystery symptoms—or that they have the wrong culprit pegged for a particular disorder. In some cases the funding just isn't there for the research that's needed, or fads take studies in the wrong direction. In other cases, it's only a matter of time (though sometimes decades) before the right diagnostic technology will be available.

Physicians are often taught that in the absence of explanations, it's a genuine help to tell patients that their conditions are psychosomatic. The health-care establishment believes this will give patients some sort of wake-up call, which would be true . . . if the illnesses were just in people's heads.

Most of the time, there's an actual, physical root to a chronic mystery condition; medical communities just haven't named it yet or figured out what makes it better. It can take years and thousands of dollars before people dealing with mystery illness find me. Friends and family may have begged them to stop the search, urged them to accept their diagnoses and the hands they've been dealt. Still, something has pushed them forward: the primal will to survive, the determination to make the most of life, the instinct that they deserve to be healthy.

There aren't any words for the relief these clients find, or how empowered they become, once they understand what was really behind their suffering.

Now it's your turn to learn: You are not to blame for your illness. It's not something you manifested or attracted. It's not your fault. You certainly don't deserve to feel unwell. You have a God-given right to heal.

If you've dealt with chronic illness, then I'm sure you've dealt with the people who say, "But you look perfectly healthy." You've no doubt stopped giving an honest answer to, "How are you?" because you can't bear to hear, "You're *still* not better?" It's less emotionally damaging to pretend you're fine than to listen as someone insists that a particular therapy will solve all your problems—as though you haven't already gone to the ends of the earth trying to find answers. You've probably listened as countless people have described their family members' struggles with illness—as though those experiences trump your own.

When you're healthy, it's easy to spout theories about how those who are sick just need to change their mind-sets. When you don't understand the true nature of illness, it's easy to think it's because a person is holding herself or himself back with a fear of healing, or that she or he is a malingerer who secretly enjoys the attention this malady brings.

Anyone who's told you these are the reasons for your illness hasn't been there. These ideas make things so much worse for those who suffer from mystery illness. They cause people to feel ashamed of their problems and avoid asking for help—to feel like they have to hide their suffering out of worry they'll be called out as fakes.

Let's make it crystal clear: Nobody wants to be sick or compromised. Nobody has a fear of healing.

What people fear is being ill, and that's what causes healthy people to utter insensitive remarks. What they're really saying is, "I'll never have to go through what you're going through, right?"

What you need them to say is, "I hear you, I see you, I believe you, and I believe *in* you. What you're going through is valid, *and* there must be some way to triumph over it. I'll hang in there with you for the long haul."

In the process of healing, knowing the cause of your condition (and knowing what *isn't* the cause) is half the battle. The next step is learning how to make it better. If you follow the guidelines for how to use the chapters ahead that I laid out in the introduction, this book will help you do both.

Spirit has the answers. He wants you to learn the secrets behind mystery illness. He wants you and your loved ones to get better, to have a clear sense of direction on how to move forward, to have control over your life.

Spirit understands, with the utmost compassion, what people suffer on this earth.

God granted me the ability to access vast, highly advanced healing information through Spirit. Because of this, countless men, women, and children who've come to me have found the solutions to their chronic mystery illnesses and regained control over their health, achieving complete recovery. In the chapters that follow, you can find solutions, too.

CASE HISTORY:
The Real Heal

Lila* was a 34-year-old real estate agent when she started to experience mental fogginess, weakness, fatigue, pressure in her ears, and numbness in her extremities. Her symptoms soon got in the way of her job. She could tell that her fellow agents had noticed she was dropping the ball with some of her clients—forgetting appointments and staging second-rate open houses. Lila frequently failed to recall addresses and names and found herself so fatigued after a day at work that the next morning, she would sleep through her alarm. At property closings, she was on edge, unable to think through the mortgage details coherently, and fuzzy on the numbers, which had once been her strength.

Finally, Lila had to admit to herself and her employer that she was sick. She sat down with her supervisor, who recommended a doctor. At her first appointment, Lila listed her symptoms, but after an exam, the physician couldn't pinpoint a physical cause and declared her perfectly healthy. Depression, he said, was probably behind her ailments.

Lila tried to work with this. Determined to ward off her tiredness, mental fog, and other complaints with a sunny disposition, she returned to her job. Anything that felt like a symptom, she told herself, was a manifestation of her frame of mind. Maybe she'd just been craving attention.

But she started missing more house showings because she was unable to rise from bed, her hands felt too numb to drive, or she was embarrassed that she'd been too weak to bathe. It soon became apparent to Lila and those at her office that no matter her outlook, she was unable to do her job and needed to take a leave of absence. She dragged herself back to the doctor and reiterated her plight. He examined her again and once more concluded that she was perfectly fine. "I'm not going to be the doctor who lets you collect disability," he said.

Devastated and now in survival mode, Lila sought out a second opinion. She submitted to a battery of tests, only to have her new M.D. play it safe and back up the first doctor's ruling. He, too, refused to provide the documentation she needed to receive disability benefits.

---

* Names and other select client details throughout have been changed to protect client privacy.

This was just the beginning of Lila's years-long journey through the conventional and alternative medical worlds, searching for explanations of her mystery illness. Along the way, she had a few glimpses of hope, but every time she thought she'd found a name for her condition or a shot at getting better, she found herself right back where she'd started—or worse.

That is, until she came to me. Spirit provided the long-awaited insights that Lila knew existed, including the underlying cause of her downward spiral and instructions to regain her health. Before long, Lila felt better than she had since she could remember. Her renewed energy brought her renewed trust and delight in life, and she was able to devote herself to her job once more—as well as explore passions she'd neglected for years.

In this book, you'll read about many cases such as Lila's. You might notice a pattern, and you may identify with it: the years of being ill with no validation, the doctor-shopping journey, the isolation, confusion, and frustration. You may resonate with the stories where someone *does* get validation for her or his illness—but it's a misleading validation, either in the form of a misdiagnosis or a prescribed path of healing that leads nowhere fast.

None of the stories end there. You don't have to get stuck in the endless cycle of guesswork. Just like Lila, you can solve the mystery—and real healing can happen.

PART II

THE
HIDDEN
EPIDEMIC

CHAPTER 3

Epstein-Barr Virus, Chronic Fatigue Syndrome, and Fibromyalgia

The *Epstein-Barr virus* (EBV) has created a secret epidemic. Out of the roughly 320 million people in the U.S.,[1] over 225 million Americans have some form of EBV.

Epstein-Barr is responsible for mystery illnesses of every category: For some people, it creates fatigue and pain that go unnamed. For others, EBV symptoms prompt doctors to prescribe ineffective treatments, such as hormone replacement. And for so many people walking around with EBV, it gets misdiagnosed.

Among the reasons EBV is thriving: so little is understood about it. Medical communities are aware of only one version of EBV, but there are actually over 60 varieties. Epstein-Barr is behind several of the debilitating illnesses that stump doctors. As I said in the Introduction, it's the mystery illness of mystery illnesses.

Doctors have no idea how the virus operates long-term and how problematic it can be. The truth is, EBV is the source of numerous health problems that are currently considered mystery illnesses, such as fibromyalgia and chronic fatigue syndrome. EBV is also the cause of some major maladies that medical communities think they understand but really don't—including thyroid disease, vertigo, and tinnitus.

This chapter explains when the Epstein-Barr virus arose, how it's transmitted, how it operates to create untold havoc in strategic stages no one knows about, and the steps (never revealed before) that can destroy the virus and restore health.

EPSTEIN-BARR ORIGINS AND TRANSMISSION

Though Epstein-Barr was discovered by two brilliant physicians in 1964, it had actually begun taking hold in the early 1900s—over half a century before. EBV's initial versions—which are still with us— are relatively slow to act, and might not even create notable symptoms until late in life. Even then, they're only mildly harmful. Many people have these nonaggressive EBV strains.

Unfortunately, EBV has evolved over the decades, and each generation of the virus has grown more challenging than the one before.

Until the publication of this book, those with EBV would typically be stuck with it for the rest of their lives. Doctors seldom recognize EBV as the root cause of the myriad of problems it creates; plus doctors have no idea how to address the Epstein-Barr virus even when it is recognized.

There are many ways to catch EBV. For example, you can get it as a baby if your mother has the virus. You can also get it through infected blood. Hospitals don't screen for the virus, so any blood transfusion puts you at risk. You can even get it from eating out! That's because chefs are under tremendous pressure to get dishes prepared quickly. They often end up cutting a finger or hand, slapping on a Band-Aid, and continuing to work. Their blood can get into the food . . . and if they happen to have EBV during a contagious phase, that can be enough to infect you.

Transmission can also happen through other bodily fluids, such as those exchanged during sex. Under some circumstances, even a kiss can be enough to transmit EBV.

Someone with the virus isn't contagious all the time, though. It's most likely to spread during its Stage Two. Which brings up something else that until now hasn't been revealed: EBV goes through four stages.

EPSTEIN-BARR STAGE ONE

If you catch EBV, it goes through an initial dormant period of floating around in your bloodstream doing little more than slowly replicating itself to build its numbers—and waiting for an opportunity to launch a more direct infection.

For example, if you physically exhaust yourself for weeks and give yourself no chance to fully recover, or allow your body to become deprived of essential nutrients such as zinc or vitamin B_{12}, or undergo a traumatic emotional experience such as a breakup or the death of a loved one, the virus will detect your stress-related hormones and choose that time to take advantage.

EBV will also often act when you're undergoing a major hormonal change—for example, during puberty, pregnancy, or menopause. A common scenario is when a woman goes through childbirth. Afterward, she may feel various symptoms, including fatigue, aches and pains, and depression. In this case EBV isn't exploiting your weakness, but the fact that hormones are a powerful food source for it—their abundance acts as a trigger. The hormones flooding through your body effectively does for the virus what spinach does for Popeye.

EBV is inhumanly patient. This Stage One period of fortifying itself and waiting for an ideal opportunity can take weeks, months, or even a decade or longer, depending on a variety of factors.

The virus is especially vulnerable during Stage One. However, it's also undetectable through tests and causes no symptoms, so you normally wouldn't know to fight it, because you wouldn't be aware it was there.

EPSTEIN-BARR STAGE TWO

At the end of Stage One, the Epstein-Barr virus is ready to do battle with your body. That's when EBV first makes its presence known . . . by turning into *mononucleosis*. This is the infamous mono that we all grow up hearing about as the "kissing disease." It's what thousands of college students contract every year when they run themselves down with all-night partying and studying.

Medical communities are unaware that every case of mononucleosis is only Stage Two of EBV.

This is the period when the virus is most contagious. It's therefore advisable to avoid getting exposed to blood, saliva, or other bodily fluids from someone who has mono . . . or to avoid exposing anyone to your fluids if *you* have mono.

During this Stage Two, your body's immune system goes to war with the virus. It sends identifier cells to "tag" virus cells, i.e., place a hormone on them that marks them as invaders. It then sends soldier cells to seek out and kill the tagged virus cells. This is the power of your immune system coming to your defense.

How severely this battle rages will vary from person to person, because everyone is different, and it will also depend on what EBV strain or variety a person has. You can have mono for just a week or two with a mild scratchy throat and tiredness, in which case you aren't likely to realize what's really happening, so you most likely won't visit a doctor for a blood test.

Then again, you can get hit hard with fatigue, sore throat, fever, headaches, rashes, and more that hang on for several months. If this happens, the chances are you'll go see a doctor who'll test your blood, and the Epstein-Barr virus will show up as a form of mono . . . most of the time.

It's during this stage that EBV seeks a long-term home by making a run for one or more of your major organs—typically your liver and/or spleen. EBV loves being in these organs because mercury, dioxins, and other toxins are likely to accumulate there. The virus thrives on these poisons.

One other secret about EBV is that it has a best friend, a bacterium called *Streptococcus*. In such cases your body is dealing with not only a virus, but also bacteria that further confuse the immune system and produce their own array of symptoms. This is Epstein-Barr's number one *cofactor*.

During EBV's Stage Two, *Streptococcus* can travel up to create strep throat and/or infest the sinuses, nose, or mouth. It can also travel down to create infections in the urinary tract, vagina, kidneys, or bladder . . . eventually causing cystitis.

EPSTEIN-BARR STAGE THREE

Once the virus settles into your liver, spleen, and/or other organs, it nests there.

From this point on, when a doctor tests for Epstein-Barr, she or he will find antibodies and take these to indicate a *past* infection, when EBV was in its mono phase. The doctor will not find the EBV presently active in the bloodstream. The confusion here is one of the biggest blunders in medical history—this is how this virus has slipped through the cracks. Unless you have already followed the measures outlined in this book to kill the EBV, the virus *is,* in fact, still alive and causing new symptoms . . . and it's eluding the tests. That's because it's living in the liver, spleen, or other organs, and the test to detect this has not yet been invented.

With the virus hiding undetected in your organs, your body assumes it's won the war and the invader has been destroyed. Your immune system returns to its normal state, your mononucleosis ends, and your doctor tells you that you're healthy.

Unfortunately, the Epstein-Barr virus has barely begun its voyage through your body.

If you have a typical variety, EBV could lie dormant in your organs for years—possibly for decades—without your knowing it. If you have an especially aggressive variety, though, EBV may create serious problems even while it's nesting.

For example, the virus may burrow deep into your liver and spleen, causing those organs to become inflamed and enlarged. And once again, keep in mind that your doctor does not know to connect the dots between *past* EBV and its *present* activity in the organs.

The virus also creates three types of poison:

- EBV excretes toxic waste matter, or viral *byproduct.* This becomes increasingly significant as the virus grows more cells, and its expanding army keeps eating and excreting poisonous byproduct. This waste matter is often identified as spirochetes, which can trigger false positives on tests such as Lyme titers (screening tests for Lyme disease) and lead to a false diagnosis of Lyme.

- When a cell of the virus dies—which happens often, as the cells have a six-week life cycle—the *corpse* that is left behind is itself toxic and so further poisons your body. As with viral byproduct, this problem becomes more severe as EBV's army grows, creating fatigue.

- The poisons EBV creates through these two processes have the ability to generate a *neurotoxin*—i.e., a poison that disrupts nerve function and confuses your immune system. It will secrete this special toxin at strategic periods during Stage Three, and continuously during Stage Four, to prevent your immune system from zeroing in on the virus and attacking it.

The issues that may result from an aggressive variety of EBV nesting in your organs include:

- Your liver performing so sluggishly that it does a poor job of flushing toxins out of your system.

- *Hepatitis C.* (EBV is actually the primary cause of hepatitis C.)

- Your liver's sluggish performance leading to the lowering of your stomach's hydrochloric acid and your intestinal tract starting to become toxic. This in turn can result in some food not being fully digested and instead putrefying in your intestinal tract, resulting in bloating and/or constipation.

- Your developing sensitivities to foods that never caused you problems before. This happens when the virus consumes a food it likes, such as cheese, and transforms it into something your body doesn't recognize.

The virus bides its time until it senses stress-related hormones indicating you're in an especially vulnerable state—say, as a result of burning the candle at both ends, enduring a severe emotional blow, or suffering a physical jolt such as being in a car accident—or when it senses you're undergoing hormonal upheaval, such as during pregnancy or menopause.

When the virus is nearly ready to spring, it begins excreting its neurotoxin. This adds to the burden on your system already created by EBV's byproduct and virus corpses. All this poison in your system finally triggers your immune system—and also thoroughly confuses it, because it has no idea where the toxins are coming from.

Lupus

The immune system response I've just described triggers the mysterious symptoms that doctors can diagnose as *lupus*. Medical communities have no understanding that lupus is just the body reacting to Epstein-Barr's byproducts and neurotoxins. It's the body having an allergic reaction to these neurotoxins, which then elevates the inflammatory markers that doctors search for to identify and diagnose lupus. In truth, lupus is just a viral infection of Epstein-Barr.

Hypothyroidism and Other Thyroid Disorders

While your immune system is in disarray, EBV takes advantage of the chaos by leaving the organs it's been nesting in and making a run for a different major organ or gland—which this time is your thyroid!

Medical communities aren't yet aware that EBV is the actual cause of most thyroid disorders and diseases—especially Hashimoto's, but also Graves', thyroid cancer, and other thyroid ills. (Thyroid disease is also sometimes caused by radiation; but in over 95 percent of cases, the culprit is Epstein-Barr.) Medical research has not yet uncovered the true causes of thyroid disorders, and it's still decades away from discovering that EBV is the virus that causes them. If a doctor gives you a Hashimoto's diagnosis, it really means that she or he doesn't know what's wrong. The claim is that your body is attacking your thyroid—a view that arises from misinformation. In truth, it's the EBV—not your body—attacking the thyroid.

Once in your thyroid, EBV begins drilling into its tissues. The virus cells literally twist and spin like drills to burrow deep into the thyroid, killing thyroid cells and scarring the organ as they go, creating hidden hypothyroidism in millions of women, from mild cases to the more extreme. Your immune system notices this and tries to intervene, causing inflammation; but between EBV's neurotoxin, viral byproduct, and poisonous corpses confusing things, and with EBV hiding in your thyroid, your immune system can't tag the virus for complete destruction.

While the above may sound unnerving, don't let it rattle you; your thyroid has the ability to rejuvenate and heal itself when it's given what it needs. And never underestimate the power of your immune system, which by the end of this chapter will become activated just by you learning the truth.

As a fallback option, your immune system tries to wall off the virus with calcium, creating nodules in your thyroid. However, this doesn't hurt EBV. First, most of its cells evade this attack and remain free. Second, a virus cell that your immune system successfully walls off typically remains alive and turns its calcium prison into a comfortable home, where it feeds on your thyroid, draining it of energy. The virus cell might even eventually transform its prison into a living growth, called a *cyst,* that creates further strain on your thyroid.

Meanwhile, these attacks against EBV can hurt *you* if you aren't eating enough calcium-rich foods. That's because if your immune system can't get the calcium to wall off the virus from your bloodstream, it'll extract what it needs from your bones . . . which can lead to osteoporosis.

Simultaneously, the hundreds of virus cells that *aren't* imprisoned in nodules can weaken your thyroid, making it less effective at producing the hormones your body needs to function. This lack of adequate thyroid hormones, coupled with EBV's toxins, can in turn lead to weight gain, fatigue, mental fogginess, impaired memory, depression, hair loss, insomnia, brittle nails, muscle weakness, and/or dozens of other symptoms.

Some especially rare, aggressive varieties of EBV go even further. They create *cancer* in the thyroid. The rate of thyroid cancer in the U.S. has been rising rapidly. Medical communities don't know that the cause is an increase in rare, aggressive forms of EBV.

The Epstein-Barr virus invades your thyroid for a strategic reason: it's seeking to confuse and place stress on your endocrine system. The strain on your adrenal glands produces more adrenaline, which is a favored food of EBV that makes it stronger and better able to go after its ultimate target: your nervous system.

EPSTEIN-BARR STAGE FOUR

The ultimate goal of the Epstein-Barr virus is to leave your thyroid and inflame your central nervous system.

Your immune system normally wouldn't allow this to happen. But if EBV has successfully worn you down in Stage Three by entering your thyroid, and if on top of that you abruptly get clobbered with some physical or severe emotional injury, the virus will take advantage of your vulnerability and start to cause a multitude of strange symptoms that range from heart palpitations to generalized aches and pains to nerve pain.

A common scenario is being in an accident, getting surgery, or suffering some other physical damage, and then feeling awful for much longer than would be expected from the injury alone. A typical reaction is to "feel like a truck hit me."

Blood tests, X-rays, and MRIs will reveal nothing wrong, so doctors won't be aware of the virus inflaming the nerves. Stage Four Epstein-Barr is therefore a major source of mystery illnesses—that is, problems that cause doctors massive confusion.

What's actually happening is that your injured nerves trigger an "alarm" hormone to notify your body that the nerves are exposed and need repair. In Stage Four, EBV detects that hormone and rushes over to latch onto those damaged nerves.

A nerve is similar to a string of yarn with little root hairs hanging off it. When the nerve is injured, the root hairs pop off the sides of the nerve sheath. EBV looks for those openings and grabs onto them. If it succeeds, it can keep the area inflamed for years. As a result, you can have a relatively small injury that remains flared up and causes you continual pain.

The issues that result from this viral inflammation can include muscle pain, joint pain, painful tender points, back pain, tingling and/or numbness in the hands and feet, migraines, ongoing fatigue, dizziness, eye floaters, insomnia, unrestful sleep, and night sweats. Patients with these issues are sometimes diagnosed as having fibromyalgia, chronic fatigue syndrome, or rheumatoid arthritis, all of which are collections of symptoms that medical communities admit they don't understand and for which they have no cure. In such cases the patients are given inappropriate treatments that don't begin to address the real culprit—because these mystery illnesses are really Stage Four Epstein-Barr.

One of the greatest missteps of all time is mistaking women's Epstein-Barr symptoms for perimenopause and menopause. Symptoms such as hot flashes, night sweats, heart palpitations, dizziness, depression, hair loss, and anxiety were and are frequently misinterpreted as hormonal change—which is what launched the disastrous HRT movement. (To learn more, see Chapter 15, "Premenstrual Syndrome and Menopause.")

Let's take a closer look at the chronic illnesses that have puzzled doctors for decades and are the result of Stage Four Epstein-Barr.

Chronic Fatigue Syndrome

There's a long history of womankind facing denial that there's a physical cause of their suffering. Like those with fibromyalgia (see below), people with chronic fatigue syndrome (CFS)—also known by names such as *myalgic encephalomyelitis/chronic fatigue syndrome* (ME/CFS), *chronic fatigue immune dysfunction syndrome* (CFIDS), and *systemic exertion intolerance disease* (SEID)—often hear that they are liars, lazy, delusional, and/or crazy. It's an illness that affects women in disproportionately large numbers.

And chronic fatigue syndrome is on the rise.

It's becoming common for young women in college to return home mid-semester with the condition, unable to do anything but lie in bed. Contracting CFS as a woman in your late teens or early 20s can be particularly devastating as you watch friends move on with relationships and jobs, meanwhile feeling stuck and unable to live up to your potential.

Women who get CFS in their 30s, 40s, or 50s have their own obstacles: while you're old enough at this point to have an established life and support network, you also have established responsibilities. You're likely trying to be everything to everybody, taking care of more than you can handle, and so you feel the pressure to act normal when CFS hits.

Compounding the isolation for both age groups are the feelings of guilt, fear, and shame that accompany their misdiagnoses. I'm sure that if you have CFS, you've been in the depths of physical suffering and had someone say, "But you look perfectly healthy." It is so disheartening to feel unwell and hear from practitioners, friends, or family that there's nothing wrong with you.

Chronic fatigue syndrome is real. It's the Epstein-Barr virus.

As we've seen, those with CFS have an elevated viral load of EBV, which systematically afflicts the body by creating a neurotoxin that inflames the central nervous system. This can eventually weaken the adrenals and digestive system, and create the feeling that you have a low battery.

Fibromyalgia

We've had over six decades of medical denial that *fibromyalgia* is a legitimate problem. Now, medical communities are finally accepting it as an actual condition.

The best explanation doctors are given by the establishment, though, is that fibromyalgia is overactive nerves. What this really translates to is . . . no one has a clue. It's not the doctors' fault. There's no magic book they receive that tells them what will help their fibromyalgia patients or what is genuinely causing their pain.

The medical system is still years from discovering the illness's true root—because it's viral, and it takes place at a nerve level that medical tools currently can't detect.

Those suffering from fibromyalgia are under a very real and debilitating attack. It's the Epstein-Barr virus that is causing this disorder, inflaming both the central nervous system and nerves throughout the body, which creates ongoing pain, sensitivity to touch, severe fatigue, and a host of other issues.

Tinnitus

Tinnitus, or ringing in the ear, is usually caused by EBV getting into the inner ear's nerve channel, called the labyrinth. The ringing is the result of the virus inflaming and vibrating the labyrinth and the vestibulocochlear nerve.

Vertigo and Ménière's Disease

Vertigo and *Ménière's disease* are often attributed by doctors to calcium crystals, or *stones,* becoming disrupted in the inner ear. However, most chronic cases are actually caused by EBV's neurotoxin inflaming the vagus nerve.

Other Symptoms

Anxiety, dizziness, chest tightness, chest pain, esophageal spasms, and asthma can also be caused by EBV inflaming the vagus nerve.

Insomnia, and tingling and numbness in hands and feet, can be caused by phrenic nerves becoming perpetually inflamed by EBV.

And heart palpitations can result from buildup of EBV's poisonous virus corpses and byproduct in the heart's mitral valve.

If you have EBV, or suspect you do, you may find the virus in Stage Four beyond frustrating. Take comfort. If you take the right steps—which medical communities don't know about yet, but which are covered at the end of this chapter—you can recover, rebuild your immune system, return to a normal state again, and regain control of your life.

TYPES OF EPSTEIN-BARR

As I've noted earlier, there are over 60 varieties of the Epstein-Barr virus. That number is so large because EBV has existed for well over 100 years. It's had generations of people to move through, mutating and elevating its various hybrids and strains in that time. The strains can be organized into six groups of escalating severity, with roughly ten types per group.

EBV Group 1 is the oldest and mildest. These versions of the virus typically take years, even decades, to transition from one stage to another. Their effects might not be noticeable until you're in your 70s or 80s, and then result in little more than back pain. They might even remain in your organs and never reach Stage Three or Stage Four.

EBV Group 2 moves from stage to stage a bit quicker than Group 1; you might notice symptoms in your 50s or 60s. These varieties may partially linger in the thyroid and send only some of their virus cells out to inflame nerves, resulting in relatively mild nerve inflammation. The only variety of EBV that medical communities are aware of is in this group.

EBV Group 3 will transition between stages faster than Group 2, so its symptoms might be noticeable around age 40. Also, these viruses fully complete Stage Four—that is, they entirely leave the thyroid to latch onto nerves. Viruses in this group can cause a variety of ills, including joint pain, fatigue, heart palpitations, tinnitus, and vertigo.

EBV Group 4 will create noticeable problems as early as age 30. Its aggressive actions on nerves can result in symptoms associated with fibromyalgia, chronic fatigue syndrome, brain fog, confusion, anxiety, moodiness, and everything caused by Groups 1 to 3. This group can also create symptoms of posttraumatic stress disorder, even if a person never underwent any trauma beyond getting inflamed by the virus.

EBV Group 5 will create noticeable issues as early as age 20. This is an especially nasty form of the virus because it strikes just when a young person is setting out to start an independent life. It can create all the problems of Group 4, and it feeds off negative emotions such as fear and worry. Doctors who can't find anything wrong, and perceive these patients as young and healthy, often declare "it's all in your head" and send them to psychologists to convince them what's actually happening in their bodies isn't real. Unless, that is, a patient happens upon a doctor who's up on the Lyme disease trend, in which case the patient will probably walk away with a Lyme misdiagnosis.

The worst type, however, is EBV Group 6, which can strike hard even in young children. In addition to everything Group 5 does, Group 6 can create symptoms so severe that they're misdiagnosed as leukemia, viral meningitis, lupus, and more. Plus it suppresses the immune system, which can lead to a wide variety of symptoms including rashes, weakness in the limbs, and severe nerve pain.

HEALING FROM THE EPSTEIN-BARR VIRUS

Because it's very easy to catch and hard to detect, and can cause a number of mysterious symptoms, you might understandably find the Epstein-Barr virus overwhelming and its effects disheartening.

The good news is that if you carefully and patiently follow the steps detailed in this section, and in Part IV of the book, you can heal. You can recover your immune system, free yourself of EBV, rejuvenate your body, gain full control over your health, and move on with your life.

How long the process takes varies for each individual and depends on myriad factors. Some people conquer the virus in as little as three months. However, a more typical period is a full year. And there are some people who need 18 months or more to destroy EBV.

Healing Foods

Certain fruits and vegetables can help your body rid itself of EBV and heal from its effects. The following are the best ones to incorporate into your diet (listed in rough order of importance). Try to eat at least three of these foods per day—the more the better—rotating your consumption so that in a given week or two, you get all of these foods into your system.

- **Wild blueberries:** help restore the central nervous system and flush EBV neurotoxins out of the liver.

- **Celery:** strengthens hydrochloric acid in the gut and provides mineral salts to the central nervous system.

- **Sprouts:** high in zinc and selenium to strengthen the immune system against EBV.

- **Asparagus:** cleanses the liver and spleen; strengthens the pancreas.

- **Spinach:** creates an alkaline environment in the body and provides highly absorbable micronutrients to the nervous system.

- **Cilantro:** removes heavy metals such as mercury and lead, which are favored foods of EBV.

- **Parsley:** removes high levels of copper and aluminum, which feed EBV.

- **Coconut oil:** antiviral and acts as an anti-inflammatory.

- **Garlic:** antiviral and antibacterial that defends against EBV.

- **Ginger:** helps with nutrient assimilation and relieves spasms associated with EBV.

- **Raspberries:** rich in antioxidants to remove free radicals from the organs and bloodstream.

- **Lettuce:** stimulates peristaltic action in the intestinal tract and helps cleanse EBV from the liver.

- **Papayas:** restore the central nervous system; strengthen and rebuild hydrochloric acid in the gut.

- **Apricots:** immune system rebuilders that also strengthen the blood.

- **Pomegranates:** help detox and cleanse the blood as well as the lymphatic system.

- **Grapefruit:** rich source of bioflavonoids and calcium to support the immune system and flush toxins out of the body.

- **Kale:** high in specific alkaloids that protect against viruses such as EBV.

- **Sweet potatoes:** help cleanse and detox the liver from EBV byproducts and toxins.

- **Cucumbers:** strengthen the adrenals and kidneys and flush neurotoxins out of the bloodstream.

- **Fennel:** contains strong antiviral compounds to fight off EBV.

Healing Herbs and Supplements

The following herbs and supplements (listed in rough order of importance) can further strengthen your immune system and aid your body in healing from the virus's effects:

- **Cat's claw:** herb that reduces EBV and cofactors such as strep A and strep B.

- **Silver hydrosol:** lowers EBV viral load.

- **Zinc:** strengthens the immune system and protects the thyroid from EBV inflammation.

- **Vitamin B$_{12}$ (as methylcobalamin and/or adenosylcobalamin):** strengthens the central nervous system.

- **Licorice root:** lowers EBV production and strengthens the adrenals and kidneys.

- **Lemon balm:** antiviral and antibacterial. Kills EBV cells and strengthens the immune system.

- **5-MTHF (5-methyltetrahydrofolate):** helps strengthen the endocrine system and central nervous system.

- **Selenium:** strengthens and protects the central nervous system.

- **Red marine algae:** powerful antiviral that removes heavy metals such as mercury and reduces viral load.

- **L-lysine:** lowers EBV load and acts as a central nervous system anti-inflammatory.

- **Spirulina (preferably from Hawaii):** rebuilds the central nervous system and eliminates heavy metals.

- **Ester-C:** strengthens the immune system and flushes EBV toxins from the liver.

- **Nettle leaf:** provides vital micronutrients to the brain, blood, and central nervous system.

- **Monolaurin:** antiviral; breaks down EBV load and reduces cofactors.

- **Elderberry:** antiviral; strengthens the immune system.

- **Red clover:** cleanses the liver, lymphatic system, and spleen of neurotoxins from EBV.

- **Star anise:** antiviral; helps destroy EBV in the liver and thyroid.

- **Curcumin:** component of turmeric that helps strengthen the endocrine system and central nervous system.

CASE HISTORY:
A Career Almost Lost to Epstein-Barr

Michelle and her husband, Matthew, both had high-paying corporate jobs. Michelle was a star at her firm and made a point of going to work throughout her pregnancy, leaving only when she was about to go into labor.

After giving birth, Michelle instantly fell in love with her new son, Jordan. She couldn't have been happier. *I have it all now,* she thought, *a career I love, and a family I love even more.*

But Michelle's bright future started to dim when she was struck with a fatigue she couldn't shake. No matter how many vitamins she took or how much she exercised, she felt run-down all the time. So Michelle visited her doctor. After giving her a physical, he dismissed her concerns: "You look fine to me. It's natural for a new baby to be exhausting. Just get more sleep and don't worry about it."

Michelle took care to sleep more. After another week, she felt worse than ever. Suspecting a post-pregnancy issue, Michelle went to see her OB/GYN. This doctor drew her blood for a number of tests, including several for thyroid disease. When the lab results came in, the OB/GYN correctly diagnosed Michelle as having Hashimoto's—i.e., her thyroid was no longer producing the level of hormones needed.

Michelle was put on thyroid medication to get her hormone levels back to normal. This made her feel a little better . . . though not quite as well as she had before her pregnancy. She'd been aiming to return to work a month after having her son, and now she had to postpone those plans.

After about six months, Michelle's fatigue was back—and much more severe. That's when Michelle's troubles really began. Soon she had trouble taking care of Jordan. Matthew agreed to help out until she felt better.

Instead, Michelle grew worse. On top of being tired, she started to feel aches and pains, especially in her joints. Michelle returned to her OB/GYN, who ran another set of tests. The lab results showed nothing wrong. Thanks to the thyroid medication Michelle was continuing to take, her thyroid levels were perfect. So were all her vitamin and mineral levels. The OB/GYN was baffled.

Suspecting that Michelle's symptoms were related to her thyroid condition, the OB/GYN referred Michelle to a top endocrinologist (a doctor who specializes in hormonal issues). The specialist conducted a thorough thyroid profile, and tested Michelle's other hormone levels from a variety of angles. He ended up telling Michelle she had "mild adrenal fatigue."

There was some small truth to that. Michelle's adrenal glands were being strained by the Epstein-Barr virus, which her pregnancy had triggered and which was now inflaming her thyroid.

The endocrinologist told Michelle to take it easy and avoid stress. On his recommendation, Michelle handed off the freelance consulting projects she'd been working on from home.

In reality, Michelle's job had nothing to do with her condition. Her source of stress wasn't her work, but the illness that was eating away at her life . . . and her seeming helplessness to understand it or do anything about it.

Michelle continued to get worse. Her knees flared up and swelled, making it difficult to walk. She bought knee supports . . . and decided to pursue help more aggressively. Michelle's intuition told her an invader was present in her body, so she went to see an infectious disease specialist. This would be precisely the right thing to do—if infectious disease doctors actually knew how to recognize and treat past infections of EBV.

Unfortunately, they don't. So after running an exhausting battery of tests and noticing that Michelle had an antibody from a past EBV infection, he dismissed it as a problem right away. This doctor told her she was physically fit. He added that she might be depressed, and offered to refer her to a psychiatrist.

Infuriated at being made to feel she was crazy for trying to address what she deeply sensed was a real physical problem, Michelle (painfully) rose and strode out of the room.

With increasing desperation, Michelle now visited doctors across the spectrum. They put her through ultrasounds, X-rays, MRIs, CT scans, and loads of blood tests. She was told she had *Candida*, fibromyalgia, MS, lupus, Lyme disease, and rheumatoid arthritis. None of it was right. She was put on immunosuppressant drugs, antibiotics, and loads of different supplements. None of the treatments helped.

Michelle became an insomniac, suffered heart palpitations, and developed chronic vertigo that caused dizziness and nausea. She dropped from 140 to 115 pounds.

Soon, Michelle was spending most of her days in bed. She was wasting away. Her husband, Matthew, was terrified.

After Michelle had spent four years exploring all other options, and based on the recommendation of the naturopath Michelle visited, Matthew called my office as a last resort. When my assistant answered, Matthew burst into tears. "What's wrong?" she asked.

He replied, "My wife is dying."

For our first appointment Matthew planned to do most of the talking while sitting next to Michelle, who was in bed. Less than a minute after Matthew started telling me Michelle's story, I interrupted him. "It's okay," I said. "Spirit tells me it's an aggressive form of the Epstein-Barr virus."

The virus's neurotoxin was inflaming all of Michelle's joints. Her insomnia and foot pain were the result of her phrenic nerves being perpetually inflamed. Her vertigo stemmed from EBV's neurotoxin inflaming her vagus nerve. And her heart palpitations were being caused by buildup of EBV virus corpses and viral byproduct in her mitral valve.

"Don't worry," I told Michelle and Matthew. "I know how to beat this virus."

Michelle exclaimed, with as much joyful energy as she could muster, "I knew it was a virus!"

It was the first critical step in her recovery.

I recommended a blend of celery juice and papaya, which is great for boosting someone in Michelle's condition (e.g., low weight, not being able to eat, high number of virus cells). I followed that up with the recommendations for healing in this chapter, including a list of helpful supplements, as well as the recommendations from Part IV, "How to Finally Heal."

The cleanse diet immediately stopped feeding Michelle's EBV. Within a week, there was a noticeable reduction of the swelling in her knees. The L-lysine shut down Michelle's vertigo. And the other supplements started killing virus cells and/or dampening the production of new ones.

In three months, Michelle was regularly up and walking again. In nine months, she was once again working part-time at her challenging corporate job.

And in 18 months, Michelle's pain and suffering were just a memory—she'd taken control over EBV. Today, Michelle has fully recovered her health. She's returned to juggling her job and her family energetically and happily.

CASE HISTORY:
An End to CFS Confinement

Cynthia was a mother of two. Shortly after her youngest, Sophie, was born, Cynthia began experiencing fatigue. It took everything she had to push through the day, and she relied on increasing her coffee intake just to function. Within a few years, she had to quit her part-time job at a clothing store because long naps were taking up her afternoons. She needed the rest so she could be strong enough to meet her kids at the school bus, make dinner, and help them with their homework.

Cynthia noticed herself becoming irritable, and arguments arose often with her husband, Mark, who didn't understand why she was tired all the time. After all, the tests that Cynthia's doctor had run indicated nothing was wrong. The doctor said she was healthy and concluded that maybe she was just unhappy or depressed.

This made Cynthia want to walk out of the doctor's office without another word. Any blue mood she experienced was because she was tired all the time and could barely function—not the other way around. Yet her husband sided with the doctor and became increasingly resentful toward her.

The ongoing stress put Cynthia on overload; life felt impossible to keep up with. She couldn't find the energy to brush her hair, and the mere thought of running the vacuum cleaner or washing the dishes exhausted her. From the outside, it looked like she was giving up on life. Mark got angrier—he was talking separation now. "I work too long and hard at the office all day to worry about taking care of things at home," he said. "This is supposed to be your department."

Cynthia felt more pressure than ever to get better, but the worries about her marriage and what would happen to her children put her fatigue at an all-time high. She could barely drive to the grocery store or make dinner for her family. All she could do was lie in bed or on the couch.

This is what a moderate-to-severe case of undiagnosed chronic fatigue syndrome can look like. When Cynthia called me, her life had fallen apart. Her husband had left her, and her daughter, Sophie, now seven years old, and her son, Ryan, age nine, had lost their family unit. What her doctor had misconstrued as a psychiatric condition was an actual physical problem: Epstein-Barr virus. The same story applies to far too many women.

I set to work informing Cynthia that she had a case of EBV that her doctor had missed. With an emphasis on getting her viral load under control and addressing nutritional deficiencies, I laid out the background on CFS that I described earlier in this chapter, and I explained the protocols outlined here and in Part IV. Like her life depended on it—because it did—Cynthia followed Spirit's advice.

Slowly, Cynthia began to get better. Her adrenals recovered normal function, and her stamina returned. Once again, she could tend to her children, run errands, keep the house in shape, and do her hair—all without the gallons of coffee she used to rely on. Cynthia finally had the energy to return to work, too.

After witnessing this change in his wife, Mark called Cynthia and asked her out to dinner—his mother would look after the kids, he said. When they arrived at the fancy restaurant, which had long ago been the deli where they had flirted as college students, Mark told Cynthia he'd called ahead and ordered a special healing-food meal for her—and that he'd ordered the same for himself, out of solidarity. Over sundried-tomato hummus and vegetable nori rolls, Mark didn't exactly cry (some things would always stay the same), but he did have to dab at his eyes as he apologized for how he'd behaved.

Cynthia was quiet, then answered with a playful smile: "You can make it up to me."

After a few weeks of testing the waters—Cynthia wanted to make sure Mark didn't just want her back as a security blanket and housekeeper—they moved back in together as a family. Mark now wakes up early every Saturday morning so he can get to the farmers' market before they run out of salad greens.

CASE HISTORY:
Fibro Pain Forgotten

Stacy, a 41-year-old part-time receptionist in a doctors' office, had been married to Rob, who worked at a car dealership, for over 15 years. She never had the energy to keep up with the outings Rob planned with their daughters. In fact, she couldn't remember ever feeling that well. She always felt slightly achy and more tired than her friends seemed to be. And since she'd given birth to her second child, who was now 11, the fatigue and muscle soreness had been more pronounced.

One weekend while Rob and the kids were at a museum, she went for a longer walk than usual—she'd decided to push herself to lose some unwanted weight she'd gained in the last few years. Afterward, she noticed an unusual pain in her left knee. Thinking back to her college basketball coach's advice to "walk it off," she tried to ignore it.

It didn't go away. Two weeks later, she scheduled time for an exam with a doctor at her office. Stacy limped out of the appointment with a prescription for an MRI—which revealed nothing visibly wrong with her knee.

Because Stacy's balance was off from leaning on her "good" leg, she found herself tripping easily—stairs, curbs, and corners of rugs had become major obstacles. Then her right knee started to hurt even though it hadn't gotten injured in any of her falls, and exams showed nothing amiss. Stacy's worry escalated to fear—something was really wrong. The doctors in her office ruled out rheumatoid arthritis, though, and guessed that the extra 30 pounds Stacy was carrying were to blame for her pain.

Soon Stacy started to hurt in other places. Now she couldn't raise her hands over her head without her arms and neck hurting. She was unable to work anymore, and depression set in as she started to spend hours at home on the sofa. At night, Rob would make dinner for the family and send their daughter to serve Stacy her plate of food on the couch.

A specialist concluded that Stacy had fibromyalgia. When Stacy asked what caused it, the doctor responded, "We don't know. It's what we think is oversensitive nerves. This should help, though." She handed Stacy a prescription for a medicine popular for treating depression and fibromyalgia pain. At her next visit to the specialist, when Stacy reported no progress, the doctor referred her to me.

After I explained what her fibromyalgia really was, that the real cause was the Epstein-Barr virus and that it had been in her system since childhood, Stacy recalled having a bout of mononucleosis at age 14. She finally felt she had a real answer. She understood now that poor diet, nutritional deficiencies, and increased stress had triggered the formerly dormant EBV to surface as fibromyalgia. Not knowing what was wrong with her—the powerlessness—had been scarier than knowing the true cause; the mystery of her mystery illness had been the hardest part. Now she had direction and felt confident in her ability to heal.

Within six months of our first call, following the same suggestions I describe in this chapter and Part IV, "How to Finally Heal," she was free from fibromyalgia, back to work, and living life again. She told me she felt happier and healthier than ever, and that *she'd* planned the next family outing—apple picking at an organic orchard.

KNOWLEDGE IS POWER

The first step of the healing process is to know the cause of your suffering is Epstein-Barr—and to realize it's not your fault.

Your EBV-related health problems aren't the result of anything you did wrong or any moral failing. You didn't make this happen, and you're in no way to blame. You did not manifest this; you did not attract this. You're a vibrant, wonderful human being and you have every God-given right to heal. You *deserve* to heal.

Much of EBV's effectiveness stems from hiding in the shadows so that neither you nor your body's immune system can sense its presence. This not only allows it to commit its mayhem unchecked, it leads to negative emotions such as guilt, fear, and helplessness.

Now things are different for you. If you have EBV, you now have a mind-body understanding of what's causing your health problems. From this alone, your immune system will strengthen and the virus will naturally weaken. So when it comes to fighting EBV, in a very real sense, *knowledge is power*.

CHAPTER 4

Multiple Sclerosis

Since medical science first identified *multiple sclerosis* (MS), grave confusion has accompanied the condition. Every year, far too many people receive an MS misdiagnosis.

In the 1950s, 1960s, and early 1970s, the prevalence of mystery neurological symptoms in women was escalating, yet doctors interpreted their conditions as menopause, hormonal imbalance, or just plain psychosis. Women had an almost impossible time finding a medical professional who would validate their pain, tremors, fatigue, vertigo, and more as real symptoms. The only women who could get doctors to take them seriously on the subject were either wealthy or of advanced age.

It wasn't until enough men presented with the same symptoms in the 1960s and 1970s that the medical establishment began to take all of these mystery neurological symptoms seriously. As with many other illnesses, a man's word was taken over a woman's.

Doctors were overwhelmed by the diagnostic task, though, and turned to the label MS.

Multiple sclerosis is most notable for inflaming and damaging the central nervous system's protective layer and message facilitator, called the *myelin sheath*. Your nerves carry electrical signals that direct all the parts of your body; when any portion of your myelin sheath is damaged, the messages from the nerves underneath it can become scrambled, wreaking a wide assortment of havoc (depending on which areas of the nervous system are inflamed).

MS can lead to muscle pain and spasms, weakness and fatigue, mental problems, vision problems, hearing problems, dizziness, depression, digestive issues, and bladder and bowel dysfunction. It can also partially or completely paralyze legs, forcing you to use a cane, crutches, or even a wheelchair.

Around 150,000 Americans a year—85 percent of whom are women—are actually struck by multiple sclerosis.

And roughly another 150,000 a year are *misdiagnosed* as having MS when they really have something else. (More about this shortly.)

Receiving a diagnosis of MS can turn your world upside down— and it can be especially devastating when the diagnosis is wrong.

This chapter reveals the truth about MS . . . and how you can move past it and take back your life.

IDENTIFYING MULTIPLE SCLEROSIS

If you have multiple sclerosis, the damage to your central nervous system's myelin sheath—and the resulting nerve inflammation and scarring—is likely to create most of the following symptoms. Still, realize that you can have many of these symptoms but not have multiple sclerosis. Only if you have the worst forms of these might your condition be MS.

- Early on, eye issues such as blurred vision, double vision, diminished perception of color, eye pain, and/or complete loss of vision—usually in one eye at a time

- Chronic weakness and fatigue

- Chronic pain, especially in muscles throughout the body

- Tremors

- Numbness in the arms and/or legs—first on one side of the body and then the other

- Weakness or paralysis in the legs that leads to trouble walking or—in severe cases—becoming confined to a wheelchair

- Mental fogginess, such as difficulty concentrating

- Memory issues

- Slurred speech

Beyond this symptoms checklist, there are no definitive tests to pinpoint MS. That's in part why there are so many medical misdiagnoses of the disease.

If you match at least six of the most critical symptoms above in a serious, pronounced form—and if your doctor has ruled out other possible causes for them—you can try to confirm you have MS by asking a neurologist to perform an MRI looking for lesions (i.e., scarring or other damage) on the myelin sheath in the areas of the brain and spinal cord. If two or more lesions are found, it's evidence that your symptoms could be the result of multiple sclerosis.

That said, lesions are very difficult to spot even with medical science's current 3-D imaging tools (and that's not likely to change until around the year 2030). So if your neurologist can't find any lesions, that doesn't mean they don't exist.

Another thing to consider is whether you've had a history of ear infections, throat infections, sinus infections, and/or, if you're a woman, vaginal infections. These all will typically occur in childhood and early adulthood before the development of multiple sclerosis.

One other way to get a sense of what's ailing you is to better understand what MS actually is.

WHAT MULTIPLE SCLEROSIS *REALLY* IS

Medical communities believe multiple sclerosis is an autoimmune disease resulting from your immune system somehow confusing areas of your nerve sheath with invaders and attacking them.

As I say in other chapters, this is a philosophy that will hold back the truth in medical research for decades. The human body does *not* attack itself. Pathogens are to blame.

Medical communities also believe that there's no resolution for MS. They're mistaken here, too. The truth is that multiple sclerosis can be healed—and that it is actually a version of the Epstein-Barr virus.

As explained in Chapter 3, EBV is a virus that chronically inflames nerves. Most strains of EBV are mild and less aggressive, but its multiple sclerosis varieties eat away at the myelin sheath, which is what creates the distinct set of symptoms associated with this disease.

(As for your immune system, not only is it innocent of any wrongdoing, it's your primary defense against MS. When your immune system gets what it needs, recovery is possible—and within reach.)

Something else that distinguishes MS from other forms of EBV is that it's accompanied by a unique combination of bacteria, fungi, and heavy metals. Specifically, if you have MS, you'll typically have the following EBV cofactors in your system:

- *Streptococcus* A and *Streptococcus* B bacteria

- *H. pylori* bacteria (or at least a previous case of *H. pylori*)

- *Candida* fungus

- Cytomegalovirus

- The heavy metals copper, mercury, and aluminum—
  these metals weaken the immune system's ability to
  protect the body from viral nerve damage

While these cofactors help give MS its particular characteristics, at its core multiple sclerosis is just a form of EBV—and knowing this illuminates any dark mysteries surrounding the illness. While EBV *can* be dangerous in some cases, Chapter 3 lays out in detail what you need to understand it—including the steps you can take to end the damage the virus is causing, and eliminate nearly all of the virus and its cofactors.

HEALING FROM MULTIPLE SCLEROSIS

Doctors typically treat multiple sclerosis using immunosuppressant drugs and steroids in the mistaken belief that your immune system is the problem. However, your immune system is *not* attacking you—a *virus* is. Your only hope of killing your EBV is a strong and vibrant immune system—which these medications are designed to weaken. So not only are these drugs failing to help you defeat EBV, they're significantly aiding the virus.

The best approach is to read Chapter 3 to fully understand EBV. Because the strains of EBV causing multiple sclerosis are especially aggressive toward your myelin sheath, the following supplements are recommended specifically for MS. They'll help reduce pain and protect your myelin sheath as you heal from EBV:

- **EPA & DHA (eicosapentaenoic acid and docosahexaenoic acid):** omega-3 fats to help protect and fortify the myelin nerve sheath. Be sure to buy a plant-based (not fish-based) version.

- **L-glutamine:** amino acid that removes toxins such as MSG from the brain and protects neurons.

- **Lion's mane:** medicinal mushroom that helps protect the myelin sheath and support neuron function.

- **ALA (alpha lipoic acid):** helps repair damaged neurons and neurotransmitters. Also helps mend the myelin nerve sheath.

- **Monolaurin:** fatty acid that kills virus cells, bacteria cells, and other bad microbes (e.g., mold) in the brain.

- **Curcumin:** component of turmeric that reduces inflammation of the central nervous system and relieves pain.

- **Barley grass juice extract powder:** contains micronutrients that feed the central nervous system. Also helps feed brain tissue, neurons, and the myelin nerve sheath.

Understand that MS is not a life sentence. If a doctor has given you an accurate diagnosis, there's no reason to fear it. (And most likely, if you've heard you have MS, you were one of the many handed a misdiagnosis. The real culprit behind your symptoms may be EBV, just not a strain that causes lesions on the myelin nerve sheath.)

If you stick to the recommendations in this section, and most importantly comply with all of the pertinent advice in Chapter 3 and Part IV to restore your central nervous and immune systems, then typically within 3 to 18 months (depending on various factors, such as your current state of health), you'll rid yourself of nearly all of the virus inflaming your nerves, and be able to resume a normal and symptom-free life.

CASE HISTORY:
Nursed Back to Health by the Truth

Rebecca, age 41, was a nurse in a hospital emergency room. One afternoon, at the end of a long shift, another nurse didn't show up for work, and so Rebecca had to work another 12 hours, late into the night.

As she was driving home to relieve her mother of babysitting her ten-year-old son, Nicholas, the right side of Rebecca's face went numb. The numbness began to travel down her arm. She'd never experienced anything like it before, though she'd witnessed it in many patients over the years. Rebecca tried to pass it off as a symptom of overwork, though, and went to bed when she got home, hoping it would be gone by morning.

When she awoke, the numbness was still there—on the right side of her face, her nose, part of her mouth, and her arm and hand. Concerned that it was a stroke, Rebecca's mother drove her to the hospital. A doctor she knew looked at her immediately and ran a series of tests, including an MRI with contrast and an EKG. The tests didn't show any problems, so the doctor didn't think it was a stroke. She suspected anxiety was the culprit. "Give it some time, and we'll see if the symptoms ease up," she said, handing Rebecca a prescription for benzodiazepine.

Over the next few weeks, Rebecca experienced very little change. She tried to get along with her mystery numbness, but it was a distraction. Her right arm began to weaken. Eventually she felt that she couldn't handle her normal nursing duties, which included transporting people from stretchers and lifting various pieces of medical equipment. She decided to take a leave of absence—and ask the hospital's top neurologist for a consult.

After a slew of comprehensive tests, he told her it was the beginning of multiple sclerosis—even though Rebecca's MRI and brain scan showed no evidence of the disease. The neurologist said Rebecca should start to receive regular MRIs. Over time, the MS would appear on the imaging if it progressed. Until then, he prescribed medications used to treat MS, such as immunosuppressant drugs and steroids. Rebecca could barely contain a sob as she went to meet her mother in the waiting room. How was she going to take care of Nicholas?

Over the next six months, her symptoms progressed. Now the numbness was accompanied by dizzy spells, fatigue, and—after the latest MRI with contrast—brain fog. One day a nurse Rebecca had worked with, who was a client of mine, recommended that Rebecca call me and make an appointment.

First thing in the reading, Spirit informed me that Rebecca had a viral condition—a specific strain of EBV. "But I've been tested for the Epstein-Barr virus," Rebecca said. "It showed I didn't have a present infection in my blood, only an indication that I had an infection decades ago. That wouldn't be causing my problems now."

I explained that the EBV antibodies in the blood aren't necessarily an indication that the virus has left someone's system—but rather that it's traveled deeper into the body. In Rebecca's case, the Epstein-Barr was alive indeed and now affecting her central nervous system. I assured Rebecca that she didn't have multiple sclerosis.

"I'd give anything to believe that," she said.

"It's the truth," I told her, and went on to describe how in addition to the central nervous system, the EBV was inflaming her phrenic and trigeminal nerves, which accounted for the numbness. The virus was also releasing a neurotoxin that caused the dizziness, fatigue, and brain fog.

Finally, Rebecca was convinced. "It's like a weight has been lifted."

By following the protocols outlined in this chapter and in Part IV, Rebecca made a complete recovery within six months. She was free from her medication and returned to her position at the hospital. She no longer works overtime, because she feels that the stress from the extra shifts depleted her and allowed the EBV to take advantage.

Just understanding how her condition worked—and discovering that it wasn't a life sentence—made every difference to Rebecca's healing. She told me that without the knowledge of what was actually behind her mystery illness, she's sure she would have been carrying around the wrong diagnosis for the rest of her life.

CHAPTER 5

Rheumatoid Arthritis

Medical communities use the term *rheumatoid arthritis* (RA) as if it's a diagnosis for the condition that chronically and painfully inflames the joints. A better term would be *swollen joint disease,* or *joint hurting affliction,* or *unexplainable aches and pains disorder.* Because let's be honest here. If medical research hasn't uncovered the explanation for certain sets of symptoms—which it hasn't yet with RA—then it's better to call it what doctors do know. Hiding behind fancy names doesn't help anybody, least of all the patients.

Most typically, RA affects the small joints in the hands and feet. It can also affect knees, elbows, and other large joints. Rheumatoid arthritis may afflict other parts of the body, too, such as the nerves, skin, mouth, eyes, lungs, and/or heart. Joint pain and swelling are the most notable results of this illness—and, over time, joint and bone damage and/or deformity may occur. Medical communities don't know that the actual number of Americans affected by RA is higher than reported; it's actually around 2.5 million. Their ages range broadly from 15 to 60. RA affects five times more women than men.

Medical communities believe rheumatoid arthritis is an autoimmune disease—that is, a condition in which a confused immune system regards parts of your body as invaders and responds by perpetually attacking them. This implies your body is turning against you without your say.

The medical establishment trains doctors to use explanations like this about mystery illnesses across the board. It's a decoy to make patients feel safe, to feel like their health-care providers understand what's happening to them and why it's happening, to feel like there's a measure of control over what's going wrong. This explanation of autoimmune disease is not the help the establishment thinks it is.

When a patient gets the mental image of cells turning on one another, it sends the wrong message—that the patient's body has betrayed her or him, that it can't be trusted to heal.

It's critical to know that *our bodies don't attack themselves*. Here is the truth: the inflammation in the joints is there to *protect* you from attack by a particularly common virus. Your body is working hard to stop pathogens from digging deeper into the joints and the tissue around them. When the inflammation becomes long-term and chronic, that's when it becomes the problem known as RA—but it is still your body working to ward off viral damage.

Doctors also believe that there's no way to heal from rheumatoid arthritis. They're mistaken about that, too.

This chapter explains what rheumatoid arthritis really is . . . and how you can take control and regain your health.

IDENTIFYING RHEUMATOID ARTHRITIS

If you have rheumatoid arthritis, you're probably experiencing many of the following symptoms—and with good reason. These symptoms are the result of your body using its defenses to ward off the common viral pathogen:

- Joint pain—especially in the wrists and knuckles, the knees, and/or the balls of the feet, but *any* joint can be affected

- Joint inflammation

- Stiffness in the joints, especially in the morning, that may last for hours

- Tingling and/or numbness, especially in the hands and/or feet

- Fluid buildup, especially in the ankles or behind the knees

- Fatigue, fever, and other flu-like symptoms

- Heart palpitations

- Skin burning or itching

- A roaming, burning pain
- Nerve pain

Doctors employ certain methods to try to identify RA, but none of them are definitive. Below is a list of specific tests they use. Keep in mind that these are fallible, because they are not designed to look for the true root cause of RA. These tests do not find the viral pathogen that triggers RA. Rather, they serve as benchmarks for how much inflammation is present in the body.

- **Rheumatoid Factor blood test:** this checks for antibodies doctors believe are associated with RA. However, this test can produce a positive result in entirely healthy people, or in people who have some unrelated disease, such as lupus. At the same time, it can return negative results for those who actually have rheumatoid arthritis symptoms. Therefore, it's not very useful.

- **Anti-cyclic Citrullinated Peptides (anti-CCP) Antibody blood test:** this newer antibodies test is better at identifying rheumatoid arthritis inflammation cases than the Rheumatoid Factor test, but it's still far from definitive.

- **Erythrocyte Sedimentation Rate blood test:** this tests for a high degree of inflammation. There are many causes for inflammation, so this test doesn't pinpoint rheumatoid arthritis. That said, it can be used to get a sense of how much inflammation is occurring; so if you have RA, this can help you gauge its aggressiveness.

- **C-Reactive Protein blood test:** this tests for high levels of a protein associated with active inflammation. Other factors also create this protein, though, including obesity. And again, inflammation alone doesn't pinpoint the cause as being rheumatoid arthritis.

- **Ultrasounds and MRIs:** these can be used to track inflammatory activity that has caused bone damage over time.

One other way to determine whether you have rheumatoid arthritis is to learn the truth about what the condition actually is.

WHAT RHEUMATOID ARTHRITIS *REALLY* IS

Medical communities believe rheumatoid arthritis is an autoimmune disease that results from your immune system somehow mistaking your joints and other body parts for invaders and attacking them. As I've said before, *our bodies do not attack themselves.* Our bodies only react to being attacked by *pathogens.*

Rheumatoid arthritis is a version of the Epstein-Barr virus (EBV).

EBV chronically afflicts various parts of the body, including joints, bones, and nerves. It's this virus that's creating the pain and inflammation in your joints. (As for your immune system, not only is it innocent of wrongdoing, it's your primary defense against EBV.)

As mentioned earlier, there are over 60 varieties of the Epstein-Barr virus. It will take decades for medical research to shed light on the conditions and viral mutations of EBV that create RA. When the time, energy, and resources finally go into the cause—hopefully in the next 20 or 30 years—researchers will easily discover the EBV variants that have wreaked havoc on people's joints and nerves for over a century. And when doctors dig a little deeper, they'll clue in to the real solutions for this virus.

Knowing that rheumatoid arthritis is a form of EBV eliminates any dark mysteries surrounding the illness. While EBV is compromising, it's described in great detail in Chapter 3—including the steps you can take to end the virus's damage and destroy nearly all the EBV in your system.

HEALING FROM RHEUMATOID ARTHRITIS

Doctors typically treat rheumatoid arthritis using a variety of prescription anti-inflammatory and immunosuppressant medications for crisis management, because that's all they have to offer. Given the degree of pain and inflammation caused by RA, this is understandable. However, there are two problems with this strategy.

First, medications don't address the root cause of RA—which is the Epstein-Barr virus. Because these drugs do nothing to curtail EBV, they allow the illness to continue thriving inside of you. They keep your body from reacting to the virus, as if it were not there.

Second, your main defense against EBV is your immune system—and prescription medications actually *weaken* your immune system. So not only are these medications failing to help you defeat EBV, they're significantly aiding the virus.

The best approach is to read all of Chapter 3 to fully understand EBV. I hope you'll find it liberating—and I believe you'll benefit from the recommendations you find there.

Because the EBV that causes rheumatoid arthritis can be especially uncomfortable and difficult to manage, the following *natural* anti-inflammatories (i.e., that won't weaken your immune system) are also recommended, listed in rough order of preference. They'll help alleviate pain and promote healing from EBV:

- **Curcumin:** component of turmeric that reduces inflammation and relieves pain.

- **Nettle leaf:** herb containing alkaloids that can reduce inflammation specific to EBV.

- **Turmeric:** root that reduces inflammation and relieves pain.

- **N-acetyl cysteine:** amino acid that reduces inflammation and relieves pain.

- **MSM (methylsulfonylmethane):** compound that reduces inflammation and relieves joint pain.

Finally, use cold and hot packs. Place a cold pack on painful areas for about half an hour a day to reduce inflammation and speed healing, and place a hot pack on the same areas for about ten minutes a day to loosen up any muscle tension that might be developing around the damaged joints.

If you follow these recommendations, and most importantly follow all the pertinent advice in Chapter 3 and Part IV, "How to Finally Heal," then within anywhere from a few months to two years (depending on various factors, such as your current state of health), you can rid yourself of both EBV and RA and take back control of your health and your life.

CASE HISTORY:
Taking Matters into Her Own Swollen Hands

Janet loved her work as an aesthetician. Making people feel good about themselves with in-home spa treatments and makeup application was what got Janet out of bed in the morning. At age 48, Janet had a lot of responsibility, though. As a single mom with two children in their late teens, she was constantly worried about keeping up with rent payments for their home, managing her team of traveling aestheticians, and getting her older son through college. On top of all this, her mother had been sick with cancer for the last year. Janet had needed to spend every weekend and all her spare hours in service to her mom—supervising doctor appointments, paying bills, shopping for groceries, helping with household chores, and getting her mom's affairs in order.

Janet had occasionally experienced aches and pains over the years, but she always passed them off as natural, something that happened to everyone. One night in the midst of this stressful time, after staying up late to complete paperwork for her mother following a day of booked-solid client appointments, Janet noticed a stronger pain than usual in her elbows, wrists, and hands. She told herself it would be gone by morning—but when she woke up, it was even worse.

Feeling like she was unable to perform the hands-on tasks she needed to for her job, Janet booked an immediate appointment with her doctor. After blood work and a complete examination, the doctor told her, "I think you have rheumatoid arthritis." He referred Janet to a rheumatologist, who performed another exam and additional blood tests and concluded that Janet had inflammation from certain proteins and antibodies that were associated with inflammation of the joints.

This circular reasoning didn't fly for Janet. "But what does that *mean?*" she asked.

"It means you have RA," the rheumatologist said.

"But what's causing the inflammation in the first place?"

The rheumatologist answered that her body's immune system was attacking her joints and inflaming them. He handed her a prescription for an anti-inflammatory and immunosuppressant medication.

The whole thing still made no sense to Janet. Up until now, she'd felt she could trust herself. She might not be able to trust others, like her ex-husband, or like Mrs. Ferguson, who never paid for her facials, but Janet had always trusted her body to be on her side. She didn't understand why her body had decided to start attacking itself. It felt like a betrayal.

She feared the condition would get worse over time. If this had started out of the blue, then what, she wondered, was to stop her body from continuing to hurt her? She looked at her 82-year-old mother, battling cancer, and wondered how much worse off she'd be at that age. At 48, Janet's mother had been in fine health. She'd never had to deal with this RA business. Could Janet's body even make it to 70?

Janet decided to take matters into her own swollen hands and booked an appointment with a functional medicine doctor, who looked at Janet's previous blood work, ordered additional tests, and then came up with the same diagnosis of RA. Janet asked Dr. Tanaka what was causing the rheumatoid arthritis. The doctor told Janet it was autoimmune, that is, that the body was attacking itself. Janet pressed Dr. Tanaka for a better explanation, but she didn't seem to have one. Instead the doctor instructed Janet to eliminate wheat gluten and processed sugar from her diet and to take a pile of supplements, which included fish oil, vitamin D, and B complex.

On this regimen, Janet felt a little better. The pain wasn't as aggressive in her elbow, but her hands and wrists were still far from normal. She could only perform her job on what she called "good" days, and she only got so many of those a month. Not only was she losing income; she'd also had to hire a helper for her mother, and that was draining her bank account.

One day a special client, Olivia—the woman who'd encouraged Janet to start her own business years earlier—called to book Janet to do the bridal party makeup for her daughter's wedding. When Janet told Olivia she'd have to send one of her team members in her place and explained the reason, Olivia told Janet, "You're calling Anthony."

My initial scan of Janet showed inflammation in her nerves and joints. It wasn't because her body was attacking itself, though. Spirit recognized it instead as the viral condition known as Epstein-Barr. Janet's immune system was trying to fight a battle and was working *in her favor* to fend off the virus. It was doing everything it could to prevent the virus from entering her connective joint tissue. Meanwhile, the immunosuppressant medications she'd been taking were suppressing her immune system so that her body couldn't defend itself against the virus.

When I explained to Janet that EBV takes the form of mononucleosis in one of its early stages, Janet recalled having a case of mono in college, and how all her joints had hurt in a similar manner. Finally, an explanation clicked. She understood that the virus had morphed from its original mono form and burrowed deeper into her body, remaining more or less dormant until the strain of the last year, along with stress-eating certain foods that contained hidden triggers, had brought it to the surface. It all made perfect sense. And learning this truth allowed her to trust her body. She felt her fighting spirit come back, ready to help her heal.

To bring Janet back to health, we focused on the power of fruits and vegetables, concentrating on the specific antiviral ones as listed in the protocols in Chapter 3, "Epstein-Barr Virus, Chronic Fatigue Syndrome, and Fibromyalgia." After the 28-day Healing Cleanse I describe in Chapter 21, Janet was back to working almost full-time.

Within three months, she was back to her normal workload and schedule.

Janet kept her mother's aide on part-time and started taking grocery bags of healing foods to her mom's place, showing the helper how to prepare fruit smoothies, mango salsa, spinach soup, and other dishes that would keep her mother's immune system strong.

A year after our first talk, Janet was still following the EBV protocols and staying away from trigger foods—and she didn't have one ache or pain. In fact, she felt better than she had in years. She now owned the truth that she didn't have RA, and she reveled in the fact that she'd finally conquered that little mono virus from college.

When the holidays came and Janet was twice as busy as usual, she didn't flinch when she looked at her jam-packed calendar. Instead, she said, "Bring it on."

CHAPTER 6

Hypothyroidism and Hashimoto's Thyroiditis

To truly understand thyroid disorder and disease, we have to go back in history. Stories get lost through the generations, and it's human nature to forget how things first started as the busyness of daily life distracts us. If I don't put this out there, the truth of thyroid issues' origins could be gone forever.

Thyroid disease is in fact a fairly new affliction. It wasn't until the turn of the 19th century, when the Industrial Revolution had started to change the way the world worked, that people started to have real problems with their thyroids. Until this time, goiters had been uncommon. They were a result of nutritional deficiencies in minerals such as iodine and zinc, or toxicity from heavy metals such as mercury.

Then, as newly developed industries started dumping toxic heavy metals into rivers, streams, and lakes, and as factories started to release poisonous emissions of newly born chemicals that our human bodies had never encountered, people's thyroids started to bear the brunt. They were exposed to more toxicity than ever before, and more and more cases of goiters appeared.

Then around the turn of the 20th century, industries began to strip nutrients from our grains, vegetables, and fruit—all in the name of progress—and pack our foods into lead cans. Lead was the perfect heavy metal to give someone a goiter. And without the proper nutrition in their food, people were doubly vulnerable.

At the same time, medical science made what seemed to be a huge breakthrough. It was based on a philosophy that had been popular in the Middle Ages: the practice of eating an animal's body part to help heal a person's corresponding part. In those days, if someone had heart disease, they'd be instructed to eat heart. Kidney disease was treated by eating kidney, brain disease by eating brain, and eye disease by eating desiccated animal eyeballs. It was a form of quackery that was not effective, yet it was respected as the most sensible trend of its time.

Ages later, at the tail end of the 1800s, medical researchers stumbled upon an instance in which the theory actually worked—for the first time in human history. They found that the thyroid glands of pigs, when dried and ground up, created a medicine that helped relieve the symptoms of human thyroid disorder, specifically goiters.

One reason it actually worked was that the desiccated thyroid provided people with a nutrient that they were critically lacking: iodine. Another reason it gave patients relief was that the medical establishment had accidentally discovered its first steroid compound—that is, a concentrated hormone compound that suppresses inflammation and the immune system. When the thyroid is in trouble, the body will often overreact, resulting in fluid gathering around the gland; this is part of what causes a goiter. The hormone concentration in desiccated thyroid medication acted as an immunosuppressant, slowing down the body's ability to react to the troubled thyroid.

For the first time, it seemed like a cure had emerged from the eating-matching-body-parts philosophy. In altered concentrations, desiccated bovine or porcine thyroid is still the ingredient used in thyroid medications today—which makes them antiquated at best. They still don't address the underlying health issues. So let's not start handing out posthumous medals for this fluke discovery.

We have to realize this wasn't high-minded scientific thought on display. It was a doctor who woke up one morning and thought, *Let's try that old chestnut of a theory,* then visited the butcher shop for some discarded animal parts and started riffing in his lab. *An eye for an eye, a kidney for a kidney, a thyroid gland for a thyroid gland— hey, that last one works!* He'd taken the thyroid from a pig, cured and dehydrated it, then fed it to his patients with goiters—and they'd happened to see results. It was in no way a grand epiphany based on sophisticated science.

In the 20th century, the viral upsurge began, and women started to present with thyroid-related symptoms very different from the goiters seen years before. Now, years later, this new condition has gotten tagged as *thyroiditis,* which just means an inflamed thyroid. Often these days, patients get the specific labels *Hashimoto's* and *hypothyroidism*—yet these remain mystery illnesses.

Now another wave of this thyroid illness is upon us. Tens of millions of people, mostly women, don't even realize they have a thyroid condition, yet are leading diminished lives because of it. Patients who do get attention for their thyroids still receive medications made from synthetic or desiccated animal thyroid, and when that doesn't suppress their symptoms enough, they are offered radioactive iodine treatment to try and destroy the thyroid gland.

This isn't progress. Answers have still not surfaced about what actually causes these mystery thyroid conditions, so people aren't learning how to heal, either.

In the sections that follow, I'll uncover the true reason why so many people are struggling with thyroid-related symptoms, and what you can do if you're one of them. If you're suffering, there's a reason—and a way to get better.

UNDERSTANDING HYPOTHYROIDISM AND HASHIMOTO'S

The thyroid is a small gland in the neck that plays a major role in your health. It regulates how much or how little energy you take in at any given moment. This affects every cell in the body.

When the thyroid produces plenty of its hormones, it signals cells to receive glucose and convert it into energy for activity, repair, and reproduction. When the thyroid produces fewer hormones, it signals your cells to hold off and save their energy conversion for later. This helps ensure that your body runs at a steady pace. Over time, though, lower thyroid levels cause "power shortages" throughout your body, because your cells aren't receiving the hormonal instructions to charge up that they need to function properly.

When your thyroid is operating smoothly, so do you. When your thyroid stops working the right way, though, multiple areas of your health can come crashing down.

Hypothyroidism is the name for the underproduction of thyroid hormones; it's a mild, early-stage case of thyroiditis. Hypothyroidism and Hashimoto's thyroiditis aren't the goiter conditions of the past, brought on by iodine deficiency and toxin accumulation in the thyroid. And these names don't explain what's really going on to cause people's fatigue, heart palpitations, hot flashes, brain fog, weight gain, and many other associated issues.

Medical communities believe Hashimoto's is the result of the immune system somehow going haywire, mistaking thyroid cells for invaders, and declaring war on them.

That's not correct. I've said this before, and I'll say it again: The body does not attack itself. Our immune systems do not become confused and go after our own organs. This is as true for the thyroid as it is for any other organ.

The mistaken theory of autoimmune disease is merely a blame game. It points a finger of fault at the patient's own body to distract from the truth that medical research has not yet scratched the surface of what causes thyroid conditions.

Truth is, over 95 percent of today's thyroid disorders, including Hashimoto's, stem from a *viral* infection. (The other 5 percent come from radiation.) That virus is Epstein-Barr (EBV).

As Chapter 3 explains, after a long incubation period—typically in the liver—EBV begins its journey to the thyroid, and then enters into the tissue there. Over time, the viral load will weaken the thyroid, making it less effective at producing the hormones the body requires to function. As time passes, the EBV will also slowly inflame the thyroid, leading from a case of hypothyroidism to a case of Hashimoto's thyroiditis. This is not your body betraying you. Rather, your immune system is going after a real intruder and working hard to protect you.

One major confusion is that patients think thyroid medications go after the root cause of their illness. In fact, these drugs do not treat the thyroid itself. They just add hormones to the bloodstream in hopes that the body will use them to replace the hormones the thyroid isn't producing. It's a secret that thyroid drugs are mild steroids, and that they slow the immune system down from reacting to your symptoms. It's a secret that doctors often don't even know; they just haven't been told. And typically, doctors don't explain to patients that they don't truly understand hypothyroidism or Hashimoto's or that the medications will not alleviate the conditions themselves.

If you're on thyroid medication and feel a positive difference, that's fine. It can act as a mostly harmless Band-Aid to a thyroid condition that comes from a viral load. If you've tried thyroid medications and couldn't find relief, though, now you understand your frustration was valid.

I have heard stories from hundreds of women who started on medication for their thyroid disorders and 10 to 15 years later, when they were in their 50s or 60s, went to get a thyroid exam. The nurse practitioner or doctor took a look at the results and said, "What the heck happened to your thyroid? It looks terrible." All this time, the women thought they were being responsible and proactive. They thought the drugs had been caring for their thyroids.

You don't have to be stuck with this fate. By following the program in Chapter 3, you can rid yourself of the Epstein-Barr virus. And with the advice in the sections below, you can help heal and protect your damaged thyroid, as well as fortify supporting glands. You will finally be empowered to reverse your thyroid condition, instead of being told you're addressing and treating it when you actually aren't. With the truth about what's causing your condition and how to get better, you can reclaim control over your health.

THYROID BLOOD TESTS

If you suspect you have a thyroid issue or disorder but aren't sure, have your doctor conduct blood tests for your thyroid hormone levels.

Specifically, ask to be tested for TSH, free T4, free T3, and thyroid antibodies. While they're far from perfect, these lab tests are the current gold standards.

One fad that's developed among the alternative medicine community is reverse T3 testing. Its advocates claim that it's an accurate indicator of problems, while its detractors claim it's just noise.

In a sense, they're both right. Your reverse T3 level *does* reflect genuine problems—but with so many of them all at once, it's impossible to know what any result means. So even though a reverse T3 result isn't an arbitrary value, it is still okay to have your doctor order the test.

Finally, it's important to be aware that even if all your thyroid test results are in the normal range, you could still have a thyroid problem. Many people, mostly women, feel low-grade viral hypothyroid symptoms regardless of normal test results. Sometimes it takes months or even years before a thyroid condition develops to the point where blood tests pick up on it. (Plus most lab ranges are too broad, so a mild condition can, and normally does, slip through their cracks.)

Some doctors now prescribe thyroid medications even if a patient's thyroid test results are in the normal range. It's an awareness meant to nip problems in the bud, and it's progress for women because they're finally being taken seriously and heard. However, it's just the medications' mild steroid effect that gives patients partial relief from their low-grade viral infections. Research is still a long distance away from discovering the underlying cause of thyroid disorder and what will truly help these patients.

If you're feeling thyroid symptoms regardless of what your lab tests say, make use of the programs in Chapter 3, Part IV, and in the next section below. If your suspicions are wrong, the worst that's likely to happen is you'll make your thyroid stronger. And if you've guessed right, you'll not only be working to end your thyroid disorder, you'll recover and spare yourself from future frustrating thyroid issues.

ADDRESSING THYROID CONDITIONS

This section offers foods, herbs, and supplements that heal your damaged thyroid, strengthen all its fellow glands in your endocrine system (adrenal glands, pituitary gland, pancreas, and so on)—and lower the viral load specifically within your thyroid.

"Goitrogenic" Foods

There's a new trend that's making people fearful of vegetables such as cauliflower, kale, broccoli, cabbage, collard greens, and broccoli rabe. Rumor has it that these contain goitrogens, that is, substances that cause goiters.

Don't pay this fad any mind! These so-called "goitrogenic" foods do not contain enough goitrogens to inhibit the thyroid on any level. You'd have to eat a 100-pound barrel's worth of broccoli daily to reach any level of concern.

So please consume and enjoy your favorite cruciferous vegetables. They actually help promote thyroid health.

Healing Foods

Among the most healing foods for thyroid conditions are Atlantic dulse, wild blueberries, sprouts, cilantro, garlic, hemp seeds, coconut oil, Brazil nuts, and cranberries. Variously, they can kill EBV cells, provide micronutrients, repair thyroid tissue, reduce nodule growth, flush toxic heavy metals and viral waste, and boost production of thyroid hormones.

Healing Herbs and Supplements

- **Zinc:** kills EBV cells, strengthens the thyroid, and helps protect the endocrine system.

- **Spirulina (preferably from Hawaii):** provides critical micronutrients for the thyroid.

- **Bladderwrack:** provides easily assimilated iodine and trace minerals for the thyroid.

- **Chromium:** helps stabilize the endocrine system.

- **L-tyrosine:** helps increase the production of thyroid hormones.

- **Ashwagandha:** bolsters the thyroid and adrenal glands and helps stabilize the endocrine system.

- **Licorice root:** kills EBV cells in the thyroid and aids the adrenal glands.

- **Eleuthero (aka Siberian ginseng):** bolsters the adrenal glands and helps stabilize the endocrine system.

- **Lemon balm:** kills EBV cells in the thyroid and dampens nodule growth.

- **Manganese:** critical for production of thyroid hormone T3.

- **Selenium:** stimulates the production of thyroid hormone T4.

- **Vitamin D$_3$:** helps stabilize the immune system and its responses.

- **B-complex:** essential vitamins for the endocrine system.

- **Magnesium:** helps stabilize thyroid hormone T3.

- **EPA & DHA (eicosapentaenoic acid and docosahexaenoic acid):** fortifies the endocrine system and nervous system. Be sure to buy a plant-based (not fish-based) version.

- *Bacopa monnieri*: supports thyroid hormone production and T4-to-T3 conversion.

- **Rubidium:** helps stabilize thyroid hormone production.

- **Copper:** kills EBV cells and augments the effectiveness of iodine.

CASE HISTORY:
Stronger Than Ever

Sarah's friends lived in awe (and a little jealousy) of her ability to take on the world with energy that never flagged. On weekends, she and her boyfriend, Rob, would head to the mountains to hike, and then she'd still want to go out with her girlfriends when she got home. She could eat whatever she wanted and never gain a pound. Rob, who worked as a trainer, loved to show her off at the gym where he worked.

When Sarah was 36, she noticed that she'd put on an extra seven pounds between Thanksgiving and New Year's. She could barely fit into her good jeans. At first it seemed like it might just be bloating from her menstrual cycle. But when her period passed, she was still struggling to button her waistband.

She decided she'd go full-throttle at the gym and burn off the extra weight. She also cut out all carbohydrates from her diet.

Sarah's girlfriend Jessica told her she was happy to see her weight go up a little. "You look much healthier," she said. Still, Sarah had been more comfortable at her lower weight and knew it wasn't normal to get heavier out of nowhere. She also knew that Jessica had other reasons for being happy to see Sarah fill out—namely, a history of envy.

In the second week of Sarah's extra workout and no carb regimen, she noticed that the number on the scale hadn't gone down, but her energy had dropped. Rob, who'd never had a problem keeping weight off, told Sarah she just wasn't applying herself enough at the gym. He also put her on protein shakes to try and build her muscle mass.

Yet Sarah's weight was going up at a rate of a pound every two weeks, and her energy just kept dropping. She'd once been 115 pounds. The day the scale hit 130, she called her doctor.

After a full workup, Dr. Kiernan explained that Sarah's thyroid hormone level tests showed that her thyroid levels were elevated, indicating hypothyroidism. Sarah asked what was making that happen. She'd always been healthy, she said, she ate a healthy diet, and she exercised all the time. Dr. Kiernan answered that it was just something that could happen as people aged.

This didn't compute for Sarah. "Aging" wasn't part of her vocabulary. She was still in her 30s, she wasn't even married yet, she didn't have children—and already she was getting the ailments of an older person?

Still, she took the thyroid medication that Dr. Kiernan prescribed, continued her frequent workouts, and kept avoiding carbs. Yet her weight continued to increase by two pounds every month. When she reached 140 pounds, she called her mother to vent about how disappointed Rob was in her weight gain. He no longer liked to be seen at the gym with her, because he said her body reflected poorly on his skills as a trainer. Rob had stopped inviting her out with his friends and colleagues. The one time she'd been out with them in recent weeks, he'd said a defensive, "Don't worry about Sarah. She's just been eating too many carbs," at the beginning of the evening.

Her mom groaned over Rob's behavior and said to Sarah, "I know I've told you about Anthony before and you haven't called him. I really think now's the time."

In the initial scan, Spirit helped me confirm that Sarah did have a thyroid problem—thyroiditis, just on the edge of early hypothyroidism. She wasn't yet at the point of full inflammation of the thyroid, but she was headed there. I hurried to explain that the condition wasn't a symptom of getting older. A virus—specifically Epstein-Barr—was causing Sarah's problem.

Right away, we altered Sarah's diet. We took out hormone-disrupting foods such as eggs and dairy, and minimized her animal protein to once daily. We also increased her consumption of antiviral fruits and vegetables, including papayas, berries, apples, mâche, mangoes, spinach, kale, sprouts, Atlantic dulse, cilantro, and garlic. For supplements, we concentrated on lemon balm, chromium, zinc, and bladderwrack. With this protocol, we were able to reduce the viral load on Sarah's thyroid, and it returned to producing its normal level of hormones.

At the beginning, Rob was suspicious of this new diet. He thought fruit smoothies (with no protein powder) for breakfast, a spinach salad with orange and avocado for lunch, salmon with vegetables for dinner, and fruit for snacks in between was too much sugar and not enough protein.

Within the first two weeks, though, Sarah had lost four pounds. And within the first month, a total of eight pounds.

The second month, the weight loss was more gradual, but her energy was increasing. Sarah's metabolism had bounced back. As an added benefit, she felt like she was building muscles she'd never even felt before.

After three and a half months, she was back to 115 pounds—with more muscle than the last time she'd been that weight.

Meanwhile, Sarah told Dr. Kiernan she wanted to wean off the thyroid medication. Though it went against what he'd been taught, Dr. Kiernan couldn't deny that Sarah's thyroid was restoring its normal function, and Sarah was coming back to life before his eyes. Soon, Sarah was off the medication entirely.

Now when Rob had gym clients who were having trouble losing weight, he told them all about his girlfriend's weight-loss story (implying he'd been the one to help her), and put those clients on high-fruit, low-fat cleanse diets.

Rob apologized to Sarah for his past behavior and hinted that he might be popping the question soon. Sarah told me that while Rob is easy on the eyes, she's not so quick to commit to him after seeing the way he treated her when times got hard. They remain unmarried.

PART III

SECRETS BEHIND OTHER MYSTERY ILLNESSES

CHAPTER 7

Type 2 Diabetes and Hypoglycemia

The fundamental fuel for your body is *glucose,* a simple sugar that provides all your cells with the energy they need to function, heal, grow, and thrive.

Glucose keeps us going—and keeps us alive. The central nervous system runs on it, as does every organ in the body, including the heart. Glucose is what we use to build and sustain muscle, and it performs vital functions such as repairing damaged tissue and cells.

When you eat food, your body breaks it down into glucose and places it in your bloodstream so it can travel to all your cells. However, your cells can't access the glucose directly. They need some help from your *pancreas,* which is a large endocrine gland located behind your stomach.

Your pancreas is constantly monitoring your bloodstream. When it detects a rise in glucose levels, it responds by producing a hormone called *insulin.* Insulin attaches to your cells and signals them to open up and absorb the glucose from your blood. Insulin therefore both allows your cells to get the energy they need and ensures your blood glucose levels remain stable.

If your bloodstream has more glucose than your cells can consume—for example, if you've eaten a particularly heavy meal (maybe pork ribs slathered in syrupy barbecue sauce; in other words, a lot of fat combined with sugar)—your insulin directs the extra glucose to be stored in your liver. At some later point when your glucose levels run low—for example, in between meals, or during periods of intense physical activity—your liver will release stored glucose for use by your cells. That is, if your liver is strong and functions well.

This is normally an effective system for optimal glucose use. However, it starts to go wrong if your pancreas fails to produce enough insulin when it's needed. It also goes wrong if some of your cells start refusing to let the insulin attach and open the cells up to receive glucose; this is called *insulin resistance.*

When either or both of these problems occur, not enough glucose is removed from your blood by your cells. Your body will expel some of the excess glucose in your urine, which may cause you to urinate more frequently, and also dehydrate you and make you feel thirsty.

If your pancreas isn't creating enough insulin when your body needs it, and/or if you're experiencing insulin resistance, and if these issues lead to exceptionally high blood glucose levels, you're at risk for *type 2 diabetes.* Around 35 million people have this disease in the U.S. alone. And another 95 million have *prediabetes,* with blood glucose levels higher than normal but not yet at diabetes levels. As many as 35 percent of those with prediabetes will develop type 2 diabetes within six years.

Medical professionals don't know why type 2 diabetes happens. This is evident in the diets that physicians and dieticians recommend to diabetics; if they knew what was really happening in these patients' bodies, they'd offer completely different food advice. While doctors get some elements of treatment right, they aren't able to offer an understanding of how or why this disease starts.

This chapter will tell you precisely what causes type 2 diabetes. It'll also truly explain how insulin resistance occurs, as well as what hypoglycemia is and how to get your system back in balance enough so your body can have the chance to heal.

TYPE 2 DIABETES SYMPTOMS

If you have type 2 diabetes, you may experience one or more of the following symptoms. (Note that it's possible to be in the early stages of diabetes and not experience any symptoms.)

- **Unusual thirst, dry mouth, frequent urination:** this is because your body is using up water to expel excess glucose via your urine.

- **Blurry vision:** as you become dehydrated, your body may pull water from the lenses of your eyes to help flush out the excess glucose.

- **Unusual hunger:** this is because your cells aren't getting all the glucose they need to feed themselves.

- **Fatigue and irritability:** as you're not getting the energy you normally do when your cells are fully fueled with glucose.

- **Digestive problems:** your pancreas doesn't just make insulin; it makes enzymes to help your body break down foods. If your pancreas is underperforming, this creates not only an insulin deficiency but also an enzyme deficiency, making it harder for your body to digest anything.

- **Hypoglycemia:** these energy lows—blood sugar drops that occur as often as every other hour—are the result of weakness of the liver and underactive adrenals.

WHAT *REALLY* CAUSES TYPE 2 DIABETES AND HYPOGLYCEMIA

While medical communities are unaware of this, the causes of both type 2 diabetes and hypoglycemia typically begin with the adrenal glands.

When you're up against continual stress and experiencing difficult and unavoidable trials in life, it sets your adrenal glands to flood your body with *adrenaline,* a hormone that charges you with emergency energy. While this is a helpful response for dire straits, if you're continually operating in crisis mode and aren't able to physically burn off the corrosive adrenaline saturating the tissues of your organs and glands, the adrenaline can eventually do serious damage.

Your pancreas is normally as smooth as a baby's bottom. But chronic scorching by fear-based or other negative-emotion-based adrenaline will wear away at the pancreas, creating calluses that turn it thick and hard.

It's like this: When you're born, your pancreas is like a brand-new credit card. Some come into the world with a sweet deal—a high spending limit, a generous cash credit line, and a cache of frequent flyer miles just for signing up. Others come into the world with lower credit limits, higher interest rates, and fewer bonuses. Either way, you can use that thing up if you're not careful. When people go through life wearing themselves down and taming the stress with fried or high-fat foods, ice cream, cookies . . . they run up the balance on the pancreas and use up those frequent flyer miles.

Over time, this damages the pancreas's ability to produce enough insulin to remove all the glucose it should from your bloodstream. And this underperformance alone is enough to create type 2 diabetes.

That's not the end of it. Your entire body is damaged by chronic floods of negative-emotion-based adrenaline. Especially if you eat when you're emotional, your pancreas will produce insulin that mixes with the adrenaline in your bloodstream, leading your body to associate the insulin with the fear-based adrenaline that's hurting it. Over time, this can make many of your cells "allergic" to your adrenaline/insulin blend and cause them to shun both hormones. Medical research hasn't yet uncovered this "Franken-sulin" hybrid (as I call it), nor has it understood that the physical body revolts in this way. It's one of the primary causes of pancreatic weakness, which leads to lowered insulin production and nonacceptance of glucose in the body's cells.

Heavy, rich meals can trigger excess adrenaline production, too. That's because the adrenals are like a fire station, and fat triggers the alarm bell. When the adrenals get the signal that high levels of fat are in the bloodstream—and therefore have the potential to put the pancreas and liver in immediate danger—the firehouse (the adrenals) sends out the fire trucks (adrenaline) to address the situation. That rush of adrenaline increases digestive strength to help move the fat through your system and protect you, but you pay a price, as this process can weaken the pancreas over time.

On the flip side, your adrenal glands may be underperforming—that is, producing too *little* adrenaline. This makes your pancreas work overtime to try to compensate. If this condition is chronic, your pancreas will become inflamed or enlarged, and may eventually start underperforming as well.

Then again, you can have *adrenal fatigue,* in which your unstable adrenals are sometimes producing too little adrenaline and sometimes producing way too much. This can batter your pancreas as it becomes inflamed to compensate for dry spells of adrenaline and then gets scorched by floods of it.

Once your pancreas becomes dysfunctional, it can suffer damage from *itself.* That's because in addition to insulin, your pancreas produces enzymes that aid with digestion. Your pancreas also makes inhibitors that prevent these powerful enzymes from turning on itself as if it were a food to be dissolved. But if your pancreas grows sufficiently defective, it'll start underproducing its inhibitors, at which point the enzymes it produces will create even more damage. (On top of that, you'll start experiencing digestive problems . . .)

A precursor to type 2 diabetes is a fluctuating but low glucose level—called *hypoglycemia*—which indicates a major issue with your body's ability to manage glucose properly. This can occur if your liver becomes impaired in its ability to store and release glucose. It can also happen if you're failing to eat at least a light, balanced snack—e.g., a fruit (for sugar and potassium) and a vegetable (for sodium)—every two hours. Regularly skipping meals forces your body to use up the liver's precious glucose storage, driving the body to run on adrenaline; and as previously mentioned, this can damage your pancreas, create insulin resistance, and lead to adrenal fatigue and weight gain over time.

One other major factor is the *type* of food you eat. There's a common misconception that diabetes is caused by eating a lot of foods with sugar in them. However, it's not actually the sugar that's the problem. It's sugar and fat combined—mainly fat. For example, you could eat fruit all day and every day for the rest of your life and never get diabetes. (In fact, eating a lot of fruit is the most effective way to add years to your life, as I'll explain in Chapter 20, "Fruit Fear.")

The problem is *fat.* Most people who consume processed foods and junk foods such as cakes, cookies, doughnuts, ice cream, and so on—or people who have a seemingly healthy main dish like chicken but follow it up with dessert—typically eat a lot of fat *and* a lot of sugar at the same time. While sugar that's not attached to nutrients (e.g., that isn't coming from fruit or vegetables) is definitely unhealthy, it's the *fat* that strains your liver and pancreas.

The first thing that will happen is that instant insulin resistance from the high levels of blood fat that result from an animal protein meal—whether lean versions of pork, steak, or chicken, or fast food battered and fried in oil—will stop the body's ability to allow the insulin produced by your pancreas to drive sugar into your cells. This will mean there's a whole lot of sugar floating around the bloodstream that can't go anywhere. A strong liver will help gather up as much glucose as it can to store for a rainy day. Over time, a diet high in animal fat, protein, and processed oils can burden the liver, though. Your liver can reach a vulnerable state from the constant responsibility to clean up the excess glucose in the bloodstream, and from waiting too many hours between meals to be refueled. When the liver becomes overburdened in this way, it dumps all of its glucose storage back into the bloodstream. This can prompt the birthing stage of hypoglycemia.

Since your liver has to take the burden of processing the fat you eat, a diet high in animal fat (which hides in even the lean animal protein people tend to think of as healthy) can make the organ sluggish and unable to store and release glucose the way it should. Large, heavy meals plus glucose dry spells caused by not eating in between can eventually result in type 2 diabetes.

At the same time, your pancreas has to produce enzymes to break down the fat so you can digest it. A lot of fat makes your pancreas work extra hard; and if you've already got other factors straining your pancreas, such as severe negative emotions and/or adrenal glands flooding it with corrosive adrenaline, a diet high in fat may be all that's needed to push your pancreas over the edge and create type 2 diabetes.

The good news is that all the damage described above is absolutely reversible. Next we'll cover how to heal your pancreas, your liver, and your insulin-traumatized cells so you can bring your hypoglycemia or type 2 diabetes to an end.

ADDRESSING TYPE 2 DIABETES AND HYPOGLYCEMIA

Since medical communities don't know the real story of what causes type 2 diabetes and hypoglycemia, they don't provide the proper diet guidance. Typically, they recommend a diet with little to no sugar in it, advising patients to avoid fruit altogether and focus on eating animal protein and vegetables.

Heeding this advice will probably keep you diabetic forever—and not just diabetic and functional, but diabetic and ailing—since the fat in meat is only going to make your condition worse, while eating fruit is critical for healing diabetes. It's imperative to understand that animal fats are what weakened the pancreas and liver to begin with.

Sugar was just the messenger. And in this case, health professionals shoot the messenger. That sugar was showcasing the insulin resistance that had cropped up from a pancreas overburdened by fat.

It's easy to eat a diet high in animal fat without realizing it. Even a lean-cut four-ounce piece of meat will contain a tablespoon of concentrated fat that can burden the pancreas and liver. So when a person is insulin resistant (even from a diet that seems traditionally "healthy") and puts sugar into her or his system, that sugar is going to prompt insulin problems—and suddenly sugar is going to get all the attention, when it's not the real instigator.

Think of it like the teenager who throws a party when her parents are out of town. Say her younger brother drinks some punch he didn't realize was spiked, gets sick, and calls Mom and Dad. Then say when they return home to a trashed house and drunk visitors, the big sister (fat) tries to blame the whole thing on her little brother (sugar). But he didn't do anything wrong!

Now of course table sugar and many other sweeteners aren't good for you—I'm not recommending you eat these. Yet to address type 2 diabetes and hypoglycemia, it is *critical* to lower fat consumption and increase fresh fruit and vegetable consumption. I recommend the cleanse in Chapter 21 to help heal the liver, pancreas, and adrenal glands and stabilize blood sugar levels.

Your doctor may prescribe insulin. While insulin lowers your blood glucose level, it does nothing to address core problems such as damaged adrenal glands, a damaged pancreas, a dysfunctional liver, chronic negative emotions, and/or insulin resistance.

What follows is a more targeted daily approach that focuses on healing every likely cause of your type 2 diabetes or hypoglycemia. You'll also find guidance in Part IV, "How to Finally Heal." How long you'll need to stick with this program depends on how much damage has to be undone. You should notice improvements within a few months, and the complete process typically requires six months to two-and-a-half years.

Bolster Your Adrenal Glands

The fact that you have type 2 diabetes means it's likely you have an issue with your adrenal glands. Therefore, one step toward healing is to read Chapter 8, "Adrenal Fatigue." You can follow its advice to make your adrenal glands stable and strong.

Healing Foods

Wild blueberries, spinach, celery, papayas, sprouts, kale, raspberries, and asparagus are top foods to eat if you have type 2 diabetes or hypoglycemia. These perform functions such as detoxing the liver, strengthening glucose levels, supporting the pancreas, boosting the adrenal glands, and stabilizing insulin.

Take care to avoid certain foods as well, most specifically cheese, milk, cream, butter, eggs, processed oils, and all sugars except for raw honey and fruit.

Healing Herbs and Supplements

- **Zinc:** supports the pancreas and adrenal glands and helps stabilize glucose levels in the blood.
- **Chromium:** sustains the pancreas and adrenal glands and helps stabilize insulin levels.
- **Spirulina (preferably from Hawaii):** helps stabilize glucose levels in the blood and aids the adrenal glands.

- **Ester-C:** this form of vitamin C soothes and bolsters the adrenal glands.

- **ALA (alpha lipoic acid):** boosts the liver's ability to store and release glucose.

- **Silica:** helps stabilize the pancreas's release of insulin.

- **Purslane:** strengthens the pancreas and its production of digestive enzymes.

- **Eleuthero (aka Siberian ginseng):** enhances the body's ability to react and adapt, which helps prevent the adrenal glands from overreacting to fear, stress, and other intense emotions.

- **Panax ginseng:** also enhances the body's ability to react and adapt, which in turn helps prevent the adrenal glands from overreacting to fear, stress, and other intense emotions.

- **EPA & DHA (eicosapentaenoic acid and docosahexaenoic acid):** helps heal insulin resistance. Be sure to buy a plant-based (not fish-based) version.

- **Biotin:** helps stabilize glucose levels in the blood and supports the central nervous system.

- **B-complex:** sustains the central nervous system.

- *Gymnema sylvestre*: helps lower glucose levels in the blood and stabilize insulin levels.

- **Magnesium:** soothes digestive issues caused by an underperforming pancreas. Also calms stressed adrenal glands.

- **Vitamin D$_3$:** bolsters the pancreas and adrenal glands, and reduces inflammation.

CASE HISTORY:
Getting a New Perspective on Sugar

Starting in her teens, Morgan battled what she called emotional highs and lows. Her mother, Kim, learned that if Morgan went too long without eating, she'd start to act out with a burst of frustration or fall into tears out of nowhere.

Kim repeatedly took Morgan to the family doctor to have her blood sugar levels evaluated, but Morgan's A1C and other tests would always come back normal. The doctor passed off Morgan's inconsistent behavior as an aspect of being a sensitive—or maybe even bipolar—girl.

When Morgan was in her early 20s, Kim found an alternative doctor who said Morgan was hypoglycemic. The practitioner instructed Morgan to stay away completely from sugars and other carbohydrates, and to eat a diet of strictly protein and vegetables, with small meals every few hours to stabilize her blood sugar.

At first, Morgan felt an improvement. She and Kim took this as an indication that the diet was helpful, so all through her early adult life, Morgan stayed clear of most carbs and all processed sugars. She focused on eating doctor-recommended proteins such as eggs, chicken, turkey, cheese, fish, and nuts every few hours, as well as salads with tomatoes and cucumbers, which were allowed because they were low-carb. This gave Morgan the blood sugar and energy stability to function.

As she got into her late 20s, though, her energy levels became inconsistent again. She started to develop digestive gas and bloating, along with weight gain and fatigue. After exercising, she'd get a huge energy crash and intensely crave sugar.

Morgan had her blood drawn at the alternative doctor's office, and the A1C test showed evidence that she now had type 2 diabetes. She could barely process the information. She'd hardly eaten any sugar over the last seven years. She read every food package, every label, and she studiously sought out protein and avoided carbohydrates. This had once seemed to be saving her.

Kim vented about the predicament to her hairdresser, who was a client of mine. She told Kim I'd be able to get to the bottom of Morgan's health problem.

Within the first minute of my phone call with Morgan and Kim, Spirit confirmed that Morgan was hypoglycemic and now technically had type 2 diabetes.

"How could this happen?" Morgan asked. "I strictly avoid sugar and carbs, and I eat protein every three hours."

"Sugar isn't the issue," I said. "It's fat. Unfortunately, Morgan, you were prescribed a high-fat diet under the guise of a high-protein one."

"I was told this was all protein I've been eating," Morgan said. "Where was the fat?"

"It was *in* the animal protein," I told her. "For seven years, fat has been your main calorie source, since you weren't living off sugar or carbohydrate calories."

"And why don't doctors know about this?"

"They haven't learned yet," I said. "They're wrapped up in the high-protein trend."

Kim cut in. "Why are these foods just called high-protein? Why isn't the fat mentioned?"

"Because that's how it was first marketed back in the 1930s. If all these animal products were marketed as high-fat, they wouldn't have been as appealing."

I explained that the animal fat had burdened Morgan's liver and pancreas. "You felt stabilized for the first few years because you weren't going so long between meals, and because the high-protein/high-fat combo had forced your adrenal glands to work harder, pumping out their energy hormones." Now, as she was getting older, she was exhibiting all the symptoms of adrenal fatigue and digestive distress, because her liver and pancreas had become sluggish. This was behind the weight gain, too.

"Your liver can't store glucose anymore to provide you with energy, and your adrenals are running low on adrenaline. We need to change your diet—lower your animal proteins to one serving at dinnertime, eliminate all dairy and eggs, and start bringing in natural sugars from fruit. And you need to let go of the carbohydrate fear that's been drilled into you. Bananas, apples, dates, grapes, melons, mangoes, pears, and berries are going to make every difference in your health. You can keep some nuts and seeds in rotation, just don't eat more than a handful once or twice daily."

Kim hesitated. "You're telling a diabetic that what she needs in her life is more sugar?"

I hear this all the time. "Only the natural sugar in fruit," I said. I assured them both that if Morgan used the grazing technique and ate every two hours, using food combining to balance potassium, sodium, and sugar (as I describe in Chapter 8, "Adrenal

Fatigue"), she would do great. Any and all fruits and vegetables were wonderful components of those snacks and meals. Suggested healing food combos for Morgan were celery or cucumbers with dates, apples, walnuts, or seeds.

Within the first month, Morgan felt more energy and emotional stability than she had in the last ten years. Her weight was going down, and she could finally exercise without collapsing afterward. Smoothies with dates, bananas, and celery became her favorite post-workout meal. And even though it seemed counterintuitive to all advice on the diabetes front, she decided she was feeling so great with the change in diet that she only wanted one serving of animal protein a week.

Within four months, Morgan had reversed her type 2 diabetes. Her doctor was baffled as he presented the results of her A1C test— that it was back to normal. In the months that followed, Morgan continued to restore her pancreas, liver, and adrenal glands—and get her life back on track.

CHAPTER 8

Adrenal Fatigue

Key components of your endocrine system are your *adrenal glands,* which are small lumps of tissue located directly above your kidneys. Your adrenal glands produce hormones critical for your health, including adrenaline, cortisol, and hormones that in turn regulate the production of sex hormones such as estrogen and testosterone.

The primary trigger for your adrenal glands is stress, which causes them to produce extra amounts of hormones such as adrenaline. This is an excellent survival mechanism built into your body for short-term emergencies, as the additional hormones are likely to help you get through whatever crisis is occurring.

If the stress continues over a long period, however—for example, if you're going through a bankruptcy, a divorce, the death of a loved one, or some other cause of severe emotional turmoil—your adrenal glands will eventually become damaged from being on continual "hyperdrive." Undergoing a very substantial amount of stress in even a relatively short period can also overstrain the adrenals; a common example is childbirth, which requires an enormous amount of adrenaline.

In fact, medical communities are unaware that postpartum fatigue and depression are often the result of adrenal glands becoming so exhausted after the process of childbirth that they abruptly fail to produce enough of the right hormones at the right times to keep the mother strong, vibrant, and happy.

When your adrenal glands become overextended, they have the equivalent of a nervous breakdown and behave erratically.

Some alternative medicine doctors believe that when the adrenals partially "burn out," they simply stop producing the full amount of hormones needed. That's an oversimplification of the complex role these glands play in reacting to moment-by-moment emotional and environmental changes. What really happens is that instead of operating in a rock-steady manner that creates precisely the right amount of hormones for each new situation, exhausted adrenals may produce *too little* or *too much* hormone—something like the massive mood swings in someone with bipolar disorder.

For example, depression can result when out-of-control adrenals wildly overreact to a situation and flood you with *too much* adrenaline. The excess adrenaline may in turn burn away your brain's reserves of *dopamine,* a neurotransmitter hormone vital to your feeling happy, and so leave you feeling depressed. It's this variable behavior producing hormonal extremes on either the low or the high side at any moment that characterizes genuine *adrenal fatigue.*

While alternative doctors don't grasp all the nuances of adrenal fatigue, they're way ahead of mainstream doctors who don't even recognize that this illness *exists.*

The truth is that adrenal fatigue has been with us since the start of the human race.

What's changed is how pervasive it's become. Thanks to our fast-paced and stress-filled times, over *80 percent* of us will undergo adrenal fatigue multiple times in our lives.

ADRENAL FATIGUE SYMPTOMS

If you have adrenal fatigue, you may experience one or more of the following symptoms: weakness, lack of energy, trouble concentrating, becoming easily confused, forgetfulness, trouble completing basic tasks you could once handle easily, hoarse voice, poor digestion, constipation, depression, insomnia, not feeling rested after waking from sleep, and relying on naps during the day.

Adrenaline plays a vital role in dreams (when you're running in a dream, for example, your adrenals become stimulated and release the hormone), so in extreme cases of adrenal fatigue, some people are unable to dream enough for the needs of the mind, soul, and spirit. In very extreme cases, some people are so weak that they can't get out of bed for more than a couple of hours a day.

Fatigued adrenals will often also have effects on other glands and organs. For example, your pancreas can become inflamed and/or enlarged from working overtime to compensate for adrenal underperformance. Your heart may need to work harder as it tries to regulate unusual cortisol and blood sugar levels. If excess cortisol abruptly races through your body and destroys your liver's reserves of glucose, glycogen, and iron, your liver will have to work extra hard to create more. And your central nervous system and brain can go off-kilter from sudden floods of cortisol.

Too little cortisol can wreak its own havoc. Cortisol plays a key role in converting the thyroid storage hormone T4 into the usable hormone T3, and in allowing the T3 to penetrate and "charge up" your cells. When your adrenals underperform, they can create a thyroid hormone shortage on the cellular level. In this case, even if you have a healthy thyroid that's testing as normal, you can experience hypothyroid symptoms such as weight gain, depression, hair loss, brittle nails, rough or thinning skin, feeling cold, fluctuating blood sugar, and a myriad of other issues.

You can also have these symptoms with perfectly healthy adrenal glands but a malfunctioning thyroid (see Chapter 6, "Hypothyroidism and Hashimoto's Thyroiditis"). Then again, you can have *neurological fatigue,* which is caused by the swelling of the central nervous system as a result of such viruses as Epstein-Barr and shingles. Because there are myriad causes for energy loss, it's difficult to know whether you have adrenal fatigue based on a list of symptoms alone. Fortunately, there are some additional clues you can look for.

MORE SIGNS YOU HAVE ADRENAL FATIGUE

If you have several of the symptoms described in the previous section, and your condition also matches two or more of the scenarios that follow, then it's very possible you have adrenal fatigue.

- **You "crash" in the early part of your day and/ or throughout your day.** Again, even if you've had a normal amount of sleep the night before, you may feel the need to lie down and close your eyes before lunchtime if you lack adequate adrenal hormones.

- **You feel tired all day at work, but feel more energetic at home in the evening.** This happens when your exhausted adrenal glands hold back their limited reserve of hormones during your stress-filled day in case an emergency arises, then let go of the reserves when you're back home in a relaxed environment where you're much less likely to encounter a crisis.

- **You're exceptionally exhausted at night but have trouble falling asleep.** The act of sleeping, and especially falling into REM sleep, requires adrenal hormones. If you're short on these hormones, you may experience insomnia, unsatisfyingly light sleep, and/or dreamless sleep.

- **You feel unrested even after a full night's sleep.** Again, if you lack enough adrenal hormones to fuel REM sleep and dreaming, you won't have a satisfying night. On top of that, low hormones can rob you of so much energy that you'll feel weak no matter how much sleep you get.

- **You experience continual sweating under your armpits after performing even light tasks.** This is the result of your entire endocrine system working overtime to compensate for the lack of adequate adrenaline.

- **You're continually thirsty and can't seem to quench your thirst; or you have a continually dry mouth; or you're frequently craving salt.** This is caused by a substantial number of electrolytes in your bloodstream and nervous system getting destroyed by an abrupt flood of cortisol. Water, soda, coffee, alcohol, and most other beverages won't solve this problem. You need to replenish the electrolytes by drinking something that has the right balance of sodium, potassium, and glucose—e.g., coconut water, freshly pressed apple juice, freshly pressed celery juice, or a celery/apple or celery/cucumber juice blend.

- **Blurry vision or difficulty focusing eyesight.** This is caused by a flood of excess cortisol—which tends to dehydrate any area—affecting one or more sensitive spots near the eyes, which require a great deal of constant hydration. Other symptoms are dark circles around the eyes and/or sunken eyes.

- **Continual craving for stimulants.** If you frequently feel the need for stimulants to keep you going—such as cigarettes, coffee, caffeine-infused soda, sugary snacks such as cookies or doughnuts, or even prescription-drug "uppers" such as amphetamines—you may instinctively be seeking a substitute for your missing adrenal hormones. While stimulants will give you a quick energy boost, you'll soon "crash" after their effects fade away. Plus, by forcing your adrenals to regularly over-perform and then become exhausted, these stimulants create an up-and-down cycle that makes their already poor functioning even worse over time.

AVOIDING ADRENAL FATIGUE

The most straightforward way to keep your adrenal glands strong and healthy is to avoid extended and/or extreme stress and strain that sets them up to overproduce adrenaline. For example, if you're pushing yourself too hard physically by taking on multiple jobs and skipping sleep, consider cutting back on obligations, if that's an option, to allow your adrenals time to recover and heal.

If that's not a possibility, following the advice in this chapter will still help you recover.

Also avoid artificial stimulants, such as drugs or mega-doses of caffeine, designed to give you an adrenaline "rush." These will make you feel good temporarily, but in the long term risk burning out your adrenal glands.

Another strain on your adrenals is strong emotion. That doesn't mean you should avoid *all* powerful emotions. For example, if you're feeling extreme joy, your adrenals will generate a hormone that's *good* for your body and won't overtax the glands. If you're feeling fear, however, your adrenals will produce a form of adrenaline that's destructive, and over time it will wear down both the glands and other vital parts of your body.

You might ask, "How is it possible that some emotions are better for the body than others? Don't my adrenal glands excrete the same adrenaline in response to *any* emotion?" That's what medical communities believe—and they're mistaken. The truth is your adrenal glands produce 56 different blends in response to different emotions and situations. More specifically, they produce 36 varieties of adrenaline that address everyday situations (e.g., feeling afraid, walking briskly, moving your bowels, bathing/swimming in water, dreaming), and 20 for less common scenarios (e.g., childbirth, fighting off a physical attack, mourning a death).

As a rule of thumb, if something makes you feel bad emotionally, it's probably damaging your body and making you more vulnerable to illness; and if it persists, it's also exhausting your adrenal glands. So you ideally want to let negative feelings such as fear, anxiety, anger, hatred, guilt, and shame arise and pass by instead of suppressing or engaging with them.

Turning away from painful emotions and towards joyful ones is much easier said than done. For emotional support, you'll find a number of suggestions in Chapter 22, "Soul-Healing Meditations and Techniques," and Chapter 23, "Essential Angels." These chapters also include spiritual balance exercises you can tap into when life seems to be throwing everything at you at once.

ADDRESSING ADRENAL FATIGUE

If considering the symptoms and scenarios described earlier in this chapter leads you to believe you have adrenal fatigue, don't despair. You can take a number of concrete steps, as described below and in Part IV, to heal your adrenals and return them to their optimal strength.

If your adrenal fatigue is mild, then you might restore your health in one to three months. If it's moderate, it might take 6 to 12 months. And if it's severe, it might take one to two and a half years. Other factors that can affect this time span include your overall health and what's going on in your life—e.g., if you're in a state of crisis that's continuing to strain your adrenals, you'll require a lot more time to heal.

However long it takes, the sooner you get started on the road to recovery, the sooner you'll start feeling better and restoring your adrenals to full health.

External Cortisol: For Emergencies Only

If you're in a state of crisis, a quick fix is taking cortisol replacement medication. This will provide your body with extra hormones to take the place of the ones not being generated by your underactive adrenal glands.

While this is the treatment of choice by doctors, it isn't an ideal solution, because your body needs a variety of types and amounts of hormones from your adrenal glands throughout the day to address different situations. Taking one pill in the morning isn't comparable to adrenal glands that are actively reacting to your body's needs every moment.

Also, cortisol medication is an immunosuppressant that weakens your immune system, making you vulnerable to a host of other issues.

So medication is, at best, a temporary fix to get you functional again . . . and buy you time to heal your adrenal glands properly using the techniques that follow.

Graze Every One and a Half to Two Hours

Most of us eat three relatively heavy meals a day with long stretches in between. This is tough on the adrenal glands, because one and a half to two hours after a meal your bloodstream runs low in glucose, which means you've run out of the sugars you've consumed. Once your blood sugar drops, your adrenal glands are forced to produce hormones such as cortisol to keep you "running." This means that if you frequently go without eating for long stretches, you're putting your adrenals under a steady strain and not giving them a chance to recuperate.

Therefore, the best way to heal your adrenal glands is to eat a light, balanced meal every 90 minutes to two hours.

In other words, use a *grazing* approach to food. This is critical to know—because diet trends right now are sending people in the opposite direction. Following the fashion on this will rob you of the opportunity to heal your adrenal fatigue.

The grazing technique works because the frequent meals keep your blood sugar steady throughout the day; and as long as your glucose isn't dropping, your adrenal glands don't have to interfere. Giving your adrenal glands lots of rest allows them to devote energy to healing and restoring themselves.

Each of your meals should ideally contain a balance of potassium, sodium, and sugar. Understand that we're talking about natural sugars from fruit here, the type that contains critical minerals and nutrients, unlike table sugar or lactose, the sugar present in dairy. Some examples of great meals for healing your adrenals include:

- A date (potassium), two celery sticks (sodium), and an apple (sugar)

- Half an avocado (potassium), spinach (sodium), and an orange (sugar)

- A sweet potato (potassium), parsley (sodium), and lemon squeezed on kale (sugar)

To be clear, you can also have larger meals. The examples above needn't be substitutes for your breakfast, lunch, and dinner; rather, they can serve to keep your blood sugar levels steady in between those bigger meals.

Beyond eating frequent light meals, there are specific foods you can eat to restore your adrenal glands.

Healing Foods

Certain fruits and vegetables either help protect your adrenal glands or speed their recovery by strengthening the nervous system, reducing inflammation, easing stress, and providing critical nutrients for adrenal function. The following are among the top foods to eat to bounce back from adrenal fatigue: sprouts, asparagus, wild blueberries, bananas, garlic, broccoli, kale, raspberries, blackberries, romaine lettuce, and red-skinned apples.

What *Not* to Eat

If you have mild adrenal fatigue, you might be set with following the other advice in this chapter. If you have a moderate to severe case, however, then until you get stronger, you'll probably need to take the temporary extra step of cutting out foods that put a strain on your adrenal glands and slow them from healing. Please note that many diet experts recommend eating a lot of animal protein. This is either because they don't realize how much fat can hide in even lean animal protein or because they think that fat content is a good thing. This protein advice can seem very convincing, so beware; it's bad for *anyone,* and especially unhealthy if you have adrenal fatigue. The high fat strains your pancreas and liver and eventually creates insulin resistance, making it difficult for your body to maintain a stable level of glucose . . . which in turn creates a massive strain on your adrenal glands as they struggle to produce hormones to compensate.

Diet experts also often counsel people to cut out carbohydrates from their diets. Again, this is not good and can result in strain, because your body needs carbs for energy. Following these diet trends will slow you down and keep you from healing your adrenal fatigue. Take care to avoid such unproductive diets, and instead follow the advice in this chapter to make your adrenal glands strong again.

Healing Herbs and Supplements

- **Licorice root:** helps balance the body's levels of cortisol and cortisone.

- **Spirulina (preferably from Hawaii):** contains high levels of superoxide dismutase (SOD) and chromium, which reinforce adrenal strength.

- **Ester-C:** this form of vitamin C lowers inflammation and soothes adrenal glands that have become enlarged from overexertion.

- **Chromium:** helps balance insulin levels, and augments the strength of adrenal glands, thyroid glands, and the pancreas.

- **Eleuthero (aka Siberian ginseng):** enhances the body's ability to react and adapt, which helps protect the adrenal glands from overreacting to stress.

- **Schisandra:** helps suppress kidney spasms, which in turn reduces adrenal gland stress.

- **Ashwagandha:** helps balance the production of testosterone, dehydroepiandrosterone (DHEA), and cortisol.

- **Magnesium:** lowers anxiety and calms an overactive nervous system, reducing adrenal gland stress.

- **5-MTHF (5-methyltetrahydrofolate):** augments the strength of the central nervous system, which reduces strain on the adrenal glands.

- **Cordyceps:** renews the strength of the gallbladder and liver so these glands can more effectively process excess cortisol in the bloodstream.

- **Panax ginseng:** enhances the body's ability to react and adapt, which helps protect the adrenal glands from overreacting to stress.

- **Rose hips:** lowers inflammation, soothing adrenal glands that have become enlarged from overexertion.

- **Barley grass juice extract powder:** increases the hydrochloric acid in the stomach, which strengthens the adrenal glands.

- **Astragalus:** strengthens the immune system and the whole endocrine system.

- **Lemon balm:** replenishes the nervous system and helps regulate the production of insulin.

- **Rhodiola:** optimizes adrenal function.

CASE HISTORY:
Fatigued from Animal Fat, Fixed by Fruit

Mary, age 35, went to the doctor with the complaint that she was tired all the time. No matter how much rest she got, she couldn't seem to shake her fatigue. On the job at the shipping company where she worked, she never felt fully awake or alert. Mary's doctor performed a number of tests and called when he received the results. "Nothing is wrong," he said. "You're just a little overworked. You'll bounce back when the holidays have passed."

But the fatigue persisted and steadily worsened in the New Year. This time, Mary visited an integrative medical doctor, who diagnosed her with adrenal fatigue. He was correct. However, along with a huge list of supplements to take, he instructed Mary to remove all carbohydrates and sugars from her diet, except for one green apple a day and occasional berries. She was to stick to three meals per day, with animal protein at each, plus various vegetables.

At first, Mary felt a burst of energy and thought she was healing. Here's what was really going on: to compensate for the loss of sugars in her diet that had resulted in reduction of glucose in her bloodstream, her already exhausted adrenals were now in overdrive and flooding her system with adrenaline. Further, eating animal protein—which naturally included fat—three times a day was burdening Mary's liver and pancreas and forcing her adrenals to pump more of their hormones to keep everything in balance. This is an example of the risk associated with a fad diet that's not backed up by true understanding of what the body needs and how it operates.

After 30 days of eating this way, Mary felt a noticeable decrease in energy. The fatigue was now even worse, and it was harder than ever to drag herself to work each day. On top of this, she had an irresistible hunger for sugar; she started reaching for processed carbs and sweets from the vending machine to feed the cravings. In her bloodstream, the sugars combined with the very high animal fat levels and triggered insulin resistance. Now her adrenals started releasing even more adrenaline and reached a point of near-total exhaustion.

At this point, an intern at Mary's company told her about how I'd helped his mom, so Mary gave me a call. Right off the bat, we removed the animal fats and proteins from her diet and switched her over from three meals a day to the every-two-hour grazing technique. This kept her glucose levels active and stable and put an end to her insulin resistance. We also brought balance into her diet with sodium-rich vegetables, potassium-rich fruits, and protein-rich greens.

Very soon, Mary was back to where she'd started when she went to see the first doctor. Within a month, she was feeling functional again.

And within a year, she was full of energy.

When I checked in with her recently, she said she'd noticed blood sugar-related fatigue in others at her company, so she and the intern had started making their co-workers afternoon smoothies—which were very popular. She said she still liked to graze and felt so much better eating the way Spirit had recommended that she only ventured off her healing diet for very special occasions.

CHAPTER 9

Candida

The popularity of the *Candida* diagnosis was born out of a time when conventional medicine was in complete denial. It was the mid-1980s—practically the Dark Ages in chronic illness—and the medical model was not validating women's health concerns, except by offering hormone replacement therapy or antidepressants. Tens of thousands of women felt unheard and fed up.

Meanwhile, the alternative medicine movement had reached a turning point. An increasing number of alternative doctors and healers were rolling out practices or joining established ones. This was a time when conventional and alternative doctors were starkly divided. You wouldn't find a naturopath or a holistic doctor working in a conventional practice. Alternative doctors felt primed to trump conventional medicine—they just needed something to sink their teeth into so they could prove their knowledge.

A surge of women frustrated with their regular physicians began filling the waiting rooms of alternative practices. Problem was, the practitioners didn't know what was wrong—though they did believe the women were suffering from *something*. This was the great awakening of the mid-1980s through the early 1990s. Women and their health complaints were finally being taken seriously. It was an important time, one that should be celebrated, as women's suffrage is. Yet this historic shift in women's lives didn't make it into any history books.

By this point, the hormone movement had already made a major impact. It was a well-established practice in the conventional medical community to blame anything and everything on menopause and perimenopause. As alternative doctors attempted to diagnose the flood of patients with mystery symptoms, though, they weren't yet on the hormone train. They suspected something else was in play.

The alternative medical community landed on the fungus *Candida*. The label was a breath of fresh air to women who'd gone through decades of conventional medical care and couldn't find answers. *Candida* became synonymous with, *We finally know why everyone isn't feeling well.* It was wrong, but it was still an amazing breakthrough.

Sitting in her naturopath's office and hearing that she had *Candida*, a woman would feel the blessing of validation: "You *are* sick with something." She was still getting a side order of blame as the doctor pointed to lifestyle as the culprit, but it all seemed to make perfect sense. And she might even feel some improvement in her health as she followed the doctor's instructions to cut out fried and processed foods and rich desserts.

By the late 1990s, the popularity of the *Candida* diagnosis had spread from the alternative to the conventional medical world. Now it's mainstream, and it's one of the easiest ways to tell someone, "This is why you're sick."

Do women actually recover when they're treated for *Candida?* No. And the drastic recommended diet of no sugar but high fat and protein only provides temporary relief . . . and later backfires.

In truth, *Candida* is the most inappropriately maligned yeast of our time. We *all* have *Candida*, which is a beneficial fungus residing in the intestinal tract that aids food digestion and absorption. It's possible to be virtually riddled with *Candida* and yet be perfectly healthy. There are people with extremely high levels of it who eat and drink whatever they want without a hint of fatigue or stomach upset. *Candida* by itself is typically harmless.

What isn't yet fully understood by medical communities is that *Candida* is a frequent companion, or cofactor, of other diseases and organisms. These include Lyme disease, shingles, EBV, herpes, *C. difficile, Streptococcus, H. pylori,* diabetes, MS, HHV-6, cytomegalovirus, and many more.

For example, if you have Lyme disease symptoms (see Chapter 16), the conditions that triggered them—e.g., antibiotics, unhealthy foods, lack of sleep, stress, fear—plus the inflammation created by any type of viral and/or bacterial infection is likely to result in a higher reproductive rate for *Candida*, making it more probable that a test for *Candida* turns up positive. Keep in mind that tests for *Candida* are still fallible and inconclusive. Even if the test doesn't show a positive, you can have *Candida*. Still, what's causing the damage to your body isn't the fungus; it's everything else.

Blaming *Candida* is like shooting the messenger. A large buildup of *Candida* can be an indicator that there's something wrong that bears investigation, *not* that the problem is the *Candida* itself.

Yet it's comparatively easy for doctors to employ a handful of tests to detect *Candida*, while it's currently almost impossible for them to detect the true culprits behind fibromyalgia, MS, Alzheimer's, dementia, certain UTIs, certain types of adrenal fatigue, chronic fatigue syndrome, lupus, rheumatoid arthritis, Lyme disease, thyroid disease, and numerous other illnesses that medical communities don't yet have a handle on. *Candida* has become a convenient scapegoat.

THE TRUTH ABOUT *CANDIDA*

A number of absurd notions have arisen in medical communities regarding *Candida*, built on misinformation and reinforced by decades of fads. You'll have to read these next sections with an open mind, because they contradict everything you've been told about this relatively innocuous fungus.

Recognizing the Rare Case

Candida has been misdiagnosed as the cause behind major medical problems for hundreds of thousands of patients yearly. The truth is *Candida* plays a role in serious health issues for less than 0.1 percent of the populations of the U.S. and Europe combined.

In the less than 0.1 percent of cases in which *Candida is* doing notable harm and requires treatment, the out-of-control fungus will typically create a moderate-to-high fever that can become chronic and long term, ranging from weeks to months. Clinical blood work will also show the high levels of *Candida* in the bloodstream. These true cases of *Candida* are typically due to post-surgical complications, and there's almost always a rampant bacterial infection at the same time.

If a doctor tells you that your symptoms are from *Candida,* the odds are enormous that she or he is mistaken.

Candida and Leaky Gut Syndrome

Candida has been accused of drilling through the linings of the colon and intestinal tract, resulting in leaky gut syndrome.

This is not exactly true.

The worst that's likely to result from a high level of *Candida* is formation of calluses on irritated portions of the intestinal lining that mildly hinder food absorption. In almost all cases, that's as bad as *Candida* gets. (For the true cause of leaky gut syndrome, see Chapter 17, "Gut Health.")

The Canary in the Mine

Candida's home is the gut, but it can also appear in the liver, the spleen, the vagina, and elsewhere. This causes no notable harm beyond some slight extra strain on your immune system.

However, like a canary in a coal mine, *Candida* can be an indicator of something else truly worrisome that's spurring the fungus's growth. For instance, a vaginal *Streptococcus* infection could go unnoticed by doctors, while yeast that's also present could receive the blame for the patient's discomfort. Doctors would do well, instead, to take the *Candida* as a sign to look for the underlying strep bacteria.

Treat the Root Cause

You almost never need to treat an overabundance of *Candida* directly. Instead, address the root cause of the illness that's creating your symptoms. Once you put an end to the real illness, *Candida* levels will naturally return to normal.

One bright spot in medicine today is that popular treatments for *Candida,* such as healthier eating habits, are also components of effective treatment for many of the genuine illnesses *Candida* accompanies. When someone changes her diet to eliminate foods such as cake, bread, and diet soda, her immune system will naturally strengthen, making her body less hospitable to autoimmune disease and other conditions.

However, other aspects of the diet recommended for *Candida* can be detrimental . . .

Fear of Fruit

One of the greatest misconceptions about *Candida* has to do with what foods feed it. While it's known that *Candida* may feed on sugar, the confusion lies around what *kind* of sugar.

People often think that all sugar is the same. That's like saying all water is the same, from a glass of fresh drinking water to the water in the toilet bowl.

In fact, the fructose that naturally occurs in fruit is actually bonded with compounds and substances—including antioxidants, polyphenols, anthocyanin, minerals, phytochemicals, and cancer-killing micronutrients—that annihilate almost all diseases and actually kill off *Candida*. Even when sugar is separated from fruit and concentrated into fructose, it still doesn't have the ability to feed *Candida*.

Further, fruit sugar leaves your stomach in three to six minutes and doesn't even touch the intestinal tract. So if your fear is that fruit sugar feeds *Candida*, you needn't worry anymore. Fruit's fiber, pulp, skin, and seeds kill not only all varieties of *Candida*, yeast, and fungus but also parasites, worms, and non-useful bacteria like *E. coli* and *Streptococcus*. Fruit is your anti-*Candida* secret weapon. (For more information, see Chapter 20, "Fruit Fear.")

Sugars that *do* feed *Candida* include table sugar, processed cane sugar, processed beet sugar, sugar from sources like agave nectar, processed grain sugar of any kind, and sugar from corn (such as high fructose corn syrup). So this is where the alternative doctors were helping people—by encouraging them to lay off the chocolate cake.

The Fat and Protein Myth

It's a huge misconception that eating a high-fat, high-protein diet starves *Candida*. Fat and protein actually *feed Candida*.

Proteins, which are inflammatory, are sticky and bind to the intestinal tract. The buildup of undigested proteins in someone with a weakened digestive system can result in a breeding ground for *Candida* and other varieties of fungus, as well as parasites and bacteria.

Relying on fat as your main calorie source will result in the highest *Candida* growth. A patient may follow a doctor's outlined diet to a T and it may *seem* like everything is okay. Silently, though, the *Candida* is multiplying in the patient's system, gorging itself on the poultry and eggs and oils she consumes. The day the patient caves to a craving for ice cream at her son's birthday party, the *Candida* will expose itself— and she may be worse off than when she started.

The best anti-*Candida* approach is to eat a low-fat, low-protein diet that incorporates plenty of fruits and vegetables.

HEALING FROM *CANDIDA*

The best way to heal from a flare-up of *Candida* is to address the illness that's the real cause of your symptoms.

That said, if you have no other mystery illness symptoms, no system imbalances, no autoimmune issues, or any other health problems, and you're truly confident that you're one of the rare cases in which *Candida* is an isolated issue, then follow the advice in Chapter 17, "Gut Health." The information there will benefit anyone, including those who just want to address *Candida* as a side issue to an underlying health problem. Your goal in addressing your *Candida* is to increase levels of hydrochloric acid in the digestive fluid, rebuild the intestinal tract, and strengthen and detoxify the liver.

Also keep in mind that you should avoid both antibiotics and antifungal medications. These wipe out all bacteria in your gut— including good bacteria—which severely weakens your immune system. An impaired immune system is a trigger for viruses, bacteria, and/or fungi that are lurking in your body and highly resistant to these drugs, so they may start reproducing and reducing your quality of life.

CASE HISTORY:
Not *Candida* After All

Margaret was a 42-year-old kindergarten teacher when she started to experience extreme fatigue. Even if she got a full night's sleep, she'd wake up unrested and feel tired for the remainder of the day.

Soon her elbows, knees, and ankles began to feel tender and achy, and she had trouble getting up and down from the floor for circle time with her class. Foods that used to give her no problem were now causing gastrointestinal distress, and she constantly felt bloated. On top of all this, Margaret periodically ran hot or cold, and started to dress in layers so she could adjust at a moment's notice to her sweat spells or freezing fingers.

When Margaret returned to school yawning and with dark circles under her eyes after a long weekend of doing nothing, her assistant teacher suggested she get a checkup. At Margaret's visit to her regular MD, he took a blood sample to test for thyroid issues. After the doctor got the results, he called to say that nothing was wrong. "You're perfectly fine."

Unsatisfied, Margaret asked her sister for the name of the functional medicine doctor she'd raved about. As Margaret sat fanning herself in the doctor's air-conditioned exam room, he smiled knowingly. "The problems you've been experiencing are hormonal," he said, and added that it was possibly a disorder or the initial stages of perimenopause. Either way, the doctor insisted that the issue had coupled with *Candida* to cause her symptoms.

Margaret was so relieved she had to fight the urge to hug the doctor. She finally felt she had an answer. She bounded out of his office with prescriptions for bioidentical hormone replacement therapy (BHRT) and antifungal medication, as well as a printout explaining the need to clean up her diet and eliminate processed sugar, processed oil, and fried food.

After taking the ten-day course of the antifungal drug, she didn't feel better. She returned to the functional medicine doctor to say that, in fact, her gut felt worse. He sold her a probiotic and assured her that it would take care of the discomfort. A week later, even with the probiotics, the BHRT, and her new diet, Margaret was doubling over with stomach cramps during show-and-tell at school.

This time, Margaret decided to go to a naturopath. The naturopath nodded as Margaret recounted her story, then agreed that hormonal imbalances and *Candida* were to blame. To address the *Candida,* the doctor put her on a round of colon cleanse supplements and directed her to remove all carbohydrates from her diet. Margaret was to eat mainly animal protein and vegetables.

School was out for the summer by now, so Margaret devoted herself to applying the naturopath's recommendations, even cutting out her favorite balsamic vinaigrette and nightly glass of wine. Her aches and pains, she estimated, felt about 15 percent better from the changes. It seemed like she was on the right track . . . but she couldn't improve past that initial uptick.

The naturopath put her on another cleanse program, but now Margaret watched her progress dissipate. Her tenderness and achiness were back, she developed extreme gas, and she was more fatigued than ever (which I would later tell her was because she had no carbohydrates to carry her). Margaret longed for berries, grapefruit, and bananas—but the naturopath had scared her away from even going near fruit. Through sheer determination, she kept sugar out of her diet for another 30 days and didn't consume carbs of any kind.

Now, she feared that she was worse than before she'd sought help. She felt hopeless and sequestered from the world, completely unsure how she'd function once school started back up in a few weeks. The *Candida* she'd been diagnosed with, she felt, was destroying her quality of life.

At this stage, Margaret found me. Spirit quickly gave me the reading that *Candida* wasn't the problem at all. In fact, it was nearly nonexistent in Margaret's body. The real reason for her suffering was an undiagnosed case of the stomach bacteria *H. pylori,* coupled with the cytomegalovirus (in the herpes family). Her liver was sluggish, functioning at only 40 percent, versus the 65 percent typical for a woman her age. And she had very low hydrochloric acid in her gastric fluid, as well as a moderate amount of mercury-based heavy metal poisoning.

When I brought this up, Margaret recalled that she'd had her metal dental fillings removed six months prior to the onset of her condition. I explained that during the removal process, mercury had been released into her system, saturating and overloading her liver. This had fed and grown the cytomegalovirus and *H. pylori* and diminished the hydrochloric acid she critically needed.

To address the situation, I made a quick adjustment to Margaret's diet plan. We reduced her animal fat and animal protein intake, and allowed certain fruits back into rotation, including wild blueberries, apricots, and even dates. The rest of her diet consisted of vegetables, including leafy greens, potatoes, avocados, various additional fruits, and wild salmon—with an overall emphasis on low fat. With this change, her body was able to drive out a large amount of mercury from her intestinal tract and liver. It also shut down the growth of *H. pylori* immediately and lowered the cytomegalovirus load.

By September, Margaret had gotten better enough to greet her new class in good spirits. Within three months of our first call, she'd lost all of her symptoms—which were never *Candida* or hormone issues to begin with—and completely recovered her health.

CHAPTER 10

Migraines

Nearly 35 million Americans suffer from migraines, which are recurring headaches that cause intense pulsing or throbbing, typically focused on one side. (The word *migraine* originates from the ancient Greek term *hemikrania*, which means "half of skull.") Anyone can be struck with migraines, at any age, but they're most common among women. In the U.S., nearly 35 percent of women experience migraines at some point in their lives.

Those familiar with migraines know well that the pain may be accompanied by extreme sensitivity to light, sound, and/or smell; blurry vision; seeing flashes of light; nausea and/or vomiting; difficulty speaking; and lightheadedness that can result in fainting spells. A migraine can last anywhere from a couple of hours to several days and may rob you of the desire to do anything but lie down in a dark, quiet room until it's over.

This mystery illness can be debilitating, making it difficult to maintain a job or enjoy a social life. People with migraines often feel that they have to schedule their lives around their headaches. They're constantly trying to predict whether meetings, appointments, or lunch out with friends will be ruined by a migraine.

For some, it even becomes a superstition—they can't mention the word *migraine* for fear they'll trigger one. Some clients have told me it feels like life imprisonment. The sense that migraines rule over you and control your every move—as well as the degrading effects of physical pain—can make sufferers feel extremely vulnerable and emotionally sensitive.

This is a complex mystery illness. The combination of issues that trigger it is different for each person. Doctors try to treat migraines with drug "cocktails" on a trial-and-error basis. If one group of drugs doesn't work, your doctor will put you on another, and another, until you start to experience some symptom relief. However, side effects of the drugs can create entirely new problems; plus they might work only temporarily. In some cases, the body can develop resistance to a drug over time—yet weaning yourself off the medication can trigger migraines, too.

This chapter offers information on migraines that's never been brought to the table. It reveals the secrets behind migraines' many triggers and points you toward recovery.

MIGRAINE TRIGGERS

Medical communities don't know what causes most migraines. That's in part why they have a haphazard approach to treating them. So far, the big theory is that a neuropeptide released in the trigeminal system (cranial nerves) results in head pain for people particularly sensitive to the compound.

In fact, it's often not just one thing but a combination of issues that triggers a migraine. Below, I'll lay out the most common triggers. Read through the descriptions and do your best to identify the ones that apply to you—and fully address each one so you can begin your healing process.

Also be aware that you shouldn't stop looking after you identify a single cause. Migraines often result from a cluster of causes—two, three, four, or more issues that *collectively* act as a trigger. For example, if you're not getting enough sleep, and you're under chronic stress, but otherwise you're healthy, you probably won't get migraines. But if you also have heavy metal exposure (such as to mercury or aluminum) and on top of that you're eating dairy and eggs (foods that can be mucus-forming, acidic, and allergenic), then the lack of sleep, stress, heavy metals, and food sensitivities could combine to push your system over the edge and trigger a migraine.

The Usual Suspects

There are certain conditions that are well-known for creating migraine symptoms. A trustworthy doctor will first go through the following checklist to see if you have any of these issues. If you suffer from migraines, you've no doubt visited multiple doctors and explored a variety of contributing factors and diagnostic tests. Just for reinforcement, here's the list:

- **Concussion:** a traumatic brain injury, usually caused by a blow to the head or violent shaking of the head and upper body. If you've experienced anything that might have resulted in a concussion, tell your doctor about it. Even if you had a concussion a long time ago and the migraines didn't start until much later, it could have triggered the sensitivity.

- **Meningitis:** severe inflammation and swelling of the protective membranes surrounding the brain and spinal cord. This is typically caused by a viral infection. Other causes are bacteria and certain drugs. If you once had meningitis, even a long time ago, chances are it was a trigger for your future migraine sensitivity.

- **Stroke:** a brain injury in which the blood supply to part of the brain is interrupted or greatly reduced, causing brain cells to die from lack of nutrition and oxygen. This is the easily identified, injury-induced type of stroke.

- **Transient ischemic attack (TIA):** this results in a smaller brain injury than a stroke; it can be so subtle that it's not even felt when it happens, but it can have a substantial impact on health.

- **Brain aneurysm:** the ballooning of a blood vessel in the brain.

- **Brain tumor:** an abnormal mass of tissue in the brain. A tumor can be cancerous or benign, but both types can create migraines.

- **Brain cyst or microcyst:** a sac filled with air, fluid, or other material (usually benign) that forms in the brain.

- **Impeded cervical nerves:** the cervical nerves are eight nerves branching off from the spinal cord that help control different areas of the body. The first two cervical nerves (C1 and C2) control the head. If something interferes with them, a variety of issues can result, including migraines.

If you've gone through the battery of tests, reviewed your medical history with your doctors, and ruled out the elements on the list above, then you're in the mystery realm. What follows are explanations of migraine triggers that medical communities don't yet fully understand . . . along with triggers that I'm disclosing here for the first time.

Epstein-Barr Virus and Shingles

Doctors don't know that millions of people suffer from migraines as a result of the Epstein-Barr virus (EBV), or even the shingles virus.

As explained in Chapter 3, EBV continually inflames your central nervous system—which includes your brain. If EBV gets into your vagus nerve, the inflamed nerve can be a migraine trigger.

Alternatively, shingles can inflame your trigeminal and/or phrenic nerves, which also have the potential to trigger migraines.

To learn if you're being afflicted by the Epstein-Barr virus, read Chapter 3 and see whether you have at least several other EBV symptoms beyond these headaches. If you do, then follow Chapter 3's instructions to fight the virus. To learn whether the shingles virus may be the culprit, read Chapter 11. Taming your EBV or shingles may be all you need to do to end your migraines.

Micro-Transient Ischemic Attack Trigger

Micro-transient ischemic attack is similar to transient ischemic attack, but on a much smaller scale. Medical communities are not yet aware that this micro-stroke-like activity can occur—and trigger migraines.

Sinus-Related Migraines

Some migraines stem from chronic streptococcal infections that sit in the linings of the sinus cavity. In these cases, ear, nose, and throat specialists often recommend sinus surgery to remove scar tissue. Because strep is very difficult to remove once it gets into the sinus linings, if these surgical procedures work at all, then the relief they give patients is only temporary.

A better way to address sinus-related migraines is to strengthen the immune system so that the body can naturally fight infection. The recommendations in this chapter and in Part IV, "How to Finally Heal," will guide you through that.

Ammonia Permeability Trigger

Another major migraine culprit is a defective gut. Medical communities don't know that when your digestive system isn't working properly, ammonia gas can drift out from your gut to your vagus, phrenic, and/or trigeminal nerves. Ammonia can cross the blood-brain barrier and find its way into all parts of the central nervous system. As the gas deprives them of the oxygen they need, these nerves become inflamed . . . and this can in turn disrupt the functioning of your brain, creating migraines.

To determine whether this is happening to you—and, if so, how to fix the problem—read Chapter 17, "Gut Health."

Electrolyte Deficiency Trigger

To remain healthy, your body must maintain a certain level of *electrolytes,* ions created by salt and other components of your bodily fluids. These electrolytes are used to maintain and send the electrical nerve impulses that run your body—and especially your brain, which is the center of your body's electrical activity. When you run low on electrolytes, it can severely disrupt the activity of your brain, which puts a load on your central nervous system and sets off migraines.

The most common cause of electrolyte deficiency is dehydration. Coconut water and fresh juice are top sources of electrolytes to replenish your supply. Try to drink a daily minimum of 12 ounces of cucumber, cucumber-apple, or celery-apple juice (the blends should be half-and-half).

Stress Trigger

Everyone feels stress now and then, in both big and small ways. Some of us have a higher sensitivity to it than others. If you experience chronic stress, the continual surges of erosive adrenaline it generates are likely to create havoc in a number of areas, including your brain and many of the nerves that travel throughout the body. This can create a hypertensive reaction that can tighten specific areas such as the trigeminal nerves, resulting in a migraine trigger.

For ways to ease your mental tension, read Chapter 22, "Soul-Healing Meditations and Techniques."

Menstrual Cycle Trigger

Many female migraine sufferers complain that their migraines come on right before, during, or after their menstrual cycle. This is because when a woman is menstruating, her reproductive system requires 80 percent of her body's energy reserves and immune system functionality. If your body is fending off other triggers such as stress, food allergies, heavy metal toxicity, or dehydration, then when menstruation happens, *boom,* you can end up with a migraine, because those reserves and immune system power switch over to helping the reproductive system. This is why such a large proportion of migraine sufferers are women.

If this is the case for you, turn your attention to minimizing other possible triggers so that your monthly cycle will have less chance of overwhelming your system.

Sleep Disorders

If you aren't getting enough sound sleep (i.e., uninterrupted and complete with dreams), then over time this can create imbalances in your brain chemistry. You're unlikely to get migraines for this reason alone, but it can be a major factor when combined with one or more other problems.

If you have a sleep disorder such as insomnia, take comfort: as you lie awake in bed in the middle of the night, half of your brain is actually asleep. This means that your body is still healing and your central nervous system is still rejuvenating—so if you can, try not to get frustrated or angry when you have a wakeful night. Understanding this secret alone will make you less susceptible to sleep-related migraines.

If it's a physical illness that creates insomnia and is covered by this book—e.g., EBV, shingles, Lyme disease—use the advice in the pertinent chapter and in Part IV, "How to Finally Heal," to help recover from it.

If you're not getting enough sleep because there aren't enough hours in the day with all of your obligations, try to think about where you can cut back. It may feel impossible. Since the alternative is losing hours or days to migraines, though, carving out more hours for sleep is a better trade. You deserve to respect your body's limits.

Heavy Metals and Other Environmental Toxic Triggers

Heavy metals such as mercury, aluminum, lead, and copper can settle into the brain and other organs, such as the liver, and affect their ability to function properly. Potential consequences include anxiety, depression, obsessive-compulsive disorder (OCD), and attention-deficit hyperactivity disorder (ADHD). Another possible result is migraines.

There are also thousands of questionable or flat-out toxic chemicals that you're regularly exposed to in your office, your home, your food, your water, the air you breathe, and so on. These chemicals can eventually enter your brain and disrupt its electrical impulses. Many of us have no control over our environments—what we breathe, what we're exposed to—but we do have the power to remove these toxins from our bodies. For information on that, see Chapter 18, "Freeing Your Brain and Body of Toxins." In some cases, continual detoxing—coupled with any possible avoidance of new toxins—is enough to eventually stop migraines.

Common Migraine Food Triggers

You're unlikely to get migraines from eating a certain food if you're otherwise not sensitive and not dealing with an underlying ailment.

The chances are that *multiple* issues are contributing to your condition—and the following foods are very likely to be triggers:

- **Dairy:** mucus-forming, which adds pressure in the lymphatic system, and ultimately puts pressure on the central nervous system.

- **Eggs:** when you have a weakened digestive system, including low hydrochloric acid, eggs can cause an increase in ammonia, which can saturate and irritate the central nervous system.

- **Gluten (e.g., wheat, rye, barley, spelt):** gluten confuses the immune system and elevates histamines, which can trigger migraines.

- **Meat (e.g., beef, chicken, pork):** when you have a weakened digestive system, including low hydrochloric acid, dense proteins can cause ammonia production, which can saturate and irritate the central nervous system.

- **Fermented foods (e.g., pickles, kimchi, ketchup):** fermented or vinegar-based foods lower the pH in the intestinal tract, making your body system acidic, which can trigger migraines.

- **Salt:** Celtic sea salt and Himalayan salt are best. Do not use table salt.

- **Oils:** canola, corn, cottonseed, and palm oil are highly inflammatory.

- **Additives (e.g., MSG, aspartame):** these are neurotoxic and can be aggressive triggers for migraine sufferers.

- **Alcohol:** extremely dehydrating, and also hard on the liver.

- **Chocolate:** overstimulating and highly aggressive to the central nervous system, chocolate acts as a neurotoxin that can trigger migraines. Some people claim that chocolate and other forms of caffeine can help a migraine. They've experienced that effect because caffeine triggers the adrenals to flood the body with adrenaline, which acts as a stopgap for the inflammation that causes migraines. Over time, though, that caffeine has unproductive repercussions.

To facilitate your healing, it's highly recommended that you stop eating all of the above *at least* until your migraines go away. If that's too difficult, start with the choices you think you can handle and take it from there. It's very positive to be proactive in any way.

Allergic Reactions

When you encounter something to which you're allergic, your body makes histamine to protect you from the potentially dangerous substance. In some cases your body may overreact and produce too much histamine—and this can end up creating migraines. The reaction may be delayed, occurring days after eating an allergenic food.

Think about whether there's anything you're eating, drinking, breathing, touching, or otherwise exposed to that might be making your immune system go haywire. This can range from second-hand smoke, to pollen, to a new neighbor's dog.

If your migraines began only recently, pay special attention to anything with the potential to be allergenic that was introduced into your life shortly before your first episode. Once you identify all possible causes for an allergic reaction, try to cut them out and see if that eliminates your migraines. Your intuition about what you're sensitive to is far more accurate than doctor's office testing, which is flawed, so make a point to listen to your body and stay aware.

ADDRESSING MIGRAINES

As you've just seen, there are a dizzying number of potential triggers for migraines. If you've identified the likely causes for your headaches, then the most helpful thing you can do is eliminate the triggers from your life.

Herbs and supplements, as well as healing foods, are also important. They will help lower your pain and inflammation, mitigate allergic reactions, soothe nerves, help calm you, improve your gut health, and provide a mild detox.

Healing Foods

Specific foods can help prevent and/or heal your migraines by relaxing muscles, flushing out toxins, bolstering brain tissue, improving digestion, soothing nerves, and providing critical nutrients. Fresh celery juice, cilantro, hemp seeds, papayas, chili peppers, garlic, ginger, kale, cinnamon, and apples are among the top foods to eat for addressing migraines.

Healing Herbs and Supplements

- **Chrysanthemum tea:** calms allergy-based reactions, reducing histamine.
- **Feverfew:** helps keep blood vessel expansion balanced during crises such as migraine attacks.
- **Butterbur:** fortifies the basophils (a type of white blood cell) during migraine attacks.
- **Magnesium:** reduces the tension in and around the trigeminal nerves.
- **Ester-C:** this form of vitamin C helps remove histamines from the bloodstream to provide more oxygen to needed areas. It also strengthens the immune system.
- *Ginkgo biloba*: calms allergy-based reactions, reducing histamine.
- **White willow bark:** lowers inflammation and reduces pain. **Kava-kava:** soothes tense nerves.
- **Lemon balm:** reduces inflammation and soothes the central nervous system. Also kills viruses that may be inflaming the nerves.

- **Rosemary leaf:** helps protect the blood vessels.

- **Riboflavin (Vitamin B$_2$):** aids nerve function.

- **Coenzyme Q10 (CoQ10):** reduces inflammation and boosts the nerves' ability to send messages.

- **Cayenne pepper:** alleviates pain and helps maintain your histamine balance.

- **Skullcap:** soothes tense nerves.

- **Valerian root:** relaxes the vagus nerve and reduces hypertension associated with migraine pain.

CASE HISTORY:
In the Dark No More

Erica had been suffering from migraines since she was ten years old. She could remember the first one clearly: she'd been standing under the bright stage lights in a school play when out of nowhere, a pain developed in the back of her head that suddenly intensified and radiated to the side of her head.

After that, Erica learned that the only way to manage a migraine was to lie in a dark, silent room. Sometimes the headache would radiate to the other side of her head. Sometimes the pain would make her vomit. When she got older, migraines often hit before, during, or even shortly after her menstrual cycle. She also noticed that being a passenger in a car could trigger the headaches, as could staying out a little too late with friends. Any kind of emotional conflict could start the pulsing, too.

Now 30 years old, Erica was having problems with her boyfriend of three years.

Derek couldn't understand Erica's need for extra rest and quiet. "I don't appreciate having to tiptoe around my own apartment," he'd say. He also couldn't grasp why his girlfriend didn't join him anymore for a few drinks out on the town. Erica would tell him it was because she'd get a migraine from the late night and cocktails, and Derek would go out without her, sending texts about how noble he was for not hooking up with the cute girls at the bar. This always sent Erica into a tailspin, and they'd exchange angry texts until the familiar pain took hold and she had to go lie down.

Erica never felt relief from the many different medications her doctor prescribed. She tried to change her diet based on articles she came across, but that never seemed to be the answer, either. In search of relief, she visited neurologists, nutritionists who specialized in food allergies, and even a psychotherapist when she'd begun to feel isolated and lost. An integrative medical doctor diagnosed Erica with an overabundance of *Candida* and told her to remove all sugars from her diet . . . but she didn't get any real results.

When Erica called me, her voice was quiet. She said Derek was in the other room, and he'd make fun of her if he knew she was still looking for ways to get better. He'd told her he had a theory that she had a victim mentality, and that her "migraines" were an elaborate scheme to get more attention.

The first thing Spirit instructed me to tell Erica was that this was nonsense. Her pain was all too real.

Then I told Erica that Spirit said she had high levels of mercury in her brain and liver, due in part to heavy metal exposure when she was a child. This wasn't all: she was also chronically dehydrated, as well as allergic to eggs, dairy, and wheat gluten. She'd developed deficiencies in nutrients critical to her nervous system, including vitamin B_{12}, zinc, selenium, and molybdenum. These were also essential cofactors to electrolyte preservation.

To help Erica heal, Spirit advocated potassium-rich foods for rehydration, cilantro for heavy metal removal, and straight celery juice as a source of much-needed mineral salt for the central nervous system. Following this protocol, Erica started to balance out quickly. She stayed away from the instigative foods mentioned in this chapter, focused on staying hydrated, got plenty of rest, and started taking several of the supplements from the "Healing Herbs and Supplements" section.

For the first time in 20 years, she was now migraine-free.

And for the first time in three years, she was free of Derek. With a clear head, she'd reevaluated their relationship and decided to set her sights higher.

CHAPTER 11

Shingles—True Cause of Colitis, TMJ, Diabetic Neuropathy, and More

In the medical world, *shingles* seems like an open-and-shut case. You've got a patient with the textbook rash, nerve pain on the side or back, and that's all, folks.

If that were true, there wouldn't be any need for this chapter.

The truth is that the shingles virus is responsible for millions of people's mystery symptoms, from rashes that confound dermatologists to neurological symptoms like twitching, tingling, burning, spasms, chronic migraines, headaches, and much more. Varieties of shingles are responsible for Bell's palsy, frozen shoulder, diabetic nerve pain, colitis, vaginal burning, TMJ, Lyme disease, and even misdiagnosed MS.

Shingles is an illness that results in fever, headaches, rashes, joint pain, muscle pain, neck pain, sharp nerve pain, burning nerve pain, heart palpitations, and other highly unpleasant symptoms. The earliest shingles strains came into existence around the turn of the 20th century. Medical communities believe shingles is caused by the *zoster* virus, which is a species in the herpes family. And that's actually correct—as far as it goes.

What doctors don't yet know is that there isn't merely one type of shingles virus, but *31* varieties. This matters because different types of shingles cause different symptoms. It also matters because medical communities don't even recognize the majority of shingles cases as being the result of a virus. For example, any of the more aggressive varieties of shingles can cause Lyme disease symptoms . . . yet doctors currently believe Lyme disease is caused by *bacteria.* (For more on Lyme disease, see Chapter 16.)

This chapter covers the 15 types of shingles virus from which people most commonly suffer, and which are almost always treated improperly, sometimes with immunosuppressant drugs, steroids, and antibiotics that could damage a patient's quality of life. You'll learn about shingles symptoms, how the virus is transmitted and triggered, the unique qualities of each strain of shingles, and how to most effectively deal with the two major categories of shingles—those that cause rashes and those that don't—so you can identify and overcome whatever version of the virus you have and live a healthy life.

SHINGLES SYMPTOMS

Signs that you could be suffering from shingles include flu-like fever and chills, headaches or migraines, aches and pains, burning pain, itching, tingling, red rash, and/or pustules (blisters on the skin containing pus).

Medical communities believe that those last two symptoms—red rash and pustules—always accompany shingles. In fact, this is merely the classic presentation of one type of the zoster virus. If a patient displays pustules and blisters in unusual areas, doctors often won't consider it shingles at all. This is a common diagnostic error. Seven of the strains of shingles *do* cause rashes somewhere on the body, just not always in expected areas.

And the other eight strains cause *no* rashes. So if you're experiencing most of the symptoms of shingles but have no signs of it on your skin, and your doctor can't identify a reason for your suffering, there's a good chance you're the victim of a non-rashing shingles virus.

SHINGLES TRANSMISSION AND TRIGGERS

As with any virus in the herpes family, there are numerous ways to catch shingles. You can get it from your mother while in her womb, through a transfusion of infected blood, via an exchange of bodily fluids . . . and even from the blood of a chef's cut finger while eating out!

The Chicken Pox Myth

Contrary to the current beliefs of medical communities, one way that you *can't* get shingles is through chicken pox. Your doctor may tell you that if you've had chicken pox, sooner or later you'll get shingles. This is not the case. The only thing chicken pox has in common with shingles is that they're both viruses in the herpes family that can cause a rash. Chicken pox is an entirely different species of herpes virus from shingles. They essentially have nothing to do with each other.

Why are we being told shingles is chicken pox–related when it's not? This is a prime example of misinformation that was accepted at one point because it *sounded* like it made sense, then was perpetuated to the point where it's now ingrained.

Dormancy and Triggers

If you're infected by shingles or harboring the virus, you probably won't know it for a long time. The chances are you'll carry the virus around for at least 10 years, possibly even 50 years or more, before it strikes.

The virus hides in one of your organs—typically your liver—where it can't be detected by your immune system. It bides its time until some traumatic physical or emotional event weakens you and/or provides an environment that makes the virus stronger. Events such as financial stress or a broken heart can sometimes be enough to act as a trigger.

If you have an especially strong immune system, and/or if your lifestyle keeps you away from shingles triggers, the shingles virus might remain in its dormant state for your entire life and never cause you notable harm.

Then again, if your immune system is a bit shaky, the virus might leave its hiding place and embark on little forays into your body even before a trigger leads to a major outbreak. The virus will typically go into your lower spine, inflaming the sciatic nerve. So if you periodically feel lower back pain that seems to come and go for no apparent reason, it could be a shingles virus shuttling between your liver and spine.

The best strategy against both minor and major shingles attacks is preventative—that is, to steer clear of situations that might embolden the virus to leave its dormant state.

SHINGLES WITH RASHES

There are seven strains of shingles that cause rashes. While the resulting pustules are unsightly and painful, if they're in an easy-to-spot location that the doctor associates with the standard variety of shingles, in a sense they can be a blessing—because the rash makes it more likely that your doctor will at least realize you have shingles and not call the condition idiopathic. However, some shingles rashes may be unidentifiable to the doctor because of their location or pattern.

These seven strains have very similar symptoms. They're primarily distinguished by the different types and locations of rashes they create.

Classic Shingles

Rash appears anywhere from the chest on down to the feet. This might include a rash on the lower back or near the top of the buttocks. It can also include one side of the body or the other, or one leg or the other (but not both). This is the variety you see on TV commercials about the condition, and it's the type that's (wrongly) associated with chicken pox. This is by far the most common strain of shingles—and what doctors mistakenly believe is the only type.

Upper Body Shingles

Rash appears from the chest up—e.g., on the upper chest, shoulders, or neck—but not on the arms. This rash is the closest in appearance to the most common shingles variety.

Both Arms Shingles

Rash appears exclusively on *both* arms and on *both* hands. Also, the rash has an altered pattern, somewhat spotty, with large and small pustules sometimes spaced apart.

One Arm Shingles

Rash appears on one arm only. It can be either arm, but *not* both arms. This breakout also has an altered pattern, somewhat spotty, with large and small pustules spaced apart.

Head Shingles

Rash appears on the top and sides of the head exclusively. The resulting pustules are tinier than those of the above strains, and they sometimes have little "horns" on top. Medical communities often misdiagnose this type as a fungus that needs to be treated with anti-fungal or steroid cream.

Both Legs Shingles

Rash appears on *both* legs, but nowhere else. It has a different appearance than standard shingles, with pustules that look almost like constellations.

Vaginal Area Shingles

Affecting only women, this strain causes a rash that appears outside but near the vagina—e.g., between the rectum and vagina, or on the lower buttocks, or inside the crotch area. This strain is especially notable because doctors often misdiagnose it as sexually transmitted herpes . . . creating unnecessary emotional pain for tens of thousands of women. The primary way to tell these illnesses apart is that this strain of the shingles virus causes substantial pain, while genital herpes—i.e., herpes simplex virus 2, or HSV-2—is typically less painful. Also, this shingles virus creates pustules that are relatively spread out in the genital area and/or lower buttocks, while HSV-2 pustules tend to cluster within a small area.

Shingles Neurotoxin

One of the misconceptions about shingles is that the virus is lurking directly under the skin rash. That's never the case. The virus lies much deeper, positioning itself for the most effective inflammation possible of your nervous system.

However, the virus releases a neurotoxin; and in these seven strains, the viral poison travels outward to your peripheral nerves and your skin. It's this neurotoxin that causes the itchy, irritable red rashes and pustules for which shingles is famous.

While these seven strains create nerve damage both on the skin and far below it that can be quite painful, they're actually the mildest forms of shingles. If you have a strong immune system, and you do nothing to empower the virus, your body might drive out your shingles by itself.

SHINGLES WITHOUT RASHES

While this is entirely unknown to medical communities, there are eight strains of shingles that typically do *not* cause rashes.

As just explained, the rashes from the first seven strains result from a poison, or neurotoxin, produced by the virus that travels outward into your peripheral nerves and skin.

The eight non-rashing strains produce a neurotoxin, too. However, in these cases the poison doesn't move outward into the small peripheral nerves and skin, but instead travels *inward* into larger nerves. These nerves are already aggravated by the virus, but the neurotoxin inflames them even more and creates a greater strain on your immune system.

If you have one of these non-rashing varieties, you'll undergo more internal pain and nerve injury than you would from the strains that cause rashes. Further, you'll feel these symptoms without any outward sign to let your doctor know you're being inflamed by a shingles virus. As a result, your doctor may dismiss what you're feeling as phantom pain, accuse you of being delusional, and refer you to a psychiatrist.

That's if you're lucky.

Or your doctor may believe you and try to help—yet most conventional treatments are likely to make you *worse*.

For example, your doctor may decide you're suffering from an immune system that's mistaken a part of your body for an invader and has begun attacking it. As a treatment, your doctor may prescribe one or more immunosuppressant drugs or steroids to lessen the severity of the attack. However, as noted before, your immune system is not only entirely innocent of wrongdoing, it's your primary defense against the real source of harm. The drugs that weaken your immune system therefore give the shingles virus the opportunity to further reproduce and become substantially stronger.

An even worse situation is if your doctor decides you're being attacked by bacteria and gives you antibiotics, which create a double blow to your health, as they weaken your immune system *and* strengthen the shingles virus.

You can help protect yourself against such disasters by learning the characteristics of the eight non-rashing varieties of shingles.

Neuralgic Shingles (also known as Diabetic Neuropathy)

Neuralgic shingles—which primarily attacks the lower extremities, creating nerve pain, numbness, and/or burning in the legs and feet—is often called *diabetic neuropathy* and misidentified as a complication of diabetes. This is a huge medical myth that needs to be debunked. The sensations a patient is feeling are *not* neuropathy, which doctors believe means that the nerves in a certain area have died. Rather, the nerves are inflamed, creating neuralgia.

And the truth is, there is no link whatsoever between diabetes and so-called diabetic neuropathy. (In fact, in 50 percent of cases, this shingles variety occurs in patients *without* diabetes.) Doctors, though, have no idea that they're dealing with two separate problems, and so they either do nothing or attempt to treat the nerve issue with more medications—which makes the virus stronger.

Maddening Itch Shingles

This virus creates a continually moving itch that can't be scratched. That's because the virus is irritating nerves too far beneath the skin to be reached with fingers. There's no burning, so it's not especially painful; but having a perpetually roaming itch that you can't do anything to relieve can be maddening. If the virus is empowered by a weak immune system and/or by triggers, the severe itching can destroy your ability to get a solid night's sleep, hold a job, or otherwise lead a normal life.

Vaginal Shingles

This virus affects only women. It goes deep into the inner vaginal walls and inflames the nerves there. It also travels inside the bladder and rectum to wreak additional havoc, creating a burning so irritating it's akin to torture.

If a doctor doesn't dismiss it as being "all in your head," she or he will typically misdiagnose it once again as a hormonal imbalance and prescribe hormones to treat it. Since the shingles virus feeds on hormones, this makes an awful situation into a horrific one. Many women have truly suffered from this variety—and so far the medical industry has ignored it.

Colitis Shingles

Medical communities don't know that this virus is responsible for almost all cases of *colitis,* which is a condition that causes severe inflammation and bleeding in the inner lining of the colon. Colitis symptoms include intestinal pain, blood in the stool, weakness, and weight loss.

Colitis has always been a mystery illness and will continue to be so until medical research reveals that it's a variety of shingles. No one knows this yet! Society is once again three to four decades away from learning the truth.

Meanwhile, doctors typically try to treat colitis with immunosuppressant drugs or, even worse, antibiotics, which make the virus stronger. Steroids can put colitis in remission, but because the drugs don't address the shingles itself, the remission tends not to last.

Arm and Leg Burning Shingles

This virus creates a hot, burning pain in your arms and legs. Unlike the rash-based strains that attack arms or legs, with this strain the nerve inflammation and burning sensations all take place far below the skin, so you can't pinpoint them or relieve them.

And because no rash appears to indicate a shingles virus, doctors are likely to prescribe inappropriate medications that make the situation far worse.

Mouth Shingles, TMJ, and Bell's Palsy

This virus affects the gums and/or the area by the jaw. It's also responsible for Bell's palsy (viral inflammation of critical facial nerves) and TMJ disorders (a result of trigeminal nerve inflammation and pain). It's frequently mistaken for a dental issue, leading to unnecessary root canals. Not only does the dental surgery not help, the medications involved weaken the immune system, which allows the virus to grow even stronger.

This viral torture of the mouth can go on for years.

Frozen Shoulder Shingles

This virus aggravates the nerves in the shoulder, causing it to freeze up for anywhere from a month to a year.

This condition is often misdiagnosed as infectious bursitis and treated with antibiotics . . . which only serves to make the virus much stronger. Sometimes, unnecessary surgeries are even performed, since doctors have no idea that shingles is behind the affliction.

Body on Fire Shingles

This virus makes every part of your body feel like it's on fire, simultaneously and relentlessly. It operates by finding a central location by the ganglia deep in the nervous system and releasing its neurotoxin, which spreads throughout the body and inflames nerves everywhere. Needless to say, it creates a great deal of anxiety and fear . . . and these negative emotions produce adrenal hormones that feed the virus and make it even stronger.

This is an especially terrible shingles condition, but thankfully, relatively rare. Keep in mind that the body always has the ability to heal—even from this uncommon variety.

HEALING SHINGLES

Being struck with any kind of shingles is painful and stressful. Whether you have a variety that creates a rash or doesn't, it can be maddening.

Fortunately, there are simple yet powerful remedies for this condition. If you follow the advice in this section daily without fail, you should be able to knock the virus back into a dormant state and render it virtually harmless.

How long this process takes will depend on a variety of factors, such as the amount of time the virus has been in your system, whether you're in a healthy environment or a toxic one that feeds the virus, and whether your immune system has become damaged by inappropriate medications. Roughly speaking, the process may last from a minimum of three months to a year and a half.

Take care of yourself and your immune system by eating well, exercising, and getting enough sleep. And for additional support, read through Part IV, "How to Finally Heal."

Healing Foods

Certain foods can greatly aid the body in healing from shingles with and without rashes. They can help by, variously, attacking the different strains of the virus, supporting the body in recovery from neurotoxin flare-ups, boosting the immune system, healing nerves and stimulating nerve growth, soothing inflamed skin, and detoxifying the body. The ideal foods to concentrate on are wild blueberries, coconuts, papayas, red-skinned apples, pears, artichokes, bananas, sweet potatoes, spinach, asparagus, lettuce (varieties that are leafy and deep green or red), green beans, and avocados.

Healing Herbs and Supplements

- **ALA (alpha lipoic acid):** antioxidant that repairs and fortifies the areas of the nervous system that have been damaged by the shingles virus.

- **Magnesium:** reduces inflammation and calms nerves, which helps stop them from swelling or going into spasm. Also supports the muscles near damaged nerves.

- **MSM (methylsulfonylmethane):** restores nerves that have tightened up from inflammation to a healthy level of pliability and flexibility.

- **Vitamin B$_{12}$ (as methylcobalamin and/or adenosylcobalamin):** repairs and strengthens the areas of the nervous system that have been damaged by the virus.

- **EPA & DHA (eicosapentaenoic acid and docosahexaenoic acid):** repairs and strengthens the areas of the nervous system that have been damaged by the virus. Be sure to buy a plant-based (not fish-based) version.

- **Lobelia:** kills the virus on contact.

- **Feverfew:** reduces inflammation in the nervous system.

- **California poppy:** reduces inflammation and calms nerves, which helps stop nerves from swelling or going into spasm.

- **Licorice root:** very effective at impairing the ability of virus cells to move and reproduce.

- **Zinc:** lowers inflammatory reactions to the neurotoxin produced by the shingles virus.

- **L-lysine:** impairs the ability of shingles virus cells to move and reproduce.

- **Selenium:** restores damaged nerves near the skin.

- **Nettle leaf:** reduces the pain and inflammation of shingles rashes.

CASE HISTORY:
A Pain in the Jaw

Terrence had always experienced fairly good health. He liked to play tennis, go on adventures with his friends, and work long hours at the consulting business he owned. When Terrence was 51 years old, though, he began to develop some sensitivity in his bottom right jaw. Every time he chewed anything on that side, a pain would radiate from his jaw into his face.

His dentist noticed an old metal amalgam filling in one of his molars and pinpointed it as the potential culprit. "There's a low-grade bacterial infection in your jaw," she said. Her solution was to dig out the filling and perform a root canal.

Following the procedure, Terrence experienced a change for the worse. The pain increased, affecting his entire jaw now and making it impossible to chew. The discomfort was barely manageable with mild pain medications. One morning, Terrence woke up with tension in his jaw. It was there every morning afterward.

At a return visit to the dentist, she concluded that Terrence needed more dental work. It seemed to her that the molar next to the tooth where she had done the root canal now needed attention. She believed the root on this adjacent molar was dying, too, so she performed another root canal. Afterward, Terrence's pain didn't lessen. In fact, he now felt it spreading to his neck and shoulder.

Terrence decided to visit an oral surgeon. At first the surgeon was baffled, but he finally said that the problem must be Terrence's temporomandibular joint (TMJ). While the joint looked okay, his pain could be the beginning of a TMJ issue. In case a bacterial infection was in play, the surgeon prescribed antibiotics. After the two-week course of pills, though, Terrence still hadn't found relief.

It had been eight months since his problems started. Each night, it took hours to fall asleep. On a scale of one to ten, he called this level ten pain. To top it off, Terrence's tennis partner had found a new teammate, and the bills were piling up at work. His friends had stopped inviting him on outings, too.

One day Terrence called one of his friends, Jim, to see if they could meet for coffee, but Jim mistook Terrence's need for sympathy for an apology instead. "Don't worry, man," Jim said. "Only Reggie thinks that you've abandoned us."

When Terrence got angry at this, Jim said, "Just a joke! Calm down and get yourself better so you can come on the next hike."

Terrence felt defeated, alone, lost, and in need of answers.

That's when he found my website and scheduled a call. Right away, in the initial scan and reading, Spirit noticed a non-rashing variety of the shingles virus that was inflaming Terrence's trigeminal and phrenic nerves, causing the pain in his jaw, face, neck, and shoulder. A mechanical TMJ issue had not been the underlying cause. However, the nerve inflammation had put pressure on his jaw, which is what caused the tension he felt there at night and upon waking.

I explained to Terrence that he'd had the virus before his first root canal—in fact, he'd had the virus his entire life. When the first dentist had removed the metal amalgam filling, it had released mercury toxins, which along with the anesthetics used for the procedure, had fed and strengthened the shingles virus.

We immediately addressed the virus with the appropriate herbs and healing foods. To allow Terrence to reclaim his immune system, we also removed antagonistic foods from his diet—ones that specifically strengthened the virus, such as corn products, canola, and the whey protein powder his trainer had him consuming twice a day.

Learning the real cause of his pain took away the mystery and fear and allowed Terrence to gain back the confidence that he would heal.

Within a month on this new regimen, Terrence's pain had noticeably decreased.

After three months, he was completely out of the woods.

He'd made many new friends at the local food co-op, too, since he'd started going there for cases of organic produce. The next time a group e-mail came from his friends about a day hike, he wasn't so quick to join them. Instead he decided to sign up for a co-op workday, where he spread the gospel of fruit's healing power to anyone who would listen.

CHAPTER 12

Attention-Deficit/ Hyperactivity Disorder and Autism

Listing a dozen or more symptoms to determine if your child struggles from *attention-deficit/hyperactivity disorder* (ADHD) or *autism* is not a productive way to begin our discussion here. There's already so much confusion out there, so many books, websites, and articles about ADHD and autism indicators, that I don't want to add to the mess.

A mother's intuition is the best tool for identifying ADHD and autism. The bond between mothers and their children is a spiritual force that can never be broken. Moms know their children better than anyone else can or ever will. They know that attention issues don't arise from their children being selfish, stubborn, or insensitive. They know that their children often don't have a choice in their behavior; they know when something deeper is going on.

A mother's gut instinct overrides all clinical systems set in place to diagnose children—and all informational pamphlets, all teacher assessments, all judgments by playmates' parents. It's a mother's sense of her child that will best detect if she or he is struggling with more than just growing pains.

Tens of millions of children have ADHD and autism, and the number is growing at an alarming rate. This chapter is primarily written for parents and caregivers of children who have ADHD and autism—people who know how frustrating it can be to understand their children in the face of certain behaviors, and how challenging it can be not to get the answers and support they need from the outside world.

The chapter can also be useful if you're an adult who has one of these conditions.

Either way, it will help you better understand ADHD and autism by providing information beyond anything that medical communities know. It will also offer you options for ways to address both conditions.

THE HIDDEN UPSIDES OF ADHD AND AUTISM

You're probably familiar with the characteristics associated with ADHD and autism. You understand that it goes beyond fidgeting here and there, not paying attention now and then, and occasional difficulty communicating.

You've probably also read and heard plenty about the two types of ADHD. The first is *inattentiveness,* the type associated with the classic term *attention-deficit disorder* (ADD). This is the subset that girls are more likely to experience, and it often goes undiagnosed for them because observers categorize girls quietly suffering with ADHD as "ditzy" or "spacey" instead. The second type of ADHD is *hyperactivity* and *impulsivity.* Girls can experience this as well, though it appears more often in boys.

These traits of inattentiveness, hyperactivity, and impulsivity are considered ADHD when they're so extreme that a child has difficulty functioning in school, at home, or in other settings. When symptoms go a step beyond ADHD, they fall into the category of autism.

It's common for a child to have both types of ADHD—either to shift back and forth between the two states, or to express them both at the same time. For example, a child could continually forget his lunchbox on the bus *and* be unable to sit still through afternoon lessons at school.

There are upsides to ADHD and autism, though. Children with these conditions often have a high level of intuition, are exceptionally creative, possess an extraordinary ability to see beneath the surface, and—though this goes against traditional thinking—actually have the ability to "read" people easily. Kids with ADHD and autism often think faster, feel more deeply, and are more intuitive and artistic than the norm, in part because of their limited patience for doing things in the "standard" way. (There are also physiological reasons these traits develop in tandem with the well-known challenges of attention-deficit/hyperactivity disorder and autism; we'll cover that in the next section.)

The truth is, ADHD and autism are producing new generations of children who will grow up better equipped to solve our problems and chart the best course for humanity. A term was created in the 1970s for this new breed of kids: *indigo children*. These are children with extra special gifts, such as brilliance and exceptional intuition . . . and, in some cases, even paranormal skills like telepathy.

While being different makes life harder for indigo children—as well as for their families—it also increases their chances of living extraordinary lives.

WHAT CAUSES ADHD AND AUTISM

A popular misconception is that ADHD and autism are the result of a poor intestinal environment. The current thinking goes that an overproduction of *Candida*, yeast, mold, and non-beneficial bacteria are to blame for children's hyperactive, inattentive, impulsive, or antisocial behavior, and that improving intestinal flora will improve children's brain health and alleviate their symptoms.

This theory is a distraction from what's really in play. Anybody can benefit from cleaning up their gut health. In the case of ADHD and autism, though, improving the intestinal environment with probiotics and probiotic-rich foods is only a fraction of a step in the right direction. It doesn't address the true underlying cause of ADHD and autism: toxic heavy metals.

Specifically, ADHD and autism are born from (primarily) mercury, plus aluminum, that settles in the brain's midline cerebral canal, which divides the left cerebral hemisphere from the right.

It might occur to you that it's hard to build up significant exposure to heavy metals in just a few years of a young life. Mercury, however, is a neurotoxin that slips under doctors' noses. Medical communities are due for a massive wakeup call about obvious mercury contamination.

Mercury is a great instigator of ADHD and autism in children in the 21st century. (Mercury is also responsible for most seizure disorders.) Until mercury is addressed, the conditions will continue to affect millions of new kids each year.

It's very easy for a baby to take in heavy metals from her or his mother while in the womb, and for a father to pass along heavy metals at conception. That's because the parents have likely accumulated mercury over decades, and so did their mothers and fathers before them—and mercury tends to stay in the body generation after generation, in some cases for centuries, unless specific steps are taken to detoxify it.

Genetics are not behind ADHD and autism. Do you remember reading in other chapters about how the theory of autoimmune disease—the theory that the body sometimes attacks itself—is false and merely a way of blaming the person who's sick? The genetics theory is a similar scapegoat. Blaming DNA blames the very essence of the child who struggles with ADHD and/or autism, and that's a shame. The reason that ADHD and autism sometimes run in a family is a generation-to-generation transfer of mercury, as well as family patterns of exposure to toxic heavy metals.

It's easy to be exposed to the other toxic heavy metal typically involved in ADHD and autism. Most soda cans are made of aluminum, aluminum foil is a popular item in the kitchen, and aluminum siding is common on homes. Aluminum and mercury show up in pesticides, fungicides, and herbicides, too.

Also critical in the story behind ADHD and autism is the physical location in which the toxic heavy metals settle.

The Cerebral Midline Canal

The brain's midline is located directly between the right and left cerebral hemispheres of the brain. This midline looks like an open canal, but instead of water running through it, a channel of energy does. It's not yet documented in medical research that this canal forms a metaphysical, energetic connection between the two cerebral hemispheres and allows information to be exchanged between them. It will be many decades before this is discovered.

Children have free-flowing midline canals. It's what allows them to learn how to communicate with other people and with the metaphysical realm, and to see things adults don't see anymore, such as angels and imaginary friends.

When toxic heavy metals enter this midline canal—which is supposed to be open and free—they block the electrical and metaphysical energetic transmissions between the cerebral hemispheres. This challenges the child's brain to develop alternative ways to make that exchange happen. Adaptations set in, and the child unconsciously begins accessing areas of her or his brain that most of us never use (at least not until we're older). Metaphysical and electrical energy struggles to find its way into uncharted territory. Electrical nerve impulses begin igniting neurons and firing off neurotransmitters onto brain pathways that aren't supposed to be explored until after a person reaches age 18.

Autism is essentially a more advanced and complicated form of ADHD. Toxic heavy metals are present at higher levels in the midline cerebral canal, and gathered in uneven layers. This helps explain why there's an autism spectrum, with the syndrome displaying in different intensities depending on the child. It all has to do with the amount of heavy metals in the canal, and in what positions they have accumulated. With autism (versus ADHD), the additional layers of mercury interfere even more greatly with the metaphysical and electrical energy communications trying to cross the canal.

To understand ADHD and autism, imagine the Grand Canyon. There's a symbiotic relationship taking place in and around it, between physical and metaphysical elements. There's the water running through the canyon, the wind rising up out of it, the electrical fields from storms and the earth, and the light and heat of the sun. All of it combines just so to make the canyon a visible, energetic, and spiritual force. The brain's midline canal is like the Grand Canyon in this way—so many elements interacting at once to make it work just so.

Now what if the something altered the pristine environment of the Grand Canyon? What if someone started dropping giant boulders into it, and metal barrels? Everything would change. Wind patterns would redirect themselves. The sun would refract at different angles, no longer reaching certain areas but lighting up nooks and crannies that hadn't seen sunshine for thousands of years. Even sound within and around the canyon would change. The whole frequency of the place would be different as the elements adapted.

This is what happens when toxic heavy metals enter a child's midline cerebral canal. We see the child behaving in ways we don't expect because her or his brain is adapting to the extra materials blocking internal communication. It's learning to access different parts of itself.

Specially Evolved Brain Neurons

Children with ADHD and autism also grow specially evolved brain neurons, especially in the frontal lobe. These facilitate communication with others and intuitive abilities for "reading" people (e.g., being able to sense what someone is thinking and feeling). That might seem surprising, since children with ADHD and autism can exhibit antisocial qualities that make them appear to be shut off to others. Their laser-focus on themselves and their personal interests is actually a way to avoid being overwhelmed by the flood of information they're picking up from the people around them. The focus hides these children's powerful intuitive development.

Not only do new, evolved neurons grow in the frontal lobe, but they also develop in other parts of the brain, such as the limbic system, which processes behaviors, emotions, and desires. The new, evolved neurons are excitable—and cause most of what we witness as the issues around ADHD. This is even more true for many autistic children, who grow a greater abundance of these evolved and adaptable neurons.

Age and Brain Development

This sequence of events—the toxic heavy metals accumulating in the midline canal between the left and right cerebral hemispheres, followed by the push to access unused portions of the brain (because communication energy and information cannot pass across the canal), followed by the development of numerous evolved neurons—typically happens no later than age four. At that point, the child has become an indigo child.

However, the toxic heavy metals, such as mercury, can be removed from the child's brain through diet and other detox techniques at any point up to roughly age 18. If this is done, the child's indigo "powers" will remain, while the removal of the heavy metals will most likely end the child's ADHD or autism. This is a win-win, allowing the child to be extraordinary and yet be spared the difficulties associated with having these conditions.

At around age 18, the midline between the cerebral hemispheres closes up. The left and right cerebral hemispheres start to squeeze together, limiting the free and easy flow of energy and childlike, free-spirited information between the left and right sides of the brain. This is the normal process of growing up. It's the body's way of turning one's focus to the responsibilities of adulthood. But it also traps any toxic heavy metals such as mercury that are residing in the canal between the two hemispheres.

If you're an adult with ADHD or autism, this means you'll probably continue having some form of the condition unless you diligently try to keep removing the toxic heavy metals from your system and avoiding new exposure. For most people, ADHD and autism can be viewed not as a negative, but just as living differently from the mainstream. That said, if you have severe ADHD or autism that interferes with your life and relationships, you can follow the advice in the next section to lessen its effects.

Similarly, if you're a parent, the next section will tell you what can be done to address your child's ADHD and/or autism.

ADDRESSING ADHD AND AUTISM

Doctors typically prescribe amphetamines to treat ADHD. That's counterintuitive, because amphetamines are stimulants, which are the last things you'd think would calm down an overactive child or help one who can't focus.

Prescribing amphetamines reminds me of the practice in the late 19th and early 20th centuries of giving children Mrs. Winslow's Soothing Syrup to calm them when they were misbehaving. The concoction did quiet the children rather quickly—because it contained morphine. Eventually, when it was determined that giving children this narcotic was dangerous, the product was taken off the market.

When doctors prescribe amphetamines to help children focus for short periods, it does work most of the time—though medical communities don't know why.

The key to this mystery is the exceptional development that's taken place in your child's brain. Accessing normally unused portions of the brain and the growth of numerous evolved, adaptable neurons requires two to three times the usual amount of glucose, which is the brain's primary food. The chances are your child isn't getting enough glucose to the brain, and that's partly responsible for much of her or his ADHD-related behaviors. Amphetamines stimulate the adrenal glands to produce adrenaline, which the brain accepts in place of glucose to fuel its activities. To override the toxic heavy metals such as mercury in the brain, the adrenaline forces electrical nerve impulses to fire at an alarming rate. This helps stabilize your child's ADHD and helps your child focus, though only temporarily.

The problem is that amphetamines create a huge burden on the adrenal glands (not to mention all the organs regularly flooded with adrenaline). If this drug use goes on for years, eventually the adrenal glands are likely to "burn out" and become unstable, leading to a host of problems. I often speak with young adults who have adrenal malfunction, severe fatigue, and high anxiety as a result of prescribed amphetamine burnout.

A better long-term solution for both ADHD and autism is to make sure you provide ample fresh fruit—preferably organic—for your child to consume. This will give your child the highest quality glucose possible. (See Chapter 20, "Fruit Fear.") Get creative with making fruit a habit, for example, by blending frozen bananas to make a snack the consistency of ice cream.

Right now, a diet trend for ADHD and autism management is to cut out grains and sugar. This is a wise decision—*only* if fruit is taking the place of the other sugars being eliminated. Another trend is the high-fat ketogenic diet. Once again, doctors who fear sugar recommend this one. It's not an advisable path. Any improvement your child displays will be temporary, and only because the high levels of fat force the adrenal glands to release adrenaline, allowing your child to focus better at times. In the end, it will likely result in adrenal fatigue. If your child doesn't get fruit sugar (in its natural form), she or he will continue to struggle with symptoms of ADHD and autism.

This might give you some perspective if your child is drawn to large quantities of high-sugar foods or extremely high-calorie starches such as French fries and battered, fried foods; it's the brain telling her or him it wants glucose. The problem is that in addition to having the worst kind of nourishment-deprived sugar, junk food typically contains lard or rancid GMO oils, which stop the sugar from reaching the brain. So such "treats" do nothing for ADHD or autism.

In fact, beyond steering your child clear of traditional sweets, you ideally want to cut *all* wheat products and gluten from her or his diet. If possible, you want your child to avoid any foods and additives that have toxic qualities, such as corn, canola oil, MSG, and aspartame. (See Chapter 19, "What Not to Eat.")

You'll also want to keep your child away from any other types of poisons—especially toxic heavy metals. (See Chapter 18, "Freeing Your Brain and Body of Toxins.") Always question everything your child is exposed to.

Finally, see if you can put your child on a daily diet of the herbs, supplements, and foods that follow. In all honesty, in about 85 percent of cases, children with ADHD or autism won't want to cooperate. So if you feel your child would benefit from the items below, see if you can tap into inventive ways to make them seem appealing (or camouflage them). Engage your child in the process, too, by gearing your approach to her or his unique desires and personality. A mother or other primary caregiver has the most insight into how to speak to her or his child's best interest. Every child is wonderfully unique and amazing in every way, so just play things by ear and do your best.

Healing Foods

Diet is key to recovery from ADHD and autism. Some foods in particular are especially beneficial for, variously, flushing out heavy metals and other toxins, healing brain tissue, supporting healthy neuron signal transmission, providing glucose to the brain, calming the mind, and strengthening the central nervous system. These foods include wild blueberries, cilantro, coconut oil, celery, bananas, black-berries, avocados, strawberries, and flax seeds.

Healing Herbs and Supplements

- **Spirulina (preferably from Hawaii):** critical for removing heavy metals from the brain. Also helps grow fresh neurons and strengthen neurotransmitters.

- **Vitamin B$_{12}$ (as methylcobalamin and/or adenosylcobalamin):** bolsters the brain and central nervous system.

- **Ester-C:** this form of vitamin C helps repair damaged neurotransmitters and boosts the adrenal glands. It also helps cleanse the liver and remove toxins.

- **Zinc:** fortifies the endocrine system—including the adrenal glands, thyroid, and thalamus—which in turn supports neurotransmitters.

- **Melatonin:** reduces inflammation in the brain. Also helps repair and grow neurons.

- **Lemon balm:** reduces inflammation and soothes the central nervous system. Also kills viruses, bacteria, and funguses that may be inflaming the intestinal tract and causing food allergies.

- **Magnesium:** helps the ability to think, learn, remember, read, and speak. Also calms the central nervous system.

- *Ginkgo biloba*: helps remove mercury from the brain and reduces inflammation there.

- **GABA (gamma-Aminobutyric acid):** strengthens neuropeptides and neurotransmitters, and calms the central nervous system.

- **B-complex:** nourishes and sustains the brain and brain stem.

- **Ginseng:** fortifies the adrenal glands.

- **Probiotics:** balance and support the digestive system, which in turn boosts the immune system. Choose whatever natural and high-quality brand you like.

- **EPA & DHA (eicosapentaenoic acid and docosahexaenoic acid):** helps repair and grow neurons. Be sure to buy a plant-based (not fish-based) version.

CASE HISTORY:
Fruits of a Mother's Labors

As a child, Jonathan had a hard time communicating with friends, family, and teachers. He didn't get along with his little sister. He could never seem to sit still, and focusing was a near-impossible feat. At age five, he was diagnosed with ADHD.

Jonathan's mother, Alberta, was his major support in life. For the next 13 years, she devoted herself to getting to the root of his issues, and to promoting his health and well-being. She kept a journal of every symptom Jonathan exhibited, every health-care professional they visited, every diet, and every medicine he received, such as popularly prescribed amphetamines.

Alberta's husband liked to joke that no matter how good a day Jonathan was having concentration- and hyperactivity-wise, he was just like Rudolph—he never joined in any reindeer games. Part of it had to do with Jonathan's peers leaving him out. Another factor was that Jonathan had more advanced and intense interests than the other children his age.

While Jonathan's behavior wavered between ADHD and mild autism, Alberta knew he was a brilliant, golden, intuitive being. After coming across the phrase "indigo child" in a book, she started referring to him as one.

She always held onto the memory of Jonathan as a seven-year-old, sitting in the backseat of the car wearing jeans, his blue sweatshirt, and his favorite sneakers that he said fit just right. As Alberta sat in the front seat recording the details of the meeting she'd just had with the school counselor, Jonathan started talking to himself. "Nobody understands me," he said. "I just need a little more time to adjust here in the world."

In Jonathan's early adolescence, Alberta found a functional medicine doctor who gave them some results. Dr. Duval said that Jonathan's ADHD and borderline autistic behavior had to do with intestinal flora issues—that is, lots of unproductive bacteria and not enough good bacteria. He believed grains were part of the problem, so he recommended removing all wheat, rye, oats, barley, and so forth from Jonathan's diet. He also felt Jonathan would do best without any processed sugars or dairy products, such as milk, cheese, and butter. He advised lots of leafy greens such as kale, along with other vegetables, some nuts and seeds, and liberal servings of meat, chicken, and fish. For supplementation, Dr. Duval prescribed advanced probiotics to address what he called an unhealthy intestinal environment, as well as immune-supporting supplements.

Jonathan was the rare kid who was eager to please when it came to food. Though Alberta heard from other moms that it was near impossible to influence their children's eating habits, Jonathan didn't mind cutting out wheat and eating lots of leafy greens like kale in its place, along with nuts and seeds and other foods Dr. Duval said were brain-enhancing.

Over the years, Jonathan's focus and communication issues improved enough to get through elementary school, junior high, and eventually high school. For various periods, Alberta homeschooled Jonathan and later hired tutors. Both moves were crucial to Jonathan's scholastic success.

At the age of 18, though, Jonathan still struggled with his symptoms. He and Alberta were trying to get him into college, and both were worried (though Jonathan wouldn't admit it) about how he'd perform away from home, without Alberta's constant support. It would take a miracle for him not to have to rely on prescribed amphetamines and other stimulants.

The past 18 years had been hard on Alberta. Yet she wouldn't have traded a minute of it for anything. Whenever she got frustrated, she remembered that seven-year-old in the backseat, hoping for the world to understand him. At parent-teacher night at Jonathan's school, Alberta got talking with a mother whose child was in a similar situation. That mother gave Alberta my number, and she booked an appointment.

Alberta got on the phone for our first call, and though Jonathan wasn't on the line, I was able to perform the scan on him. I told her heavy metals, predominantly mercury, were the culprits. The functional medicine doctor and other practitioners had been able to improve Jonathan by 40 percent of his healing capacity. They'd been able to take him only so far because they were missing the most important link: the toxic heavy metals.

Substantial amounts of mercury were caught in the midline canal between Jonathan's cerebral hemispheres. (Medical research won't explore this for another two or three decades.) Since Jonathan was 18 years of age, the cerebral hemispheres were starting to squeeze together and close off the canal—but there was still space enough to get radical results.

Alberta sounded relieved that she'd called me in time, but panicked about how things would have turned out for Jonathan if she'd called me just a year later. I assured her that even if Jonathan were older, we'd still be able to get results from detox methods.

Because fats in the bloodstream get in the way of preciously needed glucose reaching the brain, we reduced Jonathan's fat consumption, which had come in the form of animal protein. All these years, the heavy metal contamination in Jonathan's brain had meant that he needed twice as much glucose as he was getting. Alberta said that Jonathan had always been drawn to sweets and frequently seemed to focus better when eating them, though it tended to last only a moment before the processed sugars brought him crashing down hard.

I agreed with her observation and confirmed that processed sugars were not the way to go. Dr. Duval had been right about something—grains and dairy were not helpful, either. What Jonathan needed most were the true brain foods: wild blueberries and other berries, apples, dates, grapes, and any other fruit that Jonathan enjoyed. Vegetables and leafy greens such as kale were also important.

For supplementation, we focused on a high dose of spirulina (mixed with coconut water for glucose and palatability) coupled with two servings of cilantro daily.

"This will be a tectonic shift," Alberta said. "All these years, Jonathan hasn't been allowed to eat fruit."

"Kale and protein as the solution to all life's problems is a well-intentioned trend," I told her. "Kale's amazing, yet it provides a fraction of the brain benefit that fruit does. And we have to be wary of the fat hiding in animal protein. This new diet, with its combination of antioxidant-rich fruit sugar, lowered fats, plus spirulina and cilantro to remove heavy metals, will change Jonathan's life."

And it did. Three weeks into the protocol, Alberta left a message with my assistant. For the first time ever, she'd had an actual, in-depth conversation with her son. Not a monologue, a dialogue. He didn't talk *at* her, or cut her off, or abruptly leave the room. Instead he listened and responded, and they went back and forth like two functioning adults. Day by day, she said, she could sense the heavy metals leaving Jonathan's system.

"My jaw is on the floor," she told my assistant, tearing up. "You know, I'm getting near the end of the latest notebook I've been using to track Jonathan's symptoms and treatments. Maybe I don't need to buy a new one."

Jonathan noticed the difference, too. Within the first month, he was able to finish his college applications without gallons of coffee. He got into a top university, enrolled, and bonded with his roommate immediately over what a mom-like thing it had been for Alberta to send him off with a 15-pound box of dates.

Alberta also started sending him weekly deliveries from an organic fruit company. Jonathan was all too happy to roll his eyes over it—but he and his roommate snacked on the fruit every day. The glucose helped Jonathan power through his classes and even a few clubs he'd gotten involved in. By the time midterms rolled around, he was at the top of his game.

CHAPTER 13

Posttraumatic Stress Disorder

Every single soul on this planet is dealing with some form of *posttraumatic stress disorder* (PTSD). This isn't just the fight-or-flight response to tragedy or the war trauma that veterans suffer from—that is, the well-known and documented form of PTSD.

There's also an epidemic of hidden PTSD.

This unknown form of PTSD, which is the focus of this chapter, is so rampant that almost everyone has it. It results from the unpleasant situations that we all have to deal with, ones that we may forget about consciously but not subconsciously. PTSD stems from millennia of hurt, too; its essence is in us from human history.

It's normal, and even healthy, to be terrified when your life or someone else's is in danger. Your fear triggers a fight-or-flight response that floods your body with adrenaline, temporarily giving you enhanced strength and heightened reflexes for dealing with the threat. Once the threat has passed you may experience emotional aftershocks. This is the classic form of PTSD that therapists and psychiatrists recognize.

A client, Jerry, once told me of his son-in-law Mike's near-death experience when they were working together in construction. On the job one day, Jerry heard Mike screaming for help from across the site. Jerry raced to see what was the matter and found Mike trapped beneath a half-ton trailer. Mike had been fixing an axle when the blocks the trailer had been resting on gave out and the trailer pinned him to the ground, nearly crushing his chest.

If he stopped to call for help, Jerry knew it would come too late. So rather than dialing 911 and later having to tell his daughter that she'd lost her husband, Jerry went into survival mode. A burst of adrenaline filled his body. He proceeded to lift the thousand-pound weight off his son-in-law's chest enough that Mike could slide out. Mike survived.

Even though a miracle had occurred and everything was okay, Mike consistently had nightmares about being trapped under something heavy and screaming for help. And Jerry couldn't look at any type of trailer without feeling nauseated. After years of this, Jerry came to me for insights into how to heal. Both men had experienced what could obviously be deemed PTSD.

Then there are the day-to-day emotional wounds that add up. Insecurities, trust issues, fears, guilt, shame, and more: These all actually stem from past negative emotional experiences. They are all a result of hidden PTSD. So, for example, when a person has a fear of committing to a relationship, it's showcasing that something happened earlier in life to create a certain level of posttraumatic stress disorder. You never know what happened in someone's past that's contributing to her or his present-day reaction.

PTSD can happen on so many different levels. I remember a hike I took once where I decided to go off the beaten path. As I veered from the trail, Spirit warned me not to do it. And yet, knowing that I was meant to go in the safe direction, I instead used my free will to follow my curiosity to a cliff. I crept to the cliff's edge and saw a terrace below that I could reach if I was careful. With no safety rails, I started to climb. Just as I was navigating the most treacherous ledge, with the ocean 100 feet below me, a fog thicker than clotted cream rolled in, and fast.

I could barely see my hands in front of me. Below, waves crashed into rock. I knew that if I slid forward or to the side just six inches, I would meet my maker. I was stuck.

For hours and hours, the fog remained. By nightfall, it was still just as dense. The temperature had dropped, and the light clothes I was wearing were soaked through from the mist. Falling asleep on the side of a cliff was not an option, so I stayed up, freezing, until dawn, when the haze lifted enough for me to see the footholds that would guide me to safety. I finally got back to the car, drove home, and tried to sleep.

As soon as I closed my eyes, all I could see was the cliff—with me on it.

Over and over, I saw the same image and felt panic at how close I'd come to the end. For someone with a daredevil streak, someone who liked to experience nature with a dose of adrenaline, the experience probably wouldn't have fazed her or him one bit. I know people who wouldn't flinch from being fogged in on a precipice—rock climbers, for instance, who regularly risk their lives free climbing with no safety equipment. That's not me, though. I was shaken.

Luckily, I knew the secrets to recovery. With time and patience and the application of Spirit's healing program, I moved on from the trauma before long.

UNRECOGNIZED PTSD

In recent times, we've become a society that's in favor of talking openly about subjects that used to be hush-hush. In the past, we pretty much had to shut up and be quiet about how we felt or we'd be sent to the asylum. If we acted out a little too much, we might even be eligible for a lobotomy.

It took centuries for war veterans to finally receive attention and treatment for the lasting stress of the traumas they had endured in battle. As a culture, we have a history of burying emotions with alcohol, drugs, food, and adrenaline-fueled activities. Expressing ourselves wasn't really an option until fairly recently, within the last 40 years. We live in a stressful age, but therapists, counselors, and life coaches abound now—and we're allowed to expand the definition and scope of PTSD.

Posttraumatic stress disorder is something that occurs from any difficult experience. There are the more severe cases of PTSD we know about, the ones that result from experiences such as abuse or tragedy or kidnapping or witnessing a violent crime.

Then there are the under-recognized triggers. A child's parents divorcing could make her avoid marriage as an adult. A teenager who doesn't get a date for prom could start disliking all school dances.

Turbulence on a plane ride could lead a person never to want to fly again. And I've heard many stories about food poisoning contracted at a restaurant franchise that lead people to squirm in their seats every time they drive by one of the chain's locations.

Other triggers include getting fired from a job, breaking up with a girlfriend or boyfriend, small fender benders that don't even result in injuries, or a moment in life when you feel like you failed at something. There are no limitations to what can cause PTSD.

A client once told me that she hadn't been able to eat green beans and meatloaf since adolescence because it had been forced on her when she was a teenager at boarding school. Just the sight or smell of either food gave her flashbacks to her coercive headmaster. I've also had many women clients afraid to conceive after enduring difficult pregnancies in the past. These are forms of PTSD, too.

Yet even in today's modern times of self-help, therapy, and emotional understanding, society isn't ready to refer to any of these under-recognized triggers as PTSD-inducing. Health professionals mostly reserve the term posttraumatic stress disorder for life-or-death experiences. This ignores the hundreds, if not thousands, of other incidents that alter (for the worse) the way someone experiences life.

That's what PTSD does, no matter the scale: it negatively influences the choices we make and changes the fabric of who we are.

One trigger that is all too rarely spoken about is illness. Many people develop PTSD just from having the flu for two weeks, never mind chronic fatigue for three months or neurological problems for years. The experience of these symptoms is one part of the story. A whole other cause for emotional damage is the doctor-shopping journey—the battery of tests, the constant MRIs and CT scans that don't reveal anything, the despair of not finding relief or validation.

PTSD tends to pile up on top of itself. Once you've been sick for any period of time, and you start believing your body is letting you down, and you're lost in a non-diagnosis or a misdiagnosis or a diagnosis that leads to no healing, and the financial strain starts to build, and maybe you feel your hold slipping on your career or relationships—it makes you a likely candidate for a unique composition of posttraumatic stress disorders.

PTSD is a very real response to the illness of a loved one, too. Watching someone lose her or his vitality and cease to be able to perform the same role she or he once did in your life can make you feel vulnerable and powerless. Overextending yourself to care for someone can be taxing, too. Even if your loved one recovers, the moment they later sound groggy or develop a benign sniffle, it can dredge up those old fears and make you feel you're reliving that dark time.

It's possible to have PTSD and not realize it. If it originates from one of those subconscious memories, you may experience unexplained feelings of avoidance, or you may shut down in certain circumstances and not know why. Perhaps you find yourself driven to overeat sweets or seek out adrenaline-rush activities. Or maybe people have given you the upsetting labels "touchy," "prickly," "fragile," "wounded," "anal," or "oversensitive." These are all signs that something once happened—or happened over an extended period—to bring about a reaction now.

The medical establishment doesn't truly know yet what PTSD is. It doesn't know PTSD's range, and it doesn't know how it occurs.

In this chapter, you'll get answers.

You are not beholden to the unpleasant parts of your personal history. You are not destined to relive the same patterns of trauma over and over again. The people who've hurt you do not hold the power to haunt you for the rest of your life. The mishaps and chronic stresses do not have to define you. There's a way forward.

With the right nutritional, emotional, and soul-healing support, you can reclaim your vitality and go back to fully living your life.

Think of it like working with a computer that's become bogged down with viruses, old files, and outdated software. It's gotten slower over time, but you're used to it. So if your niece came to visit and decided to run an anti-virus scan, to download your old files onto an external hard drive, and to update all your software, you'd be astonished at how much faster and more efficiently your computer could operate. Plus you'd have so much more storage space available.

That's what it can be like when you rid your mind and consciousness of subtle PTSD wounds. When you learn to heal, you increase your operating capacity and open yourself up to all that goodness you haven't had room to receive.

WHAT REALLY HAPPENS

What happens on a physical and emotional level to cause PTSD?

Put plainly, it's a chemical imbalance in the brain that occurs when someone experiences trauma. When there isn't enough glucose stored in the brain tissue to feed the central nervous system, emotional upheaval can create lasting effects. Contrary to popular science belief, though electrolytes do play a critical role in brain health, PTSD does not occur from a loss of electrolytes. A lack of glucose is the real cause.

Have you ever heard the expression "He has a thick skin" or "It's like water off a duck's back with her" to describe someone who goes through life untroubled by life's shocks and upsets? What's really behind these people's temperaments are ample glucose reserves in the brain. As a result, they can handle a heck of a lot of trauma without being affected.

Glucose is a protective biochemical critical to the brain because it places a veil of protection over sensitive brain and neurological tissue. Medical research has not yet tapped into an understanding of just how much glucose the brain requires to function in times of stress—and just how critical it is that there's ample glucose reserved in the storage bank of the brain. If glucose were converted into dollars, then one substantial traumatic event, like an accident, could be the equivalent of buying a new car. And a long-term trauma, such as an abusive relationship, could have the same effect on your glucose reserves that buying a new house would have on your bank account.

Glucose's protective veil is necessary for two reasons: First, glucose is needed to prevent brain cells, brain tissue, and neurons from becoming saturated by the acidic and corrosive nature of the adrenaline and cortisol released from anger, frustration, hopelessness, and fear. Second, glucose is there to stop the electrical storms in the brain that arise when trauma occurs, with electrical impulses firing off at an alarming rate, affecting brain tissue, neurons, and glial cells.

Think of the brain like a car's engine. Sweet like sugar, antifreeze runs through the engine. Without this coolant, the engine can overheat and become damaged. In the same way, when the brain doesn't have the coolant it needs—glucose—then the electrical impulses that run through the thousands of neurons in the brain can cause over-heating and burnout.

Have you ever heard of eating sugar to calm the spice of a chili pepper? Sugar acts as an antidote to the pepper's heat units, preventing the gums, tongue, and roof of your mouth from becoming burned. In the same way, glucose (sugar) protects the brain. If someone's glucose storage is low, she or he could get PTSD just from a flat tire. On the other hand, someone with a high level of glucose storage could witness an armed robbery and tell the story to a friend over dinner that same day, unruffled.

Animals have a built-in understanding of glucose's importance. Here's something else you won't find in an Internet search: when two chipmunks are running across the road and a car runs over one of them, the surviving chipmunk will dart back into the road and drink the other's blood for a quick hit of glucose. It's an innate, natural response that the chipmunk was born with to prevent brain damage from its fight-or-flight adrenaline response.

Humans also intuitively understand sugar as a calming device. It's why the doctor hands a child a lollipop as a reward for getting stuck with a needle. Or why a mom takes her kid out for ice cream after a checkup.

The problem is that, in today's world, there are so many bad sugars out there. Those lollipops and ice-cream cones aren't doing anyone nutritional favors.

Plenty of people still turn to sweets to soothe their wounds. They may just think they have an overeating problem and are particularly vulnerable to the temptations of sugary treats—whereas, really, they're subconsciously trying to address a physical debt.

And as another antidote to PTSD, people have started to replace sugar with adrenaline. There's an increasing number of adrenaline junkies who jump out of planes, engage in high-intensity sports, go zip-lining or bungee jumping, or dive off cliffs as a way of coping with suffering they may not even realize is there. Then there are rebound relationships—that new girlfriend or boyfriend someone may turn to for a boost of adrenaline following a breakup. These are all examples of using adrenaline as a quick drug to stand in for glucose.

The problem with these approaches is that what goes up must come down. A sugar high from packaged cupcakes is going to mean a crash later. And while an adrenaline high from running over fiery coals may feel healing and empowering in the moment, the surge won't last, and you'll go home depressed. These aren't the real solutions to our wounds.

We don't have to take risks in order to heal from PTSD. We don't have to gamble.

HEALING PTSD

Posttraumatic stress disorder, in its true definition, is the experience of lingering negative feelings that result from any adverse encounter, and that limit a person in any way. These feelings include fear, doubt, insecurity, worry, concern, panic, avoidance, anger, hostility, hypervigilance, irritability, distractedness, self-loathing, abandonment, defensiveness, agitation, sadness, frustration, resentment, cynicism, shame, invisibility, voicelessness, powerlessness, vulnerability, loss of confidence, lack of self-worth, and distrust.

One of the most powerful ways to heal posttraumatic stress disorder across the spectrum is to create new experiences to serve as positive reference points in your life. The more of these you create, the greater your chances of putting PTSD behind you. Every new positive experience plants a life-giving seed in a garden of nutrient-thieving weeds.

These experiences don't have to be big. They don't have to be dangerous or risk-taking (nor should they be). And they don't have to look like much to anyone else. Just taking a walk in peaceful surroundings can help you restore your brain.

It's all about how you *perceive* each new adventure, however tame. Keep a list of every new experience and journal each one, taking notes on how you felt. For example, when you took a walk, did you see any birds? What was the weather like? Was there a certain angle of light? What effect did it all have on your state of mind? It all matters. It's all part of being in the moment.

Or try putting together a puzzle. As you turn the pile of random pieces into a coherent whole, you'll be teaching yourself that order can emerge from chaos. Try painting, sketching, or drawing, too. These are powerful exercises that help orient us in the present moment and make us pay attention to beautiful details in the world around us that otherwise go unnoticed. The cathartic effects of art-making are potent.

Or perhaps call up a dear friend you haven't seen in years and ask her or him out to lunch. It will help reconnect you to essential parts of yourself. Or adopt a pet—every day will be new and filled with love. Alternatively, pick up a hobby. Surprise yourself; choose a skill area you never would have expected yourself to venture into, or one you always wanted to explore. Learn a new language. Take a vacation. One of the best things you can do is start your own garden.

No matter what you choose, journal about it all. Keep adding to your log of favorable experiences. It will help you become aware of the goodness life brings your way when you're not even looking for it, and it will help clear out the negative experiences from your consciousness. Spirit always tells me this is an exercise that will pluck one unwanted weed at a time to free up space in your garden mind. This isn't hollow advice. When you've endured emotional turmoil at one time or another, whether it's ongoing in the present or has passed, it has probably shaken you and altered your perception of the world. You may find yourself re-experiencing those old memories as though they were happening all over again—or re-experiencing the emotions they triggered without knowing why.

When you create new, constructive touch points for yourself—and pay attention to their positive effects on your state of mind—you train your brain, as though it's a radio, to access a healing frequency that is always available to you. And then when life becomes over-whelming, you can turn that internal dial to the restorative station to activate the impressions those positive experiences left on you, as though they're recordings of the original broadcasts.

When you're healing from PTSD, picture yourself as a tree that's been transplanted. Digging up the tree puts it in shock—just as whatever stressors you've experienced may have felt like they uprooted you. When you replant the tree in fresh, new soil, it's still trauma-tized, affected on all levels by losing its foothold. It will take months for the tree to recover from the change and reestablish itself.

In the same way, it can take a good three to four months on a PTSD-healing program to feel like yourself again. And just as nurser-ies offer nutrient-dense soil amendments to feed that tree in its new spot in the ground, you can nourish your central nervous system and cognitive function, as well as restore your heart and soul, with the nutrient solutions (i.e., healing foods and supplements) in this chapter.

Healing from PTSD requires support from loved ones, time, patience, and key nutritional elements. Part IV, "How to Finally Heal," will fill in more information.

Prayer, in whatever form brings you comfort, is another healing tool. You can also pray to specific angels by name to help you. The angel who best understands how the spirit and soul can be beaten down, and how they can be recovered, is the *Angel of Restitution,* and that's who you should call upon for the most direct aid with PTSD. (See Chapter 23, "Essential Angels.")

And to help mend the soul fractures that trauma can create, try the soul-healing meditations and techniques in Chapter 22. They can have a remarkable effect on the psyche by putting you back in touch with yourself, and restoring faith and trust.

You don't have to live in a tortured state of mind anymore. There's a way forward.

Healing Foods

In order to restore glucose to the brain—and build a glucose storage bin to prevent life disruptions from turning into PTSD—focus on incorporating the following foods into your diet: wild blueberries, melons, beets, bananas, persimmons, papayas, sweet potatoes, figs, oranges, mangoes, tangerines, apples, raw honey, and dates.

Note that fruit sugar and raw honey in their unadulterated states are among the only sugars the body accepts for glucose storage in the brain.

Healing Herbs and Supplements

- **L-glutamine:** helps support brain function and neural health.

- **5-MTHF (5-methyltetrahydrofolate):** supports the central nervous system.

- **B-complex:** supports cognitive function and strengthens neurotransmitters.

- *Ginkgo biloba:* feeds neurons and supports neurotransmitters.

- **GABA (gamma-Aminobutyric acid):** strengthens neurotransmitters and calms an overactive mind.

- **Spirulina (preferably from Hawaii):** helps restore brain tissue and support the central nervous system.

- **Honeysuckle:** balances and helps regulate glucose.

- **Nettle leaf:** helps regulate and support an over-reactive endocrine system.

- **Magnesium L-threonate:** boosts cognitive function and helps lower hypertension.

- **Siberian ginseng:** strengthens and balances the endocrine system.

CASE HISTORY:
Soothing the Soul from Hidden Trauma

Jacquelyn had worked in the corporate world for over a decade. During that time, she'd proven herself as an extremely loyal and disciplined employee who was easy to get along with and who cared about her co-workers. After years of commitment, she'd been promoted to her dream job, project coordinator.

Though she wasn't technically a manager, Jacquelyn had been one of the first employees hired in her department ten years earlier. Everyone knew that her experience made her the de facto boss in their division, and they respected her quiet leadership style. Whenever they finished a task, her co-workers would come to her desk to ask, "What can I do next to help you?" Every time she presented a finished assignment to the head of their corporate branch, they rooted for her to hit a home run. And she always did.

Jacquelyn's boss knew that she was one of the company's best workers, that she was eager to take on every project with a deadline of yesterday thrown on her desk, no matter how much after-hours work it required. The new position was demanding—and that was before all the drama.

Soon a new employee, Bridget, was hired in Jacquelyn's department. Bridget had worked for the company previously in human resources. Jacquelyn had been asking for more hands on deck for the busy season, and she figured the new addition would work to support her like the other people on the floor did.

At first, Bridget didn't seem to do much of anything, besides chat on the phone in a low voice and spend long stretches away from her desk. Then on the Friday of Bridget's third week, Jacquelyn arrived back at the office from a lunch break to find Bridget going from cubicle to cubicle, telling each of their co-workers, "You report to me now." If anyone asked why, she said, "I have the most experience."

Rather than confront her with everyone watching, Jacquelyn went to her desk and continued on as though nothing had changed. Her employees weren't eager to start turning in their work to this imposter Bridget, so they kept going as usual, too. Bridget approached Jacquelyn a couple of times during the afternoon to fuss about this or that detail she wasn't happy with in the checklist for their current project, but Jacquelyn just nodded each time and returned to the task at hand.

After the others had gone home, Jacquelyn approached Bridget, ready to put her in her place. Before Jacquelyn could open her mouth, Bridget told her she'd looked into Jacquelyn's past projects and they were all seriously lacking. The department needed an overhaul. Jacquelyn felt the room spin.

On Monday morning, after spending Saturday and Sunday catching up on work projects, Jacquelyn came into the office and noticed the room had been rearranged. A note was on her desk saying she was expected at her boss's office at 9 A.M. When she got there, her corporate branch manager and Bridget were deep in conversation, laughing. As soon as they saw Jacquelyn, their happy expressions faded. "Bridget, why don't you kick things off?" said Jacquelyn's boss.

Bridget proceeded to voice outlandish complaints about Jacquelyn, then produced a list of Jacqueline's unmet responsibilities. Bridget claimed that the current deadline they were working toward was destined to be a disaster and told the branch manager there was no leadership in the department. At the end of the meeting, the boss told Jacquelyn they'd been working on creating a new manager position for Bridget, and effective today, it was official.

Staving off tears, Jacquelyn rushed back to her department and inquired among her staff about issues with the project Bridget had mentioned. Several told her that, yes, it was looking like they'd blow the deadline—because Bridget had insisted they stop their tasks and start over. One staff member became incensed on Jacquelyn's behalf and led her back to the boss's office. The staff member explained to the manager about Bridget's tactics to undermine Jacquelyn, yet the boss told him he must be fabricating the story. A few days later, Jacquelyn's advocate was fired.

For the next few months, the mental abuse Jacquelyn suffered at the office was worse than that in a high school cafeteria. Bridget made up more lies about Jacquelyn, spread gossip, and acted as a taskmaster. She'd frequently assign Jacquelyn something to do, then take it away. Though Jacquelyn didn't realize it, her brain was suffering physical damage from the repeated trauma.

Jacquelyn decided she'd take her complaint to her boss one more time—but she was turned away by his receptionist and told she needed to register a complaint with human resources instead.

As Jacquelyn's weekly complaints filled a file in the HR department, nothing was done to address Bridget's abusive behavior.

One day, Jacquelyn poked her head into the HR office to make sure she'd been following the proper procedure to get Bridget disciplined. The woman she spoke with told her that the complaints hadn't, in fact, been sent on to the branch manager. "Those descriptions didn't sound like Bridget." Suddenly it dawned on Jacquelyn that this was the department where Bridget used to work, and this HR person was her friend.

Jacquelyn spent her lunch hour on a walk, working up the courage to approach her boss about the HR conspiracy. But then she walked by the window of a restaurant and spotted Bridget and their boss dining together inside, all smiles.

For about the umpteenth time, Jacquelyn went home in tears and poured her heart out to her husband, Alan. He had been her witness through the chronic nightmares, anxiety, and insomnia. She was exhausted and burned out. Whenever she tried to have a moment's peace, she heard Bridget's voice in her head, berating her. She now felt worthless, and every hour of work was torture. After ten years of effort and devotion, she might have to resign.

Jacquelyn contacted me, and before she spoke a word, both Spirit and I knew she was afflicted with posttraumatic stress disorder. When she did speak, anger, sadness, abandonment, and hurt came through in her voice.

Her identity had previously been as the hardest worker at her corporation. It was what made her feel she had a place in the world. Before her mother had died, she'd told Jacquelyn how proud she was that she'd gotten through college with flying colors and landed the job she had.

So Jacquelyn's PTSD was layered. It wasn't just about Bridget making the office an unpleasant environment; it was about Jacquelyn losing her sense of self. Jacquelyn's will and spirit were dwindling fast, and she was headed into a grave depression.

Alan got on the phone with us and said that he hadn't been able to say anything to comfort Jacquelyn. "It's like she has an allergic reaction every time I tell her she's capable."

"Do you have any vacation time?" I asked Jacquelyn. She said she had two weeks stored up, so I told her to request time off immediately.

Over the next 14 days, we implemented powerful restructuring of her spirit and soul.

To begin with, we searched for and revived things she'd once loved to do, long before her corporate identity had taken hold. We made a list of everything she'd ever enjoyed in life. Alan took out the old Scrabble set they'd played when they were courting each other. The memory-imbued game alone was a powerful first step in reigniting Jacquelyn's spirit.

Jacquelyn also started a journal of the positive experiences she was enjoying during her time off. For example, walking the dog at night had once been her task, before she'd gotten too busy and Alan had taken over. Now she made note of how calming and quiet the neighborhood was at night, of how her dog stopping to sniff every tree reminded her to breathe, and of how so many people she passed greeted her warmly.

For more positive touchstones, Jacquelyn ordered DVDs of television shows she'd once loved. Alan suggested they start learning the waltz at a local dance school. They went to favorite restaurants they hadn't had a chance to visit in years. Then they decided on a weekend getaway to a bed-and-breakfast that held positive memories.

As the list grew and the pages in Jacquelyn's journal filled, she started to feel capable again. She felt an inner strength return, the essence of who she was—her soul. On a physical level, to replenish Jacquelyn's glucose stores, Alan had been cutting up melon for her in the morning and making her all-fruit smoothies in the afternoon.

At this stage, we talked about how miserable life must be for Bridget. She must be a very injured person to be so hateful, deceitful, and angry; it must be very hard to be her. We developed a way to feel sad for Bridget. Jacquelyn realized that despite her facade, Bridget wasn't empowered at all. Just the opposite. She had no power—which was why she felt the need to trample on Jacquelyn. This allowed Jacquelyn to see Bridget in a whole new light.

We discussed how Jacquelyn's place in the office had always been hers, and it still was. Her title hadn't changed. She had been there the longest and had the most respect in the department. Instead of absorbing Bridget's negative energy each day, Jacquelyn needed to find a way to shower her with caring, love, and positive energy.

At the end of the two weeks, Jacquelyn arrived at work and noticed Bridget sitting in her car with talk radio blasting—no doubt trying to drown out the negative messages she was hearing in her head. A sorrow came over Jacquelyn as she watched Bridget sipping her coffee and frowning, and she saw how pathetic Bridget's attempts at domination truly were.

Jacquelyn knocked on Bridget's window. "Do you want to go in to work with me?"

Bridget cocked her head. "Um, sure?"

As they walked into the building, Jacquelyn put her arm around Bridget. "You're a wonderful person, you know that? I see you're struggling, and I want you to know, I'm here for you."

Bridget appeared so shocked she couldn't come up with anything to say. Over the course of the day, Jacqueline noticed Bridget didn't utter one snide remark.

After a few months, when the corporation went through restructuring, Bridget advocated for Jacqueline to become head of the new creative department. Bridget probably got a bigger paycheck in her new, vague managerial role. Still, assured in the knowledge that she was probably much more fulfilled than Bridget, Jacquelyn learned to accept the gift she had been given and move forward.

CHAPTER 14

Depression

When I lost my childhood best friend to a car accident when he was 21, I was inconsolable. This guy had been my soul brother. He'd understood my gift of hearing Spirit and what kind of pressure that put on me growing up, and he'd taken me seriously. He was one of the only people on earth who got me. When I heard the news that he was gone, I felt like a car had slammed into me, too.

No matter what words of comfort Spirit offered, my wounds couldn't be soothed. I was hurt, grief-stricken, angry, afraid. And I felt for my friend's family as well. Watching them suffer this unimaginable loss while I dealt with the aftermath of my own shock, I went into a temporary depression. It was unlike any trial I had faced yet in life, even with my struggles growing up. Nothing made sense anymore.

In the past, I'd been able to help depression sufferers because Spirit understood their plight, but I couldn't identify with them on a personal level. Now I'd been where they had been. The experience gave me a window into what others might feel when they faced their own trials.

Over time, I healed. I still look back on the loss of my friend with great sadness, but I don't reenter that headspace of despair. I learned we have to have patience with depression. Even if you've suffered with it for five years, ten years, or more, you have to keep the hope alive that it won't always be like this. Faith is essential to recovery from depression. You *must* hold on.

If you haven't experienced depression personally, then you've surely known someone who has. We've all had loved ones or friends or workmates who have uttered the phrase, "I'm depressed." Many who've never suffered through clinical depression confuse it with the everyday experience of being sad now and then, and don't understand why those struck by depression can't just "cheer up." The truth is, there's a world of difference between occasionally feeling down and having clinical depression. For some people, it's a feeling that can't quite be described, a general dampening of life. Others experience depression in its much graver form. It occurs on all different levels of severity for all different periods of time.

In medical communities, depression is still a condition with great mystery behind it. Depression has been perplexing people since humankind began. It's probably the most profound of all the mystery illnesses on the planet, never mind the universe, because it resides in the ghost of the machine—that is, the soul (which is in the brain).

In this chapter, I'll reveal key triggers of depression. I'll help you uncover the reason behind your imprisonment, and I'll help you learn how to break free.

Almost 20 years ago, a client compared the onset of her depression to being let off a train in the middle of nowhere. The train pulled away, and she was stranded all alone, with no way home. No more trains were traveling through the station. She told me the depression felt like a loneliness that wouldn't leave her. That description has stayed with me ever since.

If you suffer from depression, I want you to know: the train is coming back for you. You don't have to wander alone anymore. Let this chapter be the train's headlights, signaling that it's getting close. If you follow the recommendations here, you can find your way home to a healthy state of mind.

DEPRESSION SYMPTOMS

If you have a depressive disorder, you're probably experiencing symptoms such as sadness; loss of interest in activities that used to provide pleasure; slow thinking, speaking, and/or movement; and even thoughts of self-harm.

As these symptoms indicate, clinical depression is a very serious condition.

When you experience depression, as hard as it may be, it's important to share what you're going through with those who care about you, and to let in their love and support. You can let go of any shame you feel about your depression. There are important aspects of it that medical communities haven't yet uncovered. As you read the sections that follow, you'll gain new insights into what's behind your symptoms—and what you can do about them.

IDENTIFYING AND ADDRESSING MAJOR CAUSES OF DEPRESSION

Most people assume clinical depression comes from emotional pain, such as severe sadness and/or suppressed anger. That accurately describes one type of depression, but this is a complex condition, and it can stem from a number of different root causes. While some are based in emotion (e.g., traumatic loss), others are entirely physical (e.g., heavy metals, Epstein-Barr).

What follows are the most common reasons behind a depressive disorder. Any of these issues by itself is powerful enough to trigger depression. However, it's also possible to suffer from two or more issues simultaneously. Do your best to identify those triggers that apply to you.

Traumatic Loss

The most obvious reason for depression is a severe emotional blow or series of blows. This typically involves loss.

Examples are a family member dying (loss of a loved one); a spouse cheating on you (loss of trust, and of a close relationship); getting fired from a job that defined you (loss of security and identity); experiencing an event that demolishes long-held plans (loss of direction and purpose); suffering an injustice that makes you decide the universe is cruel (loss of faith); and having reason to believe you're soon going to die (loss of your future).

Of course, different people react to situations in different ways. A loss that sends someone else into a depressive spiral might not affect you on the same scale, or vice versa. Such dissimilar responses are due in part to variations in personality, personal history, and brain chemistry. What matters most is the effect a loss has on *you*. If it fills you with feelings of intense emotional pain, helplessness, and/or hopelessness, that can be enough to initiate severe depression.

Medical communities don't yet know that such traumatic emotions can create *micro-strokes* in your brain—that is, damage to brain tissue on a much smaller scale than that caused by conventional ischemic strokes, or even transient ischemic attack (TIA). These micro-strokes are so small that they don't show up on MRIs, CT scans, or any other imaging technology that we have today. They can result in numerous problems, including any of the symptoms of clinical depression. Fortunately, they can heal over time.

A major emotional shock can generate an actual electrical jolt in your brain. There's a reason why someone delivering bad news often warns, "You may want to sit down for this": we know intuitively that shock has a physical effect. This charge can be so intense that it effectively "blows a fuse" in your brain, causing parts of it to switch off.

This shutdown is a safety mechanism designed to protect your soul (which resides inside your brain) from being too badly injured. Whether it's a betrayal, learning you've been fired from a job, or returning to your car to find the window smashed, an alarming experience can trigger an electrical pulse in the emotional centers of the brain that's almost like a wave crashing onto shore. Depression can result when a series of upsetting events over time prompts the safety mechanism to break down and go awry.

Often, the safety measures cease proper function when upheavals add up. Picture a sand castle on the beach. The first line of defense against the rising tide is the wall you built around the castle—it stays standing against the first strong wave and holds the tide at bay for the first 20 minutes. Then a big wave hits and takes out the wall. That's okay, because you've dug a moat; the castle is still intact. For the next few minutes, all is well. And then a third swell rises—and takes out the castle.

When our mental safety measures have ceased normal operation, certain parts of the brain, the *I-can't-believe-it* emotional centers, may no longer perk back up. This can result in the feelings of numbness or pessimism that so often accompany depression.

There's good news, though: we can rebuild our mental resources. With the right nurturing, our safety mechanisms can restore themselves so that we're able to experience life in an awakened state again, and to bounce back from unexpected events. Over time, we can heal our depression.

Traumatic Stress

Another major cause of depression is severe and *sustained* stress. While we all feel such pressure now and then—it's part of being alive—when you're suffering from intense stress for a prolonged period of time, it can create a burnout effect.

Some examples are being unemployed for months and continually worrying about how you're going to pay your bills, getting hit with a lawsuit that threatens to ruin you financially, going through a combative divorce, and enduring a major illness that makes you feel afraid and helpless.

While these are serious issues that cause sustained, traumatic stress for many people, little stressors can also feel traumatic when they pile up. We have to respect that everyone has a unique sensitivity level. While something like a letter getting lost in the mail may seem like no big deal to one person, to another, it may trigger a memory of the time a critical payment went missing en route to a creditor—or maybe it's one more thing he doesn't have time to deal with in the day.

Did you ever have an elder tell you that you just needed perspective? Maybe, as a teenager, you picked up your prom dress from the tailor on the night of the dance, found it was three inches too short, and got no sympathy from your grandfather: "There are children starving in Africa, and here you are crying about a *dress?*" Or perhaps you've had a broken wrist and complained to a colleague about the difficulty of taking a shower with a cast, only for her to reply, "Well at least you still *have* your arm." Chances are, these statements (more like chastisements) didn't help.

Sure, it can be beneficial to gain perspective on our suffering, to get outside of our heads from time to time and try to see our lives in the grand scheme of things. Rational thought doesn't always help with our emotional experience of a situation, though. We go through severe stresses in our earthly lives, and we go through less severe stresses. They're hard all the same. We have to honor the different reaction levels in ourselves and in one another.

On a physical level, these events trigger a fight-or-flight response that sets your adrenal glands to flood your system with adrenaline. That would be a good thing if you were about to fight for your life against a tiger or flee down an alley as a car chased you. But when you aren't able to physically burn off the adrenaline saturating the tissues of your vital organs—and especially your brain—it eventually creates damage that can lead to major depression. The adrenaline becomes a trigger that breaks down neurotransmitters and lowers melatonin production, setting you up for feeling lost at sea in a depressive fog.

Adrenal Dysfunction

Depression can also stem from a purely physical cause. In such cases it may hit you out of the blue, leaving you dumbfounded about why you're feeling awful.

For example, as just explained, intense and/or prolonged emotions can flood your brain with corrosive adrenaline. Compare it to filling up your car at the gas station: your car needs the fuel to run, but if you overflow the gas tank, the petroleum will eat away at your paint job.

Even if you've never been rocked by such emotions, your brain can still suffer this harmful flooding if your adrenal glands are malfunctioning, and this can just as readily create depressive burnout.

To get a sense of whether this is an issue for you—and, if it is, how to heal your damaged glands—read Chapter 8, "Adrenal Fatigue."

Viral Infection

Medical communities don't know that millions of people suffer from depression as a result of a virus such as Epstein-Barr (detailed in Chapter 3) or Lyme disease (detailed in Chapter 16). The virus latches onto your nerves and continually inflames them. It also emits a poison, or *neurotoxin,* that further inflames your nerves and brain cells. This disrupts the signals to and from your brain . . . which can lead to depression. Even a mild viral load in the body that doesn't cause any other symptoms can create an underlying depression.

Heavy Metals and Other Toxins

Another type of depression is the *Everything-is-perfect* variety. Someone can have a loving family, the perfect job, a beautiful house, and feel gratitude for all of it. Yet a dark, unexplainable cloud can arrive and loom over all of it. It can cause a person to feel different, sad, not like herself or himself anymore—as though something is missing. It can make a person not want to get out of bed in the morning.

Those around such people often don't understand. "You've got everything," they say. "What's wrong with you?"

This type of depression is the result of toxins—not a bad attitude.

As a result of normal modern living, over time the body will accumulate toxic heavy metals, especially mercury, aluminum, and copper. For example, tuna and other seafood often contain mercury. Most soda cans are made of aluminum. And your tap water is probably carried into your home by copper pipes, and also filled with fluoride, a toxic aluminum by-product.

These metals may eventually settle into the area of the brain near the thalamus and the pineal, pituitary, and hypothalamus glands. If an acidic environment is coupled with a high-protein, fat-based diet, the metals will start oxidizing, which creates a poisonous chemical pool that contaminates brain cells and lowers electrical impulse activity. This disruption, in this particular area of the brain, can create a depressive disorder, which can sneak up on a person when least expected.

The oxidation isn't necessarily continuous. If the runoff from the toxic heavy metals happens on an occasional basis, you will experience depression only sporadically, with no apparent rhyme or reason for each episode.

Non-metal toxins can also create neuron and neurotransmitter damage that disrupts your brain's ability to function. The toxins most responsible for depressive disorders include:

- **Pesticides and herbicides:** you can encounter these chemicals when living near a sprayed yard, garden, farm, or golf course; walking in a recently sprayed park; eating non-organic food; and so on.

- **Formaldehyde:** this chemical is used in thousands of household products, and also used as a preservative in processed foods.

- **Solvents:** the chemicals used in carpet cleaning, household cleaning, and office cleaning create gases that you breathe in every day.

- **Food additives:** MSG, aspartame, sulfites (used as preservatives in dried fruit, potato snacks, and so on), and other unnatural additives to foods can build up in your brain. Once they've begun triggering depressive episodes, even drinking a can of diet soda can set off a new attack.

Electrolyte Deficiency

To remain healthy, your body must maintain a certain level of electrolytes, which are ions created by salt and other components of your bodily fluids. These electrolytes help maintain and send electrical impulses throughout your body—especially your brain, which is the center of your body's electrical activity. People who have higher levels of mercury and other heavy metals in the brain need higher than normal electrolytes to balance them out.

Imagine your brain as a car battery. When the chemical electrolyte solution in the battery is too low, it interrupts the flow of electricity within and keeps the car from starting. In the same way, when you run low on the electrolytes meant to be in the blood that's pumping through your brain (the battery), it can severely disrupt electrical activity and act as a trigger for depression. And like a car battery, you can recharge your brain from burnout—if you get enough electrolytes.

HEALING FROM DEPRESSION

As you've just seen, there are numerous triggers and explanations for depression. The most helpful thing you can do is address any particular cause(s) for your depression that you have identified. Just knowing what's behind your state of mind can have an enormously validating and healing effect.

It's also recommended that you take the herbs, supplements, and foods described in this section. Using exclusively natural methods, they'll bolster your brain tissue, nerve cells, and endocrine system; detoxify you; and improve your mood. For more information on nutrition—which can have a profound effect on mental health—turn to Part IV, "How to Finally Heal."

There, you'll also find Chapter 22, "Soul-Healing Meditations and Techniques," and Chapter 23, "Essential Angels." Those pages contain exercises that can help you find peace and validation as you recover from depression and reclaim your life.

Healing Foods

Specific foods can help rejuvenate the brain, remove heavy metals, replenish electrolytes, heal brain tissue, and/or address the nutritional deficiencies associated with depression. The ideal items to incorporate into your diet for the alleviation of your symptoms are wild blueberries, spinach, hemp seeds, cilantro, walnuts, coconut oil, sprouts, kale, apricots, and avocados.

Healing Herbs and Supplements

- **Vitamin B$_{12}$ (as methylcobalamin and/or adenosylcobalamin):** strengthens the brain and central nervous system.

- **Spirulina (preferably from Hawaii):** critical for removing heavy metals and other toxins from the brain and central nervous system.

- **Nascent iodine:** supports the endocrine system, including the thyroid and adrenal glands. Also kills viruses and fortifies the immune system.

- **Melatonin:** reduces inflammation in the brain. Also helps grow fresh neurons.

- **Ester-C:** this form of vitamin C repairs damaged neurotransmitters and supports the adrenal glands. It also helps cleanse the liver and remove toxins from your system.

- **Licorice root:** supports the endocrine system, including the thyroid and adrenal glands. Also impairs the ability of virus cells to move and reproduce.

- **Ginkgo leaf:** contains powerful alkaloids that nourish and grow neurotransmitters.

- **Lemon balm:** reduces inflammation and soothes the central nervous system. Also kills viruses that may be inflaming nerves.

- **Ashwagandha:** aids the endocrine system, including the thyroid and adrenal glands.

- **Vitamin D$_3$:** strengthens the endocrine system, including the thyroid and adrenal glands. Also kills viruses and reduces inflammation.

- **GABA (gamma-Aminobutyric acid):** supports neuropeptides and neurotransmitters and calms the central nervous system.

- **EPA & DHA (eicosapentaenoic acid and docosahexaenoic acid):** repairs and strengthens the central nervous system. Be sure to buy a plant-based (not fish-based) version.

- **5-HTP (5-hydroxytryptophan):** bolsters neurotransmitters.

- **B-complex:** helps protect all areas of the body from being injured by an emotional crisis. Also supports the brain and brain stem.

- **Magnesium:** calms the central nervous system and relaxes muscle tension.

- **California poppy:** calms overactive neurons and supports neurotransmitters.

- **Kava-kava:** calms the central nervous system and reduces stress.

- **Vitamin E:** supports the central nervous system.

- **Rhodiola:** strengthens the endocrine system, including the thyroid and adrenal glands. Also stabilizes the vascular system.

CASE HISTORY:
An Unexpected Answer to Happiness

Ellen had been a happy person all her life. Friends and family called her the life of the party. She knew how to comfort anyone who was down or sad, and she was the rock of her marriage. She looked forward to the sun rising and loved to plan weekends, future vacations, and her three daughters' birthday parties. Ellen treasured life and was thankful for every day. She felt her life was perfect.

Then, at the age of 44, Ellen returned home from vacation with her family and immediately began to feel strange. She couldn't quite explain it, but it felt like part of her was missing. On top of feeling extra tired, she felt like she'd lost her spunk and passion for life. A sadness started to develop.

At first Ellen passed it off as the post-vacation blues, figuring it would pass. Over the next few months, there were times when it felt like it was getting better, then it would gradually worsen again. Ellen felt like she was losing herself. Her husband, Tom, was gravely worried. "I miss your cheerleader smile," he'd tell her. She'd always given off a bright light, and now it was dim.

Searching for answers, Ellen visited her doctor, who examined her and ran a complete hormone profile test. When Ellen's hormone levels came back normal, the doctor concluded that she must be suffering from depression and handed her a prescription for antidepressants. "See if this gives you any relief."

Ellen walked out of the office more depressed than she'd been when she arrived. The diagnosis and medication felt so foreign to her. When she shared the news with her family, they were as shocked as she was. She began to take the antidepressants, but without any explanation of why these new feelings were happening to her or how long they would last, she felt as if she were a prisoner to the medication.

She decided to seek professional counseling. The therapist was positive that stored emotions were holding Ellen back. Ellen worked on digging into her past with this wonderful, supportive counselor. The process felt productive, and helped give Ellen a support system she felt was critical to keeping her afloat during her depression—but the depression was still there.

A year after its onset, Tom decided to take Ellen away from it all with another vacation. He thought maybe it would create forward movement. Off the family went for ten days—and Ellen felt a little better. She was chattering with her daughters again, planning costumes for school plays with them, and rising with the sun. She wasn't her old self, but she felt a 50 percent improvement. Sitting at the airport afterward, waiting for their flight home, Ellen told Tom the trip had been just the jump-start she needed.

As soon as she began to unpack, though, after just a few hours at home, Ellen crashed. She curled up in bed and felt the depression wash over her stronger than ever before. The feeling stayed as the days passed, and she felt as if it would never go away. She began to cry often—when she was brushing her teeth, tying her shoes, or even waking up in the morning. She no longer had the energy to sit in the living room with Tom and her daughters to watch their favorite show on Sunday nights.

Unable to get Ellen over this hump, her therapist recommended she make an appointment with me. As soon as I started the reading on Ellen, Spirit alerted me to a high level of insecticides in her organs, along with traces of herbicides. I explained the findings, and Ellen suddenly got quiet.

"Are you okay?" I asked.

Ellen started to explain that her husband had the interior and exterior of their house treated by the pest company periodically. I asked Ellen for the treatment schedule, and she had Tom pick up from another phone. He explained that every time they went away, whether for a weekend trip to his mother-in-law's or for one of their longer vacations, he'd have the neighbor let in an exterminator to spray for insects. Monthly, he had a landscaping company treat their lawn and gardens with herbicides.

I insisted that Ellen, Tom, and their children move out of the house immediately to see if Ellen improved. While they stayed at Ellen's mother's house, Ellen started a healing food, supplement, and detox regimen—as described in this section, and in Part IV of this book—to rid herself of the chemicals and heavy metals in her system that were causing her depression. (Tom joined in, too, plus we did a modified version of this program to help their daughters cleanse from the toxins.)

Ellen came back to life. With the mystery illness solved, the healing protocol in place, her renewed confidence, distance from the pesticide exposure, and the added benefit of the emotions she had processed in therapy, Ellen felt better than ever. She and Tom decided to put their house on the market and start anew.

CHAPTER 15

Premenstrual Syndrome and Menopause

Through nearly all of history, women viewed *menopause* in a positive light. Although it was a reminder of getting older, menopause gently and painlessly ended the difficulties and inconveniences of *premenstrual syndrome* (PMS) and *menstruation,* often resulted in a heightened libido, and allowed for sex without the worry of accidental pregnancy.

Women in the past didn't turn to doctors for help with menopause, because they didn't experience notable physical problems or symptoms with it. Women almost always felt *better* in perimenopause, menopause, and postmenopause than they had before. It was a normal part of life that didn't require anything beyond acceptance.

Medical literature produced up through the 1800s very seldom even mentioned menopause. When it did, it almost never referred to menopause as symptomatic or as a hardship that required a doctor's care. Hot flashes and heart palpitations were practically nonexistent.

That all changed in the modern era, around 1950. Women born from 1900 on were the first ones to experience night sweats, hot flashes, fatigue, panic attacks, anxiety, hair thinning, and joint pain when they reached a certain age. In the middle of the 20th century, a tidal wave of women ages 40 to 55 were visiting their doctors with these symptoms—and doctors didn't know what to think.

Behold, mystery illness and the autoimmune confusion were born. Medical professionals had never been so bewildered.

Physicians reported the epidemic to pharmaceutical companies, and at first, the consensus was that it was all in women's heads—it was just crazy women syndrome. They had to be making up their symptoms, because otherwise it made no sense. It was all a cry for attention, a sign they were bored. Women were told to join the PTA.

Yet through the 1950s, the wave of women experiencing memory issues, trouble concentrating, moodiness, weight gain, dizziness, and more grew larger. The pharmaceutical companies and doctors consulted again and decided that the one thing these women had in common was their age. The medical establishment decided the cause must be hormones—even though men were experiencing the same symptoms at the same time. Plenty of men were having hot flashes; they were just labeled "work sweat" (even if a man wasn't working when an episode hit) or "nervous sweat." Men dealt with other "menopause" symptoms as well—depression, growing waistlines, and forgetfulness, to name just a few. It didn't make news, though, because this was an era when men were taught to be stoic. The responsibility of being the breadwinners weighed heavily, so out of fear of losing their careers, they concealed their private physical issues.

Right away, a pharmaceutical company pursuit to exploit women and capitalize on the false discovery of female hormonal issues was born. By the late 1950s, the news was widespread that women must be suffering from hormone deficiencies. As the notion of this "women's issue" gained popularity, men felt even more pressure to keep quiet about their parallel symptoms.

Women had faced plenty of difficulties leading up to this point. They'd been oppressed and told to suppress emotions, and only in recent history had they gained the right to vote—to count as human beings. In the middle of the century, they still felt like they were fighting to have a voice. It was easy to take advantage of women by making them feel heard.

Doctors were baffled by women's mystery symptoms, but at least, finally, the doctors believed them. So even though medicine had gone in the wrong direction looking for answers, the theories were celebrated because they gave a name to women's health struggles. It was a well-intentioned effort by doctors.

To this day, doctors operate off this hormonal misinformation. Countless women hear that hormonal imbalance or menopause is behind their suffering.

It's not. Menopause is actually on your side. Believe it or not, the aging process slows down after menopause. That's not the message that's out there. Women think of menopause as the onset of aging and age-related health problems—when in fact it's just the opposite.

A woman's most rapid aging happens between puberty and menopause. Think about how quickly a girl's body starts to develop after her first menstrual cycle: that's because reproductive hormones are steroid compounds that speed up the aging process. By reducing a woman's levels of estrogen and progesterone, menopause also helps safeguard her from cancers, viruses, and bacteria, which are all attracted to and feed on reproductive hormones.

And here's the truth about *osteoporosis*: it's not that reaching post-menopause makes a woman more vulnerable to bone porousness. It's that osteoporosis takes decades to develop, so it just happens to show itself when a woman reaches a certain age. Medical communities mistake this coincidence for causation, saying that the reduced levels of estrogen in a woman's body contribute to her loss of bone mass. The reality is that *reproductive hormones* contribute to osteoporosis—because they're steroids, and steroids have a bone-dissolving effect. Combined with infections of pathogens such as the Epstein-Barr virus, nutritional deficiencies, and inadequate exercise, estrogen and progesterone are what can trigger a woman to develop osteoporosis—long before menopause.

That's not to say reproductive hormones are bad. They're the reason women are able to bear children. Without these hormones, human life couldn't continue.

Yet the body knows its limits. It's willing to pay the price for the ability to create life, so long as it restricts childbearing to the years between puberty and menopause—because it wants to keep you safe.

Women are told reproductive hormones are the fountain of youth. The irony is that your youth wasn't in your 20s, 30s, or 40s. Your true youth happened before puberty. Reaching menopause is a way of reconnecting with that time. Menopause ends the reproductive system's cycle (and its drain on your body) and brings down reproductive hormone levels. It's the body's natural way of slowing down aging so that you can live a long, healthy life.

Menopause and life after menopause aren't anything to dread. Menopause itself isn't meant to be a difficult physical process, and the wave of younger women who've begun to experience symptoms categorized as hormonal aren't going through early menopause. Other factors entirely are in play—and there are powerful ways to address them. You *can* go back to living a healthy life and embracing life at every stage.

WHAT WAS *REALLY* BEHIND THE FIRST WAVE OF "MENOPAUSE SYMPTOMS"

Here's the real story: when women started to present symptoms in the 1950s that doctors and pharmaceutical companies attributed to the change of life, they were missing three other commonalities.

The first was viral. These women had all been born in the early 1900s, just as the Epstein-Barr virus (EBV) and other viruses were beginning to take root in the population.

EBV typically enters a woman when she is young and then spends decades building itself up to the point when it's ready to make itself known in the form of inflammatory illness. It just so happened that women affected by the first non-aggressive strains of EBV were in their 40s or 50s when the viral incubation period ended and the symptoms began. (At the same time, thyroid inflammation started affecting a large number of women. For more on this, see Chapter 6, "Hypothyroidism & Hashimoto's Thyroiditis.")

So if you were born in 1905 and you'd contracted this new virus Epstein-Barr as a small child, by 1950 you'd be 45 years old and part of the first generation just beginning to experience symptoms of this epidemic viral infection. It was only a coincidence that this was the same age as perimenopause or menopause. Yet you'd probably hear that the reason for your hot flashes, night sweats, and fatigue was hormonal. If the viral inflammation presented earlier or later, you'd get the label perimenopause or postmenopause.

The second commonality among women who got the menopause tag in the 1950s was radiation exposure. Due to a colossal histori-cal blunder called the shoe-fitting fluoroscope—a mistake that's been swept under the rug—women of this time were exposed to the most radiation ever seen in history. They might have been safer if they'd lived on the border of the Chernobyl evacuation zone in 1986!

Following the fluoroscope's invention, it was all the rage from the 1920s to 1950s for a visit to the shoe store to include sticking your legs and feet into this X-ray box. The idea was that the X-ray would help salesmen understand the bone structure of customers' feet to help get them the best fit for their cork-heeled shoes. Yet the dosage of radiation was unexamined and unregulated, and there were no doctors present at the store. It was just a shoe clerk pressing a deadly button at will and whim.

It happened at every visit to the shoe store, over and over again. Plenty of women tried on shoes as therapy, making a visit to the shoe store every other week. That could mean they had something like 800 radiation treatments in a lifetime. It resulted in severe radiation poisoning for millions of women.

By the time 1950 rolled around, the fluoroscope was quietly being removed from shoe stores, as if it had never been there in the first place. Modern medicine was beginning to realize at this time that radiation was dangerous, and I'm sure someone behind the scenes made the connection between women's unprecedented health struggles and their decades-long, repeated exposure to radiation—because it was obvious that tens of thousands of women were getting foot and leg amputations due to cancer.

Rather than point to radiation, though, think tanks selected menopause as the culprit—even though for these women's mothers and grandmothers and great-grandmothers, menopause had been a smooth transition.

At the same time, a third trigger for ill health was occurring: the explosion of DDT exposure. In the 1940s, DDT was used everywhere. It was sprayed on crops, in parks, and kids would even soap themselves up with the pesticide's suds for fun as the DDT truck drove by spraying throughout the suburbs. DDT salesmen would knock on the front door of every home and sell women cans of DDT to spray on their flowers and gardens. To prove its safety, the salesmen would even spray an apple with DDT, adding that it was a nutritious supplement. By 1950, DDT use was at its height, and the central nervous systems and livers of countless women had become overloaded with the toxin.

It's amazing to think that the risk was overlooked for so long. If it hadn't been for Rachel Carson's 1962 book, *Silent Spring*, which brought attention to the dangers of chemical pesticides and eventually led to a ban on DDT and the founding of the Environmental Protection Agency, the world might have continued to overlook the harm these pesticides were causing. As it was, critics attacked Carson and called her hysterical—the very term used for women's mystery symptoms at the time. Ultimately, though, she was vindicated. Everything she went through to bring the truth to light was worth it for the lives she saved.

(By the way, it's not a coincidence that when the massive chemical industry behind DDT took a hit from public awareness about its downsides, a new industry started to emerge and dominate: hormone treatment.)

Meanwhile, menopause became the scapegoat for dozens of symptoms that really had to do with completely different causes. Symptoms misattributed to menopause included night sweats, hot flashes, fatigue, dizziness, weight gain, digestive issues, bloating, incontinence, headaches, moodiness, irritability, depression, anxiety, panic attacks, heart palpitations, trouble concentrating, memory issues, insomnia and other sleep disorders, vaginal dryness, breast sensitivity, joint pain, tingling, hair loss or thinning, dry or cracked skin, and dry or brittle nails.

It should not have made sense to anyone that a healthy and natural life process would cause these problems—especially since it never had before. But hey, why bother considering 30 years of unregulated, intense exposure to radiation, DDT, and viral pathogens?

When women started to experience what were really autoimmune or viral conditions, illnesses such as chronic fatigue syndrome, fibromyalgia, adrenal fatigue, hypothyroidism, other manifestations of the Epstein-Barr virus, lupus, heavy metal toxicity, liver dysfunction, and nutritional deficiency—all triggered by the modern era of viral, radiation, and DDT toxin exposure—medical communities couldn't understand the real answers. (Normally, they still don't consider these factors.)

It was the birth of the *It-must-be-in-your-head* argument, and when women pushed back against this non-diagnosis, because women's rights were growing stronger at this point, hormones were the perfect way to quiet women down. It was easier for doctors to say, "It's your hormones" than to admit, "I have no idea what's going on with you." Before 1950, a doctor's opinion was not considered the be-all and end-all. From 1950 on, though, modern medicine had its grip on society. For the first time in history, the doctor was heralded as God.

THE TRUTH ABOUT HORMONE REPLACEMENT THERAPY

Pharmaceutical companies actively encouraged the hormone trend when they realized billions could be made by demonizing menopause and creating drugs to "cure" it. In the early 1960s a major promotional campaign was launched claiming that "estrogen deficiencies" were the cause of most of the ills being felt by women before, during, and after menopause. Sales of products promising to replace the supposedly missing estrogen—called *hormone replacement therapy* (HRT)—skyrocketed.

HRT had actually been in the works for some time. When doctors started to diagnose women with hormone issues, pharmaceutical companies suddenly had a use for their steroid-based lab experiment. They sent patients the message, "We see your pain, so we developed this revolutionary treatment for you." In reality, they were just picking this as the perfect moment to release the products that had already been in development and hadn't had an application until now.

HRT products hardly ever produced any positive results, though. In rare cases, HRT did minimize some symptoms. However, HRT managed this not by genuinely addressing an imbalance in the body, but by acting as a steroid—that is, suppressing the immune system's response to viral inflammation, nutritional deficiencies, and exposure to toxins such as DDT.

In other words, HRT didn't make anyone healthier. On the contrary, in some cases it hid diseases by temporarily preventing the immune system from fully reacting to and combating them. So while it sometimes provided symptom relief, HRT allowed cancers, viruses, bacteria, and more to continue attacking women's bodies and aging them rapidly without their knowledge—at least, until the damage became so severe it couldn't be covered up any longer.

Suddenly, doctors were noticing cancer and strokes on the rise among the women taking HRT. It was just a glimpse of the true problems hormone replacement had been causing, yet it was enough to get attention. When the news was reported, sales dropped—for a while. Soon, another promotional campaign claimed that an adjustment to the products had addressed the problem, and HRT became popular again.

Then in 2002 an enormous clinical study called the Women's Health Initiative, which ran for over a decade and involved more than 160,000 postmenopausal women, caught on to more of the havoc that HRT had been wreaking and concluded that HRT substantially increased the risk of breast cancer, heart attacks, and strokes.[2] That is, hormone replacement therapy rapidly sped up the aging process. Once again, HRT sales plummeted.

When the findings came to light about HRT's dangers, it should have been banned. It should have prompted researchers to look into what was really behind women's mystery symptoms—and started them down the path to the discovery that hormones were never the problem.

Instead, another strategy came into the mix: *bioidentical hormone replacement therapy* (BHRT).

BHRT is safer than the previous drugs used in HRT. How much safer? No one knows. Every doctor is smart enough to know that, at this point, BHRT remains experimental. It's at the beginning of a 30-year journey of trial and error, just as HRT once was. Trends in health care are so powerful, sometimes nothing can stop them. For doctors, a trend can feel like following the Pied Piper—that is, following their best chance of keeping the peace with colleagues, protecting their livelihoods, and giving hope to patients seeking answers. It's a difficult balance. For women in a society that favors youth over wisdom, the pull is strong toward any trendy pill or cream that claims it's the fountain of youth. Not even bringing the truth to light will stop the hormone train.

No matter the reasoning or alluring language that's used to promote BHRT, the same basic issue applies: menopause is a natural part of life that doesn't need to be "cured." It's not worth taking a risk with a perilous concept that's caused tremendous damage in the past.

That said, if you're presented with both HRT and BHRT as options and still want to try one, I suggest you choose BHRT from a compounding pharmacy. Make sure you get your prescription from a highly skilled physician who's well versed in holistic health and can regulate and balance dosages with knowledge and precision—and who also views BHRT as a temporary, periodic Band-Aid rather than as an indefinite solution. Another option is to seek out an herbalist, who will provide whole herbs to balance hormones.

There are women who use HRT and get no relief, and there are women who use BHRT and get no relief. For over 25 years, I've seen women use both and get no results (except for accelerated aging, despite all claims that it will bring back their youth), and I've witnessed hundreds of frustrated doctors unable to get their patients better with hormone therapy. That's because neither form addresses the underlying health issues misattributed to menopause. When people feel like they're experiencing improvement with hormone therapy, it's because it's never prescribed by itself anymore; it's prescribed alongside loads of supplementation and an overhauled diet, and it's the supplements and new diet that make women feel better.

Hormone therapies, because they're steroids, act as immunosuppressant drugs. A patient's viral symptoms such as heart palpitations and hot flashes (which the doctor doesn't identify as viral) may calm down on BHRT, tricking everyone into believing it's working. And consider the symptom vaginal dryness, which sometimes improves on BHRT. Vaginal dryness is a symptom of adrenal fatigue, not perimenopause or menopause—that's why this discomfort can trouble even women in their 20s and 30s. The BHRT steroids can potentially prompt the adrenal glands to churn out adrenaline; this is what temporarily brings some women relief, along with the risk of longer-term adrenal issues.

Yes, it's possible to have hormonal imbalances. The symptoms doctors call menopause don't have to do with the reproductive hormones, though. Normally, they're related to the hormones of the adrenal and thyroid glands.

Saliva, blood, and urine tests are not an accurate way to determine if a woman's hormones are balanced. These testing methods are fallible and often grossly inaccurate. If the thyroid is underproducing hormones (that is, it's a hypothyroid), then the adrenal glands overproduce hormones to compensate. The destructive nature of the overproduction of adrenaline destroys the viability and accuracy of blood tests that look at progesterone, estrogen, and testosterone levels.

Body temperature fluctuations, bloating, dizziness, night sweats, heart palpitations, fatigue, and other issues listed in the previous section—these symptoms, viewed collectively, are brand-new to womankind as of the last 60 years. Reproductive hormones aren't to blame. There's a bigger picture being overlooked. I'm not trying to rain on anyone's parade here, poke the bear, or accuse well-meaning doctors of having anything but the best intentions for their patients. We are all working toward the same goal: women's health. We all want women to truly heal. That's all the information here is about.

It would be easier for me to repeat the conjecture and advice that's already out there. I can't do that in good conscience, though. The only way I sleep at night is knowing that I've listened to Spirit, that I've offered people real answers. Revealing the information in this chapter is worth it to me if it means it could protect you. I want to support you in your health, to help you avoid chronic illness, cancer, and stroke, like I've successfully done for women all these years. I want you to live to 90 or 100. I want you to be happy and free.

Your life is precious. Your soul is precious. It's critical for every woman to know the truth about menopause. It's about having options, making informed decisions. Because if you don't understand the real story, how can you make the judgment call that's right for you?

Our choices get taken away from us when we are not given the proper options, information, and truth. There's a saying, "You always have a choice." Not when all the options aren't available to you! If the truth is hidden in a vault that you don't have access to, or lost in the past and forgotten, how can you make the right choice?

The details I provide in this chapter are meant to unlock that vault.

If just one person connects with this chapter and uses these secrets that have been hidden away from womankind to keep herself safe and guard herself from the peer pressure to go with the crowd, then at least one person can live a better life.

UNDERSTANDING MENOPAUSE TODAY

The disconnect between menopause and the symptoms I've described in this chapter has become clearer recently as the current-day illnesses affecting women have grown more aggressive. Rather than waiting several decades to strike until a woman is in her 40s or 50s, some viral strains and toxic loads are now affecting women in their 30s, 20s, and even in their teens. If this had been the case in the 1940s and early 1950s, if women of all ages had been presenting with mystery symptoms, maybe health professionals would have thought twice about blaming their troubles on menopause. Or maybe pharmaceutical companies and researchers would have concocted another game.

Why are doctors still not making the connection? They have no explanation for why an 18-year-old girl has "perimenopause symptoms"— or why a 25-year-old does, or a 30-year-old. Yet it's happening to these young women at an alarming rate; they're experiencing the same set of issues that used to only affect women in their 40s and 50s. These are the symptoms of Epstein-Barr virus, thyroid disorders, and more—the same conditions that were behind the hormone, perimenopause, and menopause blame game that began in the 1950s. It was never menopause to begin with.

The prevalence of the same suffering in younger and younger women makes that clear. While shoe-fitting fluoroscopes and DDT have been phased out, women today are still surrounded by environmental toxins, pesticides, herbicides, heavy metals, and other technological-era pollutants—plus, old toxins passed down from previous generations still reside in us. At the same time, we've suffered epidemics of new forms of cancers, viruses, bacteria, and other illnesses born from the poisons of our modern age. Yet the truth gets buried deep beneath ego, greed, status, and stupidity.

Doctors don't give 18-year-olds HRT or BHRT, by the way. They *do* prescribe birth control pills for them—which have a similar steroid-like effect of suppressing symptoms without addressing their cause. (Most likely, 18-year-olds will be prescribed HRT and BHRT in the future. Already, women in their early 30s with adrenal fatigue or thyroid disorders that don't show up on blood tests are being offered BHRT.)

Something else important to understand is that your doctor can't accurately test your hormone levels when you're suffering with the symptoms I described earlier, because they throw your system out of whack. When adrenals are underactive, it will knock the hormonal test off its tracks, too. The readings of estrogen and progesterone levels will not be accurate. Millions of women with underactive adrenals are getting back inaccurate hormone test results.

When a woman is prescribed BHRT and begins to improve, BHRT gets some of the credit. However, a doctor who recommends BHRT is often holistic-minded to begin with, and so she'll recommend a better diet and plenty of nutritional supplements to clear up deficiencies at the same time. Again, the patient's switch to a healthy lifestyle is usually the real factor in her improvement. If you're experiencing symptoms like those described earlier in the chapter, you should aim to uncover the illness that's actually causing them. Reading the other chapters in this book is likely to help. So is the advice in the pages ahead. You deserve to be free from illness. You deserve to reclaim your life.

UNDERSTANDING PREMENSTRUAL SYNDROME

Symptoms such as depression, diarrhea, bloating, anxiety, insomnia, migraines, and mood swings are often blamed on PMS.

That blame is inaccurate.

These symptoms, like the supposed symptoms of menopause, are actually from underlying health conditions such as a sensitive central nervous system, IBS, food allergies, or heavy metal toxicity. They make themselves known at this particular time in a woman's cycle because the menstruation process takes up 80 percent of her body's reserves. The 20 percent left over cannot manage the health conditions that the immune system normally keeps at bay.

It's another prime example of how far medical communities still are from understanding women's health. Rather than pointing to the reproductive system as the reason for a woman's suffering at her time of the month, we should look at it as a messenger.

If you struggle with issues you've always thought of as PMS, use this book to explore what could really be causing your symptoms, and address that true cause. It's your key to a stress-free menstrual cycle.

ADDRESSING THE SYMPTOMS ASSOCIATED WITH PREMENSTRUAL SYNDROME, PERIMENOPAUSE, MENOPAUSE, AND POSTMENOPAUSE

The symptoms in this chapter that are usually, and falsely, ascribed to menopause are so broad that they can be caused by nearly any health condition. These include adrenal fatigue, food allergies, viral load, liver dysfunction, and hypothyroidism. They paint a much bigger picture than just hormone problems. This section provides a set of herbs, supplements, and foods that address a wide range of viruses, bacteria, fungi, and other toxins that *probably* include whatever's creating your symptoms.

This section also offers herbs and supplements that help stabilize your reproductive hormones and system, in case you feel you need support in that area.

And keep in mind that diet can play a profound role in minimizing the symptoms discussed in this chapter. You'll find more information on how to support your body and overcome illness, including details on detoxification, in Part IV, "How to Finally Heal."

Healing Foods

When you're looking to boost the immune system and support the reproductive system, the best foods to concentrate on are wild blueberries, sesame tahini, avocados, black beans, asparagus, apples, spinach, black grapes, and cucumbers. They'll help by variously providing antioxidants, preventing hot flashes, providing critical nutrients to fortify vital organs, reducing inflammation, and keeping hormone levels balanced.

Herbs and Supplements to Address General Symptoms

- **Silver hydrosol:** kills viruses, bacteria, and other microbes on contact and supports the immune system.

- **Zinc:** kills viruses, boosts the immune system, and helps protect the endocrine system.

- **Licorice root:** aids the adrenal glands and helps balance the body's levels of cortisol and cortisone.

- **L-lysine:** impairs the ability of virus cells to move and reproduce.

- **Vitamin B$_{12}$ (as methylcobalamin and/or adenosylcobalamin):** strengthens the central nervous system.

- **Nascent iodine:** stabilizes and strengthens the thyroid and the rest of the endocrine system.

- **Ashwagandha:** fortifies the adrenal glands and helps balance the production of cortisol.

- **Barley grass juice extract powder:** cleanses the liver, aids digestion, and promotes alkalinity.

- **Olive leaf:** kills viruses, bacteria, and fungi. Also promotes blood circulation.

- **Monolaurin:** kills viruses, bacteria, and other bad microbes.

- **Spirulina (preferably from Hawaii):** provides critical micronutrients to bolster the endocrine system.

- **Ginseng:** boosts the adrenal glands.

Herbs and Supplements for Reproductive Systems

- **Nettle leaf:** reduces inflammation in the reproductive system.

- **Wild yam:** helps stabilize levels of estrogen and progesterone.

- **Schisandra berry:** helps flush excessive estrogen from the body.

- **Hawthorn berry:** aids the ovaries.

- **Vitex (chaste tree berry):** helps stabilize the menstrual cycle (if you're still menstruating).

- **Red clover blossom:** helps flush out unhelpful hormones stored in the organs.

- **Sage:** helps protect the cervix from abnormal cell growth.

- **Folic acid:** helps replenish the uterus.

- **B-complex:** provides essential vitamins for the reproductive system.

- **Vitamin D$_3$:** helps stabilize the reproductive and immune systems.

- **Vitamin E:** promotes blood circulation and strengthens the central nervous system.

- **EPA & DHA (eicosapentaenoic acid and docosahexaenoic acid):** nourishes deep tissue in the reproductive organs. Be sure to buy a plant-based (not fish-based) version.

CASE HISTORY:
No More Sleepless Nights

Valerie was 48 years old when she began to notice unusual symptoms. To begin with, she was having trouble sleeping through the night. At 3 A.M, she'd wake up and then lie in bed unable to sleep until 5:30 or 6, when she'd sometimes be able to nod off again. Valerie also started to experience occasional heart palpitations, daytime hot flashes, and night sweats, along with moodiness. She found herself being short with her assistant and co-workers at her interior design firm, and one day she overheard her 17-year-old daughter, Molly, on the phone with her older daughter, who was away at college. "Mom has gotten super-insensitive. She seems angry all the time, and I swear it's not my fault."

Valerie decided to make an appointment with her general practitioner, Dr. Fitzgerald. He performed a complete exam and ran blood work. Everything, including Valerie's thyroid hormone levels, came back normal. Dr. Fitzgerald reported that he was pretty confident Valerie was experiencing the symptoms of perimenopause onset. He ordered a comprehensive hormone chemistry panel, the results of which indicated slight imbalances of her DHEA and testosterone levels, as well as declining progesterone and estrogen.

The prospect of trying hormone replacement didn't sit well with Valerie. She remembered her mother becoming sick from HRT in the 1980s. It had seemed to age her mother by 15 years in just a short time. Dr. Fitzgerald was aware of HRT's history, though, and assured Valerie that he only prescribed BHRT from a compounding pharmacy. Valerie agreed to give it a try, and for three months, she took the bioidentical hormones with no results. Dr. Fitzgerald made adjustments to the prescription and recommended another three months.

Though she agreed to continue with the BHRT, Valerie also decided to see another doctor for a second opinion. This physician advised Valerie to go on thyroid medication, even though her thyroid hormone levels were within normal range. Valerie opted to try it for six months, but soon after she started, she began to experience symptoms such as fatigue, depression, brain fog, more sleepless nights, and more frequent heart palpitations.

At this point, a friend recommended that Valerie give me a call. The first thing that came through in my reading was that, yes, Valerie had a thyroid condition. However, the thyroid medication wasn't addressing the issue—because the issue was viral.

The *virus* was causing her fatigue and brain fog. It was overburdening her liver, which was resulting in her sleep issues, hot flashes, and night sweats. It was creating a drain on her nervous system, which was affecting her emotions. And the viral by-product in her bloodstream had created a substance called biofilm, which was getting caught in her mitral valve and causing Valerie's heart palpitations. It was a classic case of viral load being passed off as perimenopause.

Valerie immediately weaned herself off the BHRT and thyroid medications. She also started on a powerful antiviral food regimen—which included eliminating eggs and dairy—and used supplementation to correct deficiencies in the minerals such as zinc and iodine that truly mattered to her condition.

After one month with these changes, Valerie's health improved by 80 percent.

After three months, she was back to feeling normal.

Because we'd addressed the underlying issues causing her symptoms, Valerie's health restored itself.

Too often, doctors don't know about these root causes of people's illness, and so they get swept up in the hormone trend. Valerie had decided to ignore her hormone test panels and go by the results of how she felt. She and her family are happier for it.

CHAPTER 16

Lyme Disease

For so long, I've wanted to bring the truth about Lyme disease to the public.

Yet even now, after decades of helping people recover from Lyme, I'm almost reluctant to write this chapter. That's because Lyme comes with so much baggage—suitcases filled with mistaken theories, clinical misjudgments, and trendy misconceptions.

What I'm about to reveal could cause controversy. That's not what I'm after. I just want people to understand what Lyme disease really is, and how they can get better from it. I've been working and waiting patiently, teaching so many practitioners and clients about Lyme, all the while hoping that medical research would uncover the truth. But another year goes by, and another, and medical communities just follow more false leads.

No one has decades of their life to waste while they wait for answers about why they're ill.

If the real story doesn't surface soon, before Lyme disease gets to the next level, the truth will never have a chance to reach people. We are headed to the point in the next two decades where anyone who has a set of symptoms associated with rheumatoid arthritis, multiple sclerosis, fibromyalgia, chronic fatigue syndrome, Epstein-Barr virus, adrenal fatigue, intestinal tract disorders, or thyroid disorders will be tested for Lyme disease with fallible tests—and told they have Lyme.

To understand the Lyme confusion out there, imagine a snowball. Many years ago, it started rolling down a mountainside, getting bigger and bigger. Soon it started to engulf trees, wildlife, telephone poles, cabins—anything in its wake—picking up speed along the way. With enormous, almost unstoppable momentum gained from ignorance and confusion, it has swallowed up well-meaning practitioners and those who suffer from its symptoms—and it just keeps going. Now it's poised to set off an avalanche on the town of humanity.

The easiest thing for me to do would be to stand out of the way. But that's not how I work.

For the sake of the millions of people who could get swallowed up by the Lyme madness over the next 20 years—our daughters and sons, and the new generations of practitioners, doctors, and healers who will continue to operate with outdated hypotheses—I must do what I can to prevent the avalanche.

In this chapter, you will learn the truth about Lyme disease— and you'll learn how to protect yourself from the Lyme trap of the 21st century.

A LOOK BACK

Let's travel back in time for a moment to November 1975, when "several cases of arthritis in Lyme children" were first reported to the Connecticut State Department of Health. This referred to residents of Old Lyme, Lyme, and East Haddam, Connecticut—the area that gave Lyme disease its name.[3]

First let's remind ourselves of the technology back then: rotary phones on the kitchen wall, no such thing as voice mail, and Sony was just releasing its first VCR for sale in the United States. In the medical world, kids were getting their tonsils plucked out as if they were apples on trees, with no understanding of the underlying cause of tonsillitis. Even today, there's no clinical understanding of what's behind tonsillitis. While technology has made leaps and bounds, advancements in chronic and mystery illness have been at a near standstill. The symptoms that children and a few adults in the Lyme area started to experience—chronic fatigue, headaches, joint pain, and so on—were symptoms that had been seen for decades in every other town in Connecticut, not to mention every state throughout the entire country. Yet somehow in this area around Lyme, the illness was treated as something new and unrecognizable. Doctors, researchers, and townspeople began looking for a culprit—and landed on the deer tick, because one of the patients reported seeing a tick a few weeks before he fell ill. That's like a train derailing for reasons unknown, and a passenger mentioning a deer he saw grazing 50 miles back. The clues don't add up in either scenario. Even though no one could explain *why* a tick would give someone Lyme disease, a 17th-century-style witch hunt began. Based only on rumor, deer and the ticks that lived on them became the targets.

In 1981, an entomologist announced he'd discovered the missing link—a bacterium named *Borrelia burgdorferi* that the ticks passed along to humans through their bites. He was lauded for his discovery, which led to a series of bacteria-focused tests and treatments for Lyme disease.

It was the perfect "out" for medical authorities. No one liked ticks anyway, and the theory of a tick-borne illness fed into the fear of nature already present in society. Medical authorities felt they could give up on digging for the answer.

Unfortunately, all these "discoveries" were wrong.

This is what you won't hear anywhere else: Lyme disease is *not* caused by ticks.

And Lyme disease is *not* caused by *Borrelia burgdorferi* bacteria.

When the research was taking place in the 1970s and 1980s, you'd suppose researchers would have realized the problem was happening nationwide—and globally. And today, you'd think someone would wake up and realize that hundreds of thousands of people who have never been near a deer tick receive Lyme disease diagnoses.

As for *Borrelia burgdorferi*, it's a normal part of our environment that's carried by every human being and animal on this planet—including entirely healthy ones. Truth is, this bacteria poses no health risk . . . and has zero connection to Lyme disease. If someone with Lyme disease tests positive for *Borrelia burgdorferi*, it's meaningless.

Nonetheless, virtually all the efforts of medical communities for the past decades to devise methods of diagnosing and treating Lyme disease have been based upon the false premise that it's caused by ticks and bacteria.

When a mistaken theory starts to take on a life of its own, no one's going to want to admit the mistake and disprove it. It's the equivalent of building a house using a poorly drawn set of blueprints. A worker might recognize an issue with the plans, but second-guess himself because he doesn't want to cause a problem or jeopardize his job. In this situation, no matter how skilled the builders you hire, and no matter how intricate and beautiful the decorations, the first strong wind that comes along will blow the house down.

Similarly, medical communities' acceptance of false assumptions in the 1970s and 1980s has resulted in untold misery for patients who not only aren't helped, but in many cases are gravely harmed by well-meaning doctors acting on tragically inaccurate information.

Something else medical communities don't know is that there are multiple reasons that people experience symptoms associated with Lyme disease. The earliest version, which dates back to 1901, produced relatively mild symptoms. The disease mutated into more varieties and strains by the 1950s. It then began mutating into even more aggressive varieties, which leads us to the Lyme symptoms of the 1970s.

By that time, the disease had actually been disrupting the lives of people worldwide for nearly 60 years, with its symptoms always attributed to other illnesses, or simply considered "a mystery."

We still deal with these ailments today, and have names now for many of them, including chronic fatigue syndrome; fibromyalgia; Epstein-Barr virus; multiple sclerosis; ALS; thyroid disorder; lupus; Parkinson's, Crohn's, and Addison's diseases; and many more. Yet they still cause widespread puzzlement and often account for Lyme diagnoses.

LYME DISEASE SYMPTOMS

The confusion about Lyme disease symptoms is vast. At this point, every autoimmune disease or mystery illness in this book and in existence has symptoms that have been linked to Lyme disease.

If you visit a Lyme specialist with *any* symptoms, or even a diagnosis, of MS, lupus, fibromyalgia, RA, CFS, or ME/CFS—we're talking mild to extreme and/or persistent fatigue; muscle pain, weakness, twitching, or spasms; restless leg syndrome; mental fog; joint pain or swelling; or tingling in the hands and feet—you could be deemed to have Lyme whether tests come back positive or negative. Yet if you visit a doctor who doesn't focus on Lyme, you may get a totally different diagnosis. It all has to do with where the doctor's interest and attention lies.

I often tell my clients that visiting a Lyme specialist is like visiting a broom store—without realizing all they sell is brooms. You tell the clerk that you need supplies to scrub your shower tiles, clean up spills in the kitchen, and get rid of the streaks on the living room windows. It won't matter that all these tasks are beyond the scope of what the store sells; you'll walk out carrying a broom.

WHAT LYME DISEASE *REALLY* IS

As mentioned previously, medical communities originally believed that Lyme disease was caused by a bacterium named *Borrelia burgdorferi* transmitted by a bite from a deer tick.

Recently, doctors and researchers have started to realize they may have focused on the wrong bacteria for the last three and a half decades. New patients are now hearing about different decoy bugs such as *Bartonella* and the microscopic parasite *Babesia*. And the new patients aren't being told about the long road others have been down with the *Borrelia* tag, about the traps along the way. They don't have the benefit of that perspective.

You should know, by the way, that *Bartonella* and *Babesia* are also harmless, and most of us carry them. They're once again bait-and-switch theories that promise an answer but deliver only conjecture. In case you're wondering, *Bartonella* and *Babesia* have yet to be clinically found in a tick.

Truth is, Lyme disease isn't the result of ticks, parasites, or bacteria. Lyme disease is actually *viral*—not bacterial or parasitical. When medical communities finally awaken to this fact, there will be hope for Lyme patients.

The true cause of what's being called Lyme disease varies in each individual. People who have different varieties of Epstein-Barr can have Lyme symptoms, as can people who have HHV-6 and its various strains. People who carry any of the different strains of shingles can exhibit Lyme symptoms, with the non-rashing varieties causing the most severe cases, including symptoms such as brain inflammation and other central nervous system weaknesses. It's the same for any number of viruses. So many Lyme patients' blood work also tests positive for EBV or cytomegalovirus—and so many patients have viruses that don't even show up in tests. Any of the more aggressive varieties of these viruses can be behind a patient's Lyme symptoms. All the viruses I list above are in the herpes family and can cause fever, headaches, joint pain, muscle pain, fatigue, neck pain, burning nerve pain, heart palpitations, almost any neurological symptom, and/or other symptoms that doctors think of as so-called Lyme disease. They can dramatically decrease a patient's quality of life and pose serious challenges if not properly treated.

Even if you're experiencing symptoms of any number of these viral infections, you might be able to avoid experiencing a full-blown mystery illness that gets the Lyme disease tag by keeping the virus in a dormant state. And if you're already suffering from more severe symptoms tagged as Lyme, there's a great deal you can do to combat and overcome the illness.

HOW LYME DISEASE IS TRIGGERED

If you're experiencing an onset of viral infection and your immune system is unusually weak, you can come down with Lyme symptoms in a matter of days. Much more typically, however, you'll carry a virus without knowing it's in your system for years—possibly even decades—before it strikes.

Any number of the viruses we've talked about tend to hide in your liver, spleen, small intestinal tract, central nervous system ganglia, or other areas where they can't be detected by your immune system. A virus can bide its time until some traumatic physical or emotional event, poor diet, or other trigger (which you'll read about shortly) weakens you and/or provides an environment that makes the virus stronger. It then emerges to inflame your central nervous system—which weakens your immune system's ability to fight it off.

For example, if you accumulate a heavy metal such as mercury in your system, it will poison you and impair your immune system. At the same time, a virus that can cause the Lyme disease symptoms *loves* heavy metal toxins; they're favored foods that make it stronger. This double blow triggers the virus to leave its dormant state and begin growing its "army" of virus cells.

As another example, if you experience a death in the family, your stressful and painful emotions lower the defenses of your immune system. At the same time, they cause your adrenal glands to produce hormones that are another favored food for the virus. Severe stress is therefore a very common trigger for Lyme disease.

A tick bite is at the *bottom* of the list of common triggers—*not* causes—of Lyme disease, accounting for less than 0.5 percent of Lyme cases.

It's also worth noting that your overall health can play a major role. Even if two people have the exact same type of viral infection and are struck by the same trigger, the one who eats well, exercises regularly, and gets enough sleep might not become sufficiently weakened to activate the virus, while the one who takes poor care of herself or himself might rapidly come down with Lyme symptoms.

Millions of people globally come down with symptoms of Lyme disease due to the following triggers (listed in order of prevalence). All of these triggers can send you doctor-shopping and eventually land you with a Lyme specialist, who, regardless of your test results, may give you the Lyme disease tag—without truly understanding what Lyme even is.

Most Common Lyme Triggers

The substances and circumstances below do not create Lyme disease. Rather, they can *trigger* existing viral conditions that have previously been dormant in the body—viral conditions that surface in the form of the symptoms medical communities collectively call Lyme disease. The triggers are listed in order of prevalence, with the most common at the top and the very least common at the bottom.

1. **Mold:** if you have mold in a home or office, you're spending many hours each day inhaling the fungi. This can wear away at your immune system until a breakdown occurs.

2. **Mercury-based dental amalgam fillings:** if you have old mercury fillings in your teeth (also called *silver fillings*), a well-meaning dentist may decide to remove them all at once for your safety. That's a mistake. It

overstresses the immune system and should be handled one filling at a time, as the mercury tends to be stable where it is, while there's a strong chance the removal process will end up sending the toxic mercury into your bloodstream.

3. **Mercury in other forms:** mercury from *any* source is poisonous. For example, frequently eating seafood, especially large fish such as tuna and swordfish that tend to contain significant amounts of mercury, can eventually push your immune system past the breaking point and lead to a viral infection. Always be mindful about mercury exposure. Even in today's modern times, we're always vulnerable to coming into contact with it, especially in the medical field. Do your research, and question what's being offered to you, your children, and the rest of your family.

4. **Pesticides and herbicides:** if you have poisons on your lawn or in your garden, or you live near a sprayed farm, park, or golf course, you're spending time every day inadvertently inhaling their fumes. This both damages you and feeds the viral infection with toxins that strengthen it.

5. **Insecticides in the home:** flying bug spray, ant spray, roach spray, and other poisons meant to kill insects end up poisoning you, too, and also fueling viral infection.

6. **Death in the family:** the emotional trauma of losing a loved one both weakens your immune system and strengthens viral infections—which feed on the resulting "negative emotion" hormones produced by your adrenal glands.

7. **Broken heart:** betrayal by a loved one, an unexpected breakup, a messy divorce, or anything that causes similar emotional trauma is a common trigger for viruses.

8. **Taking care of a sick loved one:** again, the emotional trauma both weakens the immune system and strengthens viruses.

9. **Spider bite:** spider bites are actually much more common triggers for Lyme disease symptoms than tick bites, accounting for about 5 percent of cases from this list. If the bite leaves some of the spider's venom in your skin, an infection can result that weakens your immune system. Roughly 1 out of 5 times, it'll also produce a bull's-eye-like red rash.

10. **Bee sting:** like spider bites, bee stings are much more common triggers for Lyme disease symptoms than tick bites, accounting for about 5 percent of cases from this list. If the sting leaves some of the bee in your skin, an infection can result that weakens your immune system. Roughly 1 out of 5 times, it will also produce a bull's-eye-like red rash.

11. **"Virus-friendly" prescription medications:** viruses thrive on antibiotics, which at the same time weaken the immune system. Medications such as benzodiazepines have a similar effect. If you suspect you have a viral infection, see your doctor and reassess the medications you're on.

12. **Overprescribed medications:** even if a medication is necessary for you in moderation, a prescription for too much can throw your immune system off-kilter, opening the door for a viral attack. Or if you have multiple doctors prescribing different medications, they can combine into an overwhelming cocktail for the immune system.

13. **Recreational drug abuse:** illegal drugs that contain toxins can simultaneously throw off your immune system and provide fuel for a viral infection.

14. **Financial stress:** worrying about losing your job, not being able to pay bills, and even possibly becoming homeless can lead to a number of strong negative

emotions—including fear of failure, fear of dying, loss of self-image, stress, and shame—that can weaken your immune system's ability to fend off a viral infection.

15. **Physical injuries:** if you twist your ankle, are in a car accident, or experience some other physical injury, it can wear down your body to a point where the virus feels emboldened to strike. That's doubly true if you require an operation to fix the damage—because surgery is usually accompanied by antibiotics.

16. **Summer swimming:** when the weather is warm, red algae can accumulate in lakes or along the ocean shore. The loss of oxygen they create encourages the growth of bacteria, which can weaken your immune system and trigger a virus to come out of dormancy.

17. **Runoff:** heavy metals and other toxins can run off from old land dumps into nearby lakes, especially during hot summer weather. Swimming in these lakes exposes you to the toxins, and lowers your immune system's ability to fight off viral infection.

18. **Professional carpet cleaning:** traditional carpet cleaners use chemicals that are highly toxic for you. Plus many carpets contain toxins already, so the "cleaning" is adding poisons on top of poisons. If you spend a lot of time indoors, you'll breathe these toxic fumes for most of each day, which can both weaken your immune system and feed viruses. Avoid this by buying "green" carpets and organic cleaners, and/or by using a modern "green" carpet cleaning service. Even these are questionable. If you're very sensitive, consider removing your carpets.

19. **Fresh paint:** most fresh paint fills the air with toxic fumes. If you're in a home or office without a lot of circulation, you can end up weakening your immune system and triggering a viral infection.

20. **Insomnia:** any sleep disorder disrupts your body, which over time can trigger a viral infection.

21. **Tick bite:** while medical communities are wrong in
    believing ticks *cause* Lyme disease, tick bites can be
    triggers for Lyme symptoms. As with spider bites and bee
    stings, an attack that leaves some of the creature in your
    skin can result in an infection, which in turn weakens
    your immune system. And if you have an underlying
    virus and the timing is perfect, a bite can be all you
    need to instigate a breakout of viral infection. This
    infection has nothing to do with *Borrelia burgdorferi;*
    Borrelia is *not* the bacterium that's in this infection.
    Again, contrary to popular belief, the tick is the *least*
    common trigger on this list, accountable for less than
    0.5 percent of Lyme disease cases.

Even if one of these triggers awakens a dormant virus, it may
take a while before the virus completes its war preparations—such as
growing an army of "soldier" cells—and launches its initial assault.
Not one of these triggers can actually infect you with the viruses that
cause Lyme symptoms, nor can they infect you with the various bacteria that are falsely associated with Lyme disease.

If you're suffering with what doctors call Lyme disease, then
chances are you were harboring a virus in your body for years before
you got sick. There's a roughly 75 percent chance that one or more
of the above triggers occurred within three months to a year of the
onset of your symptoms.

ANTIBIOTICS

Medical communities' mistaken belief that Lyme disease is
caused by bacteria (and recently parasites) is one of the greatest mistakes in modern medical history. It has kept so many generations
dealing with viral infections from getting the true help they need. I
call this the Lyme trap.

The way doctors usually deal with Lyme disease is to prescribe
antibiotics, because they're aiming to destroy *Borrelia burgdorferi* and
other bacteria such as *Bartonella,* as well as parasites such as *Babesia*—
which actually have nothing to do with Lyme disease and aren't a
health threat. *Borrelia, Bartonella,* and *Babesia* do not attack the central

nervous system, and symptoms of an inflamed central nervous system are the number-one issue among all Lyme patients. Until medical communities learn this truth, they will continue to prescribe antibiotics that yield no positive results and leave a wake of damage. That's not merely ineffective. It's dangerous.

Powerful varieties of antibiotics hammer a Lyme patient with a double blow. And because Lyme patients usually have inflamed neurological systems from viral infections in the herpes family, these harsh antibiotics bruise the nerves. Some doctors are under the mistaken impression that the pain and other symptoms a patient experiences in this circumstance are a sign of progress—an indication of a beneficial *Herxheimer reaction,* that is, bacterial die-off as the body detoxifies. In reality, the symptoms indicate something is very wrong.

Antibiotics tend to kill *all* bacteria, not just the ones that are bad for you. The good bacteria in your gut are vital for your health, and their destruction can wreak havoc with your immune system, as well as with your digestion. If a doctor places you on an aggressive antibiotic for two or more weeks, then even if you take probiotics daily, your gut might need a year or more to recover from the damage. Some guts will never be the same, even if the antibiotic is administered intravenously. (For more on gut health, see Chapter 17.)

The viruses that cause Lyme disease symptoms *love* antibiotics. And aggressive antibiotics do for viruses what mother's milk does for a baby: make them grow bigger and stronger.

Because the only significant natural enemy of the viral infections that cause Lyme symptoms is the immune system, taking an antibiotic that both compromises the immune system and super-charges the virus is like trying to put out a fire by pouring a barrel of gasoline on it. Yet it's the standard way doctors have always treated Lyme disease. Taking large doses of aggressive antibiotics can transform a relatively mild case of Lyme disease into a severe health crisis . . . and over time, a potentially dangerous one. Tragically, this happens every day.

With integrated Lyme specialists now comprehending the damage that aggressive antibiotic treatment has caused over the last 25 to 40 years, they're starting to lower dosages of antibiotics and couple them with natural nutritional support, including natural intravenous vitamins. Before we give them a medal for the realization, though, we need to recognize that medicine is still decades away from understanding that *no* antibiotics are needed—because Lyme is viral. Popular alternative treatments such as ultraviolet blood irradiation therapy (UBI) don't help either, because they work on the misguided theory that the problem is bacterial and in the bloodstream. In fact, the viruses that cause Lyme disease symptoms are mostly neurological, and they never cause Lyme symptoms when they're in the blood. It's when the viruses are in the organs and central nervous system that they cause their trouble.

As long as doctors believe the problem behind Lyme symptoms is bacterial, they'll be lost at sea in a fog, chasing a ghost ship—at the expense of potentially millions of people. It's worth noting that viruses that create Lyme disease symptoms do have many cofactors. These include: *Streptococcus* A and B, *E. coli, Mycoplasma pneumoniae, H. pylori,* and/or *Chlamydophila pneumoniae*; plus toxic molds and the fungus *Candida. Bartonella* and *Babesia,* the bugs that have become popular recently in the Lyme field and which are no more harmful than *Candida,* are also cofactors.

Note that these cofactors do not *create* the symptoms known as Lyme. To understand how medical communities misunderstand these cofactors as causes, imagine two armies in battle, one army (the medical communities) chasing down a retreating army (bacteria). When the first group of foot soldiers finally reaches the troops they've been pursuing and has them surrounded on all sides, they'll discover that those weren't bayonets they saw in the distance—they were flagpoles, trumpets, and drumsticks. The army went after the wrong guys. All this time that the foot soldiers thought they were chasing down their enemy, they were really following an infantry band. In this same way, medical research has been pursuing the messengers (bacteria), while the real adversary (viruses) sneaks by unnoticed.

Most of the real damage is caused by the viral infections that are not discovered in the patient—or, if they are discovered, pushed aside as a nonissue. The cofactors aren't the threat.

Further, the particular bacteria that are cofactors for the viruses behind Lyme disease symptoms are usually resistant to antibiotics, and become even more highly resistant over time. If you have Lyme symptoms, this is all the more reason to strenuously avoid antibiotics.

There's one exception to this rule: It's okay to use mild antibiotics to fight an infection. For example, when a normal skin infection occurs from a spider bite, bee sting, or a tick bite that leaves part of the creature lodged in your skin, your body fights against infection by creating a ringed rash, or red "bull's-eye," around the area. (This bull's-eye is the ultimate misconception about Lyme disease.)

In this situation, taking a less aggressive antibiotic is okay; the long-term risks of antibiotics are trumped by the short-term risk of the infection. Let's be clear, though: The infection itself is not Lyme disease. And it is *not Borrelia burgdorferi* within the infection. These bull's-eye infections are just normal staph infections that result from foreign debris getting beneath the skin's surface through a puncture wound. For the record, *Borrelia* has never been found and cultured from a bull's-eye, nor has *Babesia* or *Bartonella*.

TESTING FOR LYME TODAY

There are two primary tests medical communities use to diagnose Lyme disease: *Enzyme-Linked Immunosorbent Assay* (ELISA), which detects antibodies to the *Borrelia burgdorferi* bacterium; and *Western Blot*, which seeks to find antibodies to several proteins of *Borrelia burgdorferi*. Both are based on the false assumption that Lyme disease symptoms are caused by *Borrelia burgdorferi* . . . which they're not. It's therefore common for a patient to have Lyme symptoms but receive negative results from these tests.

Advanced laboratories have started to discover that these tests never worked to begin with. As they try to develop better tests, though, they are still operating under the same old theory that bacteria and/or parasites are the cause of Lyme. If we go back to that faulty blueprint analogy, it's like trying to build a whole new house with the same plans as before—without fixing the critical mistakes in the plans' conception.

If you've recently received a Lyme diagnosis from an integrative or functional medicine doctor, there's a good chance she or he mentioned they no longer rely on ELISA or the Western Blot. Your doctor may have said, "We need to send your blood to more advanced Lyme labs." When the results came back, your doctor most likely said that the Lyme titers (measures) of your blood work indicated antibodies, or that partial positives appeared for bacteria such as *Bartonella* and parasites such as *Babesia*. (If you have the flu, a staph infection, EBV, or even *Candida,* there's a good chance you'll trip a false positive test result for Lyme.)

This is the sly way of diverting from the fact that patients have been wronged for decades, as medical communities went after the incorrect culprit. What these doctors don't realize is that these new *Bartonella* and *Babesia* leads aren't really progress—because they work off the same mistaken premise as always. Rather than understanding the bacteria and parasites as harmless cofactors, they point to them as the disease itself.

And since it's exceedingly rare for a patient with Lyme symptoms to have actually been bitten by a tick, medical professionals now tell stories about how Lyme disease can come from a mosquito, deerfly, or horsefly that may have bitten a patient years ago.

There's an off chance that a bite from a deerfly or horsefly could act as a trigger for viral symptoms to come to the surface, in the manner that the other insect bites mentioned earlier can. However, pointing to these insects as actual causes of Lyme disease is once again acting on the old, misguided theory—and adding to people's fear of being out in nature. It's no more advanced than saying ticks are to blame.

The only upside to these recent developments is that medical communities are broadening the scope of what they look for with Lyme. They're coming to see it's not just one thing, and that *Borrelia burgdorferi* was a faulty hypothesis. Yet researchers are still looking in the wrong neck of the woods—literally. I predict that as the years go by, still other bacteria will be blamed for Lyme, and the true viral culprits will be ignored.

And if you're sick with Lyme disease symptoms, do you have 20 years for research to figure out the real cause?

The truth is that medical communities haven't yet discovered most of the genuine cofactors of Lyme. And in the case of *Babesia* and *Bartonella,* beyond the fact that doctors don't realize their part in Lyme disease symptoms is minimal, there are multiple problems with testing for them.

First, you can have a viral infection that causes Lyme disease symptoms but not have these cofactors, in which case you'll test negative. Second, you can harbor these cofactors but not have them picked up by the tests—which are far from infallible—and so again receive a negative result.

But the biggest issue is that 60 percent of Americans carry around *Babesia* and *Bartonella* (which are usually not harmful by themselves). As a result, you can be entirely healthy and yet test positive. Since medical tests often give a patient who has Lyme symptoms negative results and a patient without Lyme symptoms positive results, they're not very useful.

If you tested 100 healthy people with the newest, most advanced Lyme tests from the best labs, more than 50 of them would test positive for Lyme. The titers for those 50-plus study subjects would indicate antibodies present for the bacteria medical communities say are behind Lyme disease.

The most effective way to determine if you have a viral infection causing Lyme symptoms is to focus on your history and symptoms. If you've experienced one of the common triggers by which viral infection is activated; *and* you are or have been experiencing viral symptoms such as twitching, spasm, fatigue, brain fog, memory loss, nerve and joint pain, and other neurological symptoms; *and* you've eliminated other likely causes for how you're feeling—then there's a strong chance you're suffering from a virus that creates Lyme disease symptoms. As I mentioned earlier, it's most likely one of the many strains in the herpes family such as shingles, HHV-6, Epstein-Barr, or cytomegalovirus.

These viruses can all trigger false positives in the new, progressive Lyme disease lab tests. The viruses create by-products, debris, viral biofilm, and the famous spirochetes (which are viral casings mistaken for bacteria), all of which trip up the fallible testing systems of Lyme labs by making a patient's illness appear to be bacterial. Blood labs are like any other company—they're open for business. They want to stay afloat, protect their livelihoods, and so a certain amount of profit-minded perspective guides their motivation. We can't trust claims about amazing new lab tests as absolute fact. And there's a big disconnect between blood labs and the doctors who order tests from them; doctors often aren't told how the labs come up with their results. Keep this in mind, and be cautious about what "facts" you believe.

If you have taken antibiotics and experienced the viral backlash, or if you haven't undergone treatment but experience the symptoms I've described in this chapter, the odds are immense that you can recover your health by patiently and scrupulously following the directions in the next section. Over time, you should be able to destroy 90 percent or more of the virus's cells, allowing your immune system to send the virus back into a comatose-like, dormant state . . . and free yourself of Lyme.

ADDRESSING LYME DISEASE

When chronic symptoms of Lyme disease interrupt people's lives, it can be devastating. Most patients have seen multiple doctors and have received either no answers or a diagnosis such as MS, fibromyalgia, RA, Sjögren's syndrome, migraines, lupus, CFS, or ME/CFS. When one of these patients finally visits a Lyme specialist, the Lyme disease diagnosis can feel like a relief; it can feel like they've finally uncovered the mystery.

In the U.S. alone, over 500,000 people a year with symptoms of what are really viral infections are instead being treated as if their illnesses are bacterial—and they're receiving the Lyme label. It's becoming the most grievously misunderstood affliction of our time. As it gains momentum, it will become the most popular diagnosis of the future. Patients and doctors alike will be overwhelmed by the validation that this designation seems to provide, even if it doesn't make sense.

The tag "Lyme disease" will remain a label for a mystery illness that no one realizes is due to viral infection. The tag is not an answer to what's ailing you. Any name could have been put in the place of Lyme. For all the insight that name gives, you might as well just call it *cheese disease,* or *I-don't-feel-well disease.*

As we've explored in this chapter, it's critical to understand what's truly behind Lyme symptoms so you can protect yourself and your loved ones from the Lyme trap.

If you're 40 years old today, it won't be until you're 65 or 70 that the medical establishment starts to realize the mistake in how it's been conceiving of and treating Lyme disease—and that's being optimistic. However, if you follow all the steps described in this section daily without fail, you can force your viral infection back into its dormant state and render it harmless.

How long this process takes will depend on a variety of factors, such as whether you have a more or less aggressive strain of virus, have recently taken antibiotics, are in a healthy environment or a toxic one that can be a trigger and feed the virus, and are in the early or later stages of the illness. Roughly speaking, the program requires six months to two years to be fully effective.

And don't stop with the recommendations in this chapter. Also turn to Part IV, "How to Finally Heal," where you'll find details on heavy metal detox and everything else you need to rid yourself of Lyme symptoms. All the information you need to free yourself from the Lyme trap—or sidestep it altogether—is in this book.

You have the ability to heal. Your body *wants* to truly heal, and to be well. If you give your body what it needs and take away the unproductive elements, you can tap into your core healing power and recover.

Healing Foods

Certain healing foods can help your body ward off or recover from the viruses behind Lyme disease symptoms. Star anise, asparagus, wild blueberries, radishes, celery, cinnamon, garlic, apricots, and onions are among the best to focus on, as they can variously aid in killing viral cells, detoxification, repairing brain cells, recovering the central nervous system, and other healing processes.

Healing Herbs and Supplements

- **Thyme:** kills viruses on contact. Thyme is especially important because it crosses the blood/brain barrier— that is, it travels beyond the bloodstream to attack virus cells that have invaded the brain stem and spinal fluid.

- **Lemon balm:** kills cofactors of the viruses behind Lyme symptoms, including the bacteria *Streptococcus*, *E. coli, Bartonella, Babesia, Mycoplasma pneumoniae,* and

Chlamydophila pneumoniae, plus the fungus *Candida.* This reduces the strain on the immune system.

- **Zinc:** lowers inflammatory reactions to a neurotoxin produced by viruses in the herpes family.

- **Licorice root:** very effective at impairing the ability of virus cells to move and reproduce.

- **L-lysine:** impairs the ability of viral cells to move and reproduce.

- **Lomatium root:** helps flush viral and bacterial excrement and toxins, and the toxic corpses of dead virus and bacteria cells, out of the body's system.

- **Reishi mushrooms:** builds up lymphocytes, platelets, and neutrophils, which strengthen the immune system.

- **Silver hydrosol:** kills viruses on contact.

- **Astaxanthin:** an antioxidant that helps restore brain tissue and nerves damaged by viruses.

- **Nascent iodine:** stabilizes and strengthens the endocrine system.

CASE HISTORY:
The Lyme Trap

Stephanie was a happy stay-at-home mom who took care of her husband, Edward, and their two children. When Edward left her for a younger woman, Stephanie was forced to get a job selling cosmetics. Unfortunately, her boss enjoyed torturing staffers with the threat that they'd be fired if they didn't produce daily results.

The pain of betrayal by her husband, the physical and emotional toll of working a day job while also trying to raise her kids on her own, and the stress of worrying about losing that job and becoming homeless, provided multiple triggers for the onset of infection by a virus that had been lurking in Stephanie for years. Within a month, it woke up from its dormant state.

The virus left its hiding place in Stephanie's liver and invaded her central nervous system. Stephanie started to feel exceptionally tired and sluggish, and her mind became foggy.

Concerned, Stephanie went to her family doctor for a checkup. Her doctor conducted a physical exam and ran blood tests, but found nothing unusual. "It's just stress," the doctor told her. "Simply stop worrying, and you'll be fine."

Stephanie's high level of fatigue and mental confusion persisted. And as the virus reproduced and worked its way into the nerves of her legs, arms, and shoulders, Stephanie began to feel neurological symptoms she'd never experienced before. She was especially troubled by pain in her left hip and knee, which was interfering with her daily routine of jogging. All of a sudden she was almost tripping on her left leg, as if it no longer worked properly.

Stephanie returned to her family doctor, who still couldn't find anything wrong. With her joint pain in mind, he sent her to a rheumatologist.

The rheumatologist gave Stephanie another careful physical exam and blood tests, with a focus on rheumatoid arthritis. He couldn't find anything wrong either. "You're perfectly healthy," the rheumatologist concluded. "Stay calm, get enough rest, and these issues will go away by themselves."

As much as Stephanie wanted to believe this, her symptoms not only persisted but expanded. Stephanie felt tired all the time, no matter how much she slept. The pain in her left shoulder became acute. Her left hip and leg grew weaker, giving her a slight limp. And she developed a mild case of anxiety.

While sharing her woes with her friends, one of them said, "What you're describing sounds a lot like what my cousin Shelly has. She was diagnosed with Lyme disease."

"Lyme disease?" Stephanie said. "I live in the city. I haven't been in a forest or within miles of a deer for years. How would I get bitten by a tick?"

"I don't know," said her friend. "But no one else is helping you, so you might as well see a Lyme doctor. What do you have to lose?"

This made sense to Stephanie, so she saw Dr. Nartel, a Lyme specialist.

Dr. Nartel took Stephanie's blood to run two types of tests: ELISA and Western Blot. Both tests primarily look for antibodies reacting to the presence of *Borrelia burgdorferi* bacteria. Stephanie's problem wasn't *Borrelia burgdorferi,* though; it was a *virus,* so the results of both of her tests were negative.

Dr. Nartel was experienced enough to know these tests can't be counted on, even though he didn't understand why. So unlike Stephanie's previous doctors, he took her symptoms seriously. "What you're describing is consistent with Lyme disease," he told her. "I recommend you go on a 30-day treatment of antibiotics, which you'll take daily in pill form. If you really do have Lyme disease, this will kill the bacteria causing your illness."

That made sense to Stephanie: finally, a diagnosis and validation. She readily agreed.

During the next month, Stephanie felt no difference. However, the antibiotics killed not only the bad bacteria, but the good bacteria in Stephanie's gut, which actually *weakened* her immune system long-term. The antibiotics also inflamed the walls of Stephanie's intestinal lining, causing painful gastritis and spasms.

Dr. Nartel had anticipated some of these issues by also prescribing probiotics. They weren't enough to counteract the side effects of the medication. Stephanie had trouble digesting food, lost her appetite, and periodically felt a burning sensation in her stomach.

After another month, Stephanie's fatigue and joint pain were worse than before her treatment. So was her memory fog . . . which now also included periodic memory loss.

Seriously concerned, Stephanie conducted extensive research via books and the Internet. If she didn't have Lyme, she concluded that she might have CFS, fibromyalgia, lupus, or even MS. Since Dr. Nartel couldn't help, she decided to try a different Lyme specialist, Dr. Maizon.

Dr. Maizon ran a broader range of blood tests than Stephanie's previous physicians and also used a lab that tested more extensively. One of the results turned up positive for *Babesia* and *Bartonella*—which wasn't surprising, considering the different types of bacteria and parasites a person can carry around even without Lyme disease symptoms. Still, Stephanie didn't know that *Babesia* and *Bartonella* are harmless and had nothing to do with her central nervous system issues, so she relaxed because she felt she was in more experienced hands.

When Dr. Maizon told her, "We need to do a one-to-three month course of intravenous antibiotics, and we'll use a substantially stronger medication this time," Stephanie readily agreed.

The stronger antibiotic, which was much more aggressive, took her to a whole new level of pain and suffering. It fed and strengthened the viral infection the way coal fuels a fire.

After two months on this more aggressive antibiotic, Stephanie's fatigue, joint pain, brain fog, and memory loss became so severe that she had to quit her job. She also developed nerve pain and spasms throughout her body. She couldn't fully care for her kids, as she needed to spend a large portion of each day in bed.

Dr. Maizon assured Stephanie that her getting worse wasn't cause for concern. "It just means the antibiotics are working," he said. "We call this situation a Herxheimer reaction. It happens when dying bacteria release their toxins faster than your system can flush them."

What Dr. Maizon didn't know was that if the problem had been bacterial, as he thought, the antibiotics would have made a substantial difference for the better. The explanation he offered is actually a trendy rationalization that medical communities have concocted to explain why patients get *worse* under a treatment that's supposed to make them better.

In reality, Stephanie was experiencing sensitive, inflamed nerves being further irritated by aggressive antibiotics, as well as an increased viral load. Still, Stephanie believed her doctor . . . and grew increasingly ill.

After a third month on antibiotics, Stephanie had a deep feeling that if she continued the treatment much longer, she'd die. She dropped Dr. Maizon. But with her immune system compromised and the viral infection greatly strengthened, she stayed chronically ill.

Stephanie turned to yet another Lyme specialist, who prescribed natural treatments: multivitamins, vitamin D, co-enzyme Q10, and lots of fish oil. This doctor knew from past experience not to be so heavy-handed with antibiotics, so when Stephanie noticed no change with just the supplements, the specialist recommended adding only low dosages of the antibiotic medication. He argued that she'd been on too high a dosage before, but low dosages daily for three months would bring about her recovery.

Stephanie's Lyme had begun as a mild case, and might have stayed that way if she had steered clear of antibiotics. But the more she took, the more she paved the way for her Lyme symptoms to reach their full potential. Now, choosing to give antibiotics yet another try effectively handed her unidentified virus a loaded gun. After six weeks, Stephanie experienced brain inflammation and nerve pain so extreme that it brought her to what she felt was beyond crisis management. She had to struggle to even speak.

She let go of her current doctor, and in a panic visited a series of new alternative doctors.

Considering the gravity of her symptoms, one of them decided she didn't really have Lyme disease after all, but Lou Gehrig's disease (ALS).

Another declared she had multiple sclerosis.

And yet another told her she had Guillain-Barre. (In fact, Stephanie *did* have a form of Guillain-Barre—which medical communities think is a distinct disorder, but is actually just another name for viral nerve inflammation that affects the brain. This is a prime example of how much confusion revolves around Lyme.)

Finally, Stephanie went to an alternative doctor who happened to be a client of mine. He referred Stephanie to me as an emergency case.

After doing a reading and scan, the first thing I did was ease Stephanie's mind about her condition. "Yes," I said, "I'm very familiar with this illness. It wasn't caused by a tick, horsefly, or spider bite—or by bacteria. Spirit says it's a strain of a non-rashing shingles virus in the central nervous system causing brain inflammation, and the antibiotics you've been taking have been making it much stronger."

Just knowing what was really going on lifted a great weight from Stephanie and gave her the opportunity to start healing. At the same time, she was furious with the doctors who had transformed a relatively mild unidentified viral infection into a nearly fatal condition. Had she been treated with the appropriate natural methods, she would've been spared a full year of agony.

"You're entitled to be angry," I said. "You should also know that your doctors were genuinely trying to help. They were operating under the wrong assumptions that started 40 years ago about the nature of this illness. Thousands of others have gone through the same trials. What matters now is that you know the truth and can recover and heal."

Stephanie went on the foods, herbs, and supplements recommended in this chapter, and followed the instructions in this book for the 28-Day Healing Cleanse. There was a great deal of damage to undo. After six months, she resumed normal household chores, and required only a two-hour nap midday to maintain energy. After nine months, she was active outdoors again: walking without limping, driving her kids to soccer practice, gently romping around with her dog. After a year on her natural program to eliminate the viral symptoms behind her Lyme diagnosis, Stephanie felt better than she had before starting on the aggressive antibiotics.

Over time, she was stronger than she had been before the very first mild antibiotic. Stephanie finally recovered her full health, started jogging again, and resumed her normal life.

What Stephanie went through was a nightmare. Tens of thousands of people with Lyme disease undergo a similar ordeal every year. Tragically, many of them end up suffering greatly.

The good news is that virtually all of this pain and suffering can be avoided when the true nature of Lyme disease is understood . . . and the actual illness is addressed with the on-target methods covered in this chapter and the rest of this book.

PART IV

HOW TO FINALLY HEAL

CHAPTER 17

Gut Health

No one knows what really happens when food enters the stomach. The digestive system is a miracle and phenomenon beyond anything that anyone can perceive. Even with a medical understanding of the way some of it functions, the digestive system remains a great mystery.

Everyone knows we bite into a piece of food, chew it, swallow it, then it enters the gastrointestinal tract, some sort of breakdown occurs, and we expel it. We know that this is how we get nutrients. And we know that sometimes the process doesn't go so well, and stomachaches develop, or intestinal discomfort, or worse.

Just because medical science has discovered digestive enzymes, though, doesn't mean it has developed a comprehensive understanding of digestion. It doesn't mean medical science knows the difference between Jack the Ripper and Santa Claus when it comes to what we eat and how our bodies process it.

Digestion is the least founded part of the study of human physiology. While we walk around pretending that it's straightforward and science has it all figured out, it remains the most enigmatic element of how our bodies operate.

Unlike certain illnesses, where I can tell you that in a few decades, research will most likely make the discoveries it needs to make—discoveries of the information that's in this book—gut health is another story. Its secret workings may never be uncovered by medical communities on this earth—which is why this chapter is essential.

Your gut is one of the key foundations of your health. That makes caring for your digestive system the perfect place to start your journey of healing from the inside out.

Your gut includes the stomach, small intestine, large intestine (which includes the colon), liver, and gallbladder. The gut is responsible for ensuring that you absorb the nutrients of the food you eat, properly expel waste and toxins, and maintain a strong immune system.

Yet not only is it critical for these everyday functions, your gut also holds a life force of its own. Food does not digest just from the physical process of food breakdown (a process scientific study hasn't fully pieced together); there are also critical spiritual and metaphysical factors involved in digestion. That's why enlightened beings on the planet employ eating techniques such as slow and thorough chewing; mindful, present eating; prayer before, during, or after meals; and becoming one with your food.

Imagine a river flowing inside your colon. Deep in the riverbed (the colon's lining), thousands of different strains of bacteria and microorganisms are there to maintain a homeostatic balance so that the river water doesn't become toxic (i.e., so the gut doesn't become septic and poisonous).

Just as a river has a spirit, the gut harbors much of the human spirit, too. That spirit is your essence of self, your will, and your intuition.

Have you ever heard the term "gut instinct"? Or "gut reaction" or "gut feeling"? Then there's "What does your gut tell you to do?" and "What are you, gutless?" and "I felt gutted." There's "I just about busted a gut," "I hate his guts," "I ran my guts out," and "You've really got guts." How many gut-related idioms are out there? It's because we understand on some level just what an integral role it plays in our lives, far beyond physicality. We understand that it's part of the core foundation of who we are emotionally and intuitively.

Your gut is where your strength is. It has emotional pores, and because of this, emotions can actually control how much good or bad bacteria flourishes there. Poor gut health can greatly hinder intuition.

People are kind of like apples. You can have a shiny, perfect-looking apple that has a rotten core. That's like when someone's gut is spawning a lot of harmful bacteria, and maybe she or he has an immoral character, but you'd never guess from appearance. You can also have an apple with imperfections on the outside, yet on the inside it may have the most solid, healthy core you can find. Such a salt-of-the-earth, decent person may not have a happy resting face, or may not dress in vogue or seem like much fun on the surface, yet may possess a gut filled with good bacteria.

People can have anywhere from 75 to 125 trillion bacteria residing in the gut. This opens the door to infection by toxic and unproductive bacteria, microbes, mold, yeast, fungus, mycotoxins, and viruses. If not properly dealt with, these pathogens can alter and block your natural instincts and create a breeding ground for an unlimited variety of illnesses—unless your gut has a balance of good bacteria to counter these effects.

This chapter covers what most commonly goes wrong with the gut, including leaky gut syndrome, poor digestion, acid reflux, intestinal infections, irritable bowel syndrome, gastric spasms, gastritis, and general pain in or near your stomach. It provides critical information about these conditions well beyond what's known by medical communities. It also debunks a number of unproductive gut health fads and trend "remedies" and offers simple steps you can take to genuinely heal your gut and restore your health.

UNDERSTANDING LEAKY GUT SYNDROME

One very confusing condition in medicine is *leaky gut syndrome,* also called *intestinal permeability.* The names themselves are perplexing; they're terms that different medical communities use to describe different conditions and theories.

When it comes down to it, there are three sides to the leaky gut syndrome story. Let's look at the first side: the conventional medical community's understanding. Most conventional doctors and surgeons use the term "leaky gut" for a critical intestinal disease that perforates the lining of the intestinal tract or stomach and causes severe blood infections, raging fevers, and/or sepsis. They have that right. True leaky gut is a very serious ailment that causes extreme pain and misery.

Leaky gut could stem from ulcers embedded deep in the stomach lining. Or it could result from bacterial strains of *E. coli* developing pockets in the intestinal tract lining; or superbugs like *C. difficile* causing *megacolon*; or from *hemorrhaging, abscesses,* or *diverticulosis.* The name "leaky gut" is applied when one of these conditions breaks through the lining of the gastrointestinal tract and allows the pathogens to leach into the bloodstream.

Another way that leaky gut can occur is when a colonoscopy goes wrong and punctures the colon. (Clients have come to me who had very long hospital stays due to this.)

No matter the cause, true leaky gut results in dire symptoms.

The second side of the story is the alternative, integrative, and naturopathic understanding of leaky gut syndrome. These medical communities use the term to describe a condition in which mold, funguses like *Candida,* or unproductive bacteria burrow tiny holes in the linings of the intestine and cause micro levels of toxins to leak directly into the bloodstream, resulting in a multitude of symptoms.

This theory needs some adjustment.

While it's true that a toxic gut environment, including unproductive bacteria and fungus, can contribute greatly to ill health, referring to this as leaky gut is misleading. If these pathogens were truly breaking through the gastrointestinal lining in even the slightest way, then severe symptoms such as high fever, blood infection, extreme pain, and/or sepsis would result. "Leaky gut" should only be used to describe actual perforation of the digestive tract walls.

So why are tens of thousands of people who have fatigue, aches and pains, constipation, digestive discomfort, and acid reflux being told they have leaky gut or intestinal permeability by alternative practitioners?

Because there's something real going on, and this misunderstood catchphrase is the best theory the practitioners can offer. In the conventional medical world, millions of patients receive the tags IBS, celiac, Crohn's, colitis, gastroparesis, or gastritis to label these sorts of symptoms—yet the conditions remain mysterious. Or they experience gut symptoms and receive no diagnosis.

There *is* an explanation for these mystery gut problems that aren't actual leaky gut. I call it *ammonia permeability,* and it's the third side to the story.

Ammonia Permeability

Please do not confuse ammonia permeability with the recently trendy term "intestinal permeability." Intestinal permeability is just a new name, meant to give the illusion of progress, for the old theory of leaky gut.

Ammonia permeability is a real occurrence. To comprehend what it is, you must first learn a few things about how your body processes food.

When you eat, the food quickly travels down to your stomach so it can be digested. (If you're chewing slowly enough for saliva to mix with the food, digestion will begin its initial stage in the mouth.) For dense protein-based foods—e.g., animal meat, nuts and seeds, and legumes—digestion in the stomach largely occurs through the action of your stomach's *hydrochloric acid* coupled with enzymes, which break the protein down into simpler forms that can then be further digested and assimilated by your intestines.

This is a relatively smooth process if your stomach contains normal levels of hydrochloric acid.

If your hydrochloric acid levels have become low, however, your food won't be sufficiently digested in your stomach. This is common when you're eating under stress or pressure. When the proteins reach your lower intestine, they won't be broken down enough for your cells to access their nutrients, and instead the food will just lie there and rot. This is called *gut rot*—putrefaction that creates *ammonia gas* and can result in symptoms of bloating, digestive discomfort, chronic dehydration, or oftentimes no symptoms at all. That's just the start.

In some people, good hydrochloric acid diminishes and bad acids take its place. A person could live with this condition for many years and not notice. Eventually, though, the bad acids can travel up the esophagus. (If you're experiencing acid reflux, these rogue acids are causing it, not your stomach's hydrochloric acid. This is a very common confusion; the medical world sees all stomach and intestinal acids as the same.)

A related issue is that the lining of your gut creates mucus in an effort to protect you from the bad acids. If a lot of mucus is coming up your throat for no apparent reason, it's probably your gut struggling to keep you safe because the rogue acids are trying to eat away at your stomach and esophagus lining . . . and it's a signal that you've got a problem that needs to be addressed. The mucus can also travel down the intestinal tract and stop proper absorption of nutrients.

Let's go back to that ammonia gas, though. This is the key piece of information: when food decomposes in your intestinal tract and produces ammonia, this toxic gas has the ability to float, ghost-like, out of your intestines and directly into your bloodstream. This is what's called ammonia permeability.

It's the ammonia gas that creates most of the havoc associated with leaky gut syndrome. It doesn't have to do with infections or punctures of the small intestines or colon. And it isn't *Candida* yeast expelling toxins through the intestinal walls, either.

Millions of people walk around with digestive health problems, and the culprit is ammonia permeability. As I've said, what many alternative doctors diagnose as leaky gut syndrome has nothing to do with holes or other imperfections in your gut; it has nothing to do with acids or bacteria leaking out.

Rather, ammonia gas in your intestines is drifting into the bloodstream . . . which then carries the gas throughout your body. Besides the gut symptoms I mentioned earlier, ammonia permeability can result in malaise, fatigue, skin problems, restless sleep, anxiety, and so much more.

At this point you might reasonably ask, "If this all happens because of too little hydrochloric acid in the stomach, what causes *that?*" The number one reason for a deficiency of hydrochloric acid is *adrenaline.*

What is not known is that there isn't just one form of adrenaline. Your adrenal glands produce 56 different blends in response to different emotions and situations. And the ones associated with negative feelings such as fear, anxiety, anger, hatred, guilt, shame, depression, and stress can be severely damaging to a variety of areas of your body—including your stomach's supply of hydrochloric acid. So if you've been chronically stressed or upset, that can be enough to slowly break down your hydrochloric acid—and your ability to properly digest food. Different levels of stress and emotions that we experience in our everyday lives can hinder good bacteria and grow bad bacteria.

Also often wreaking havoc with your stomach's hydrochloric acid are *prescription drugs.* Antibiotics, immunosuppressants, antifungals, amphetamines, and a variety of other medications our bodies haven't adapted to can disrupt the chemical balance in the stomach.

Your hydrochloric acid is likely to be damaged if you overeat any type of protein, such as animal meat, nuts, seeds, and/or legumes. (If the protein comes from greens, sprouts, or other vegetables, it doesn't have the same effect.) Eating a lot of foods that combine fat and sugar (such as cheese, whole milk, cakes, cookies, and ice cream), can have the same harmful effect on hydrochloric acid.

Both these categories of food require much more work to be digested than fruit or vegetables do, placing a huge strain on your gut. This can eventually "burn out" your stomach's hydrochloric acid and weaken digestive enzymes. If you're eating high-protein meals (for example, chicken, fish, or meat) and you're experiencing symptoms of low hydrochloric acid such as bloating, stomach discomfort, constipation, sluggishness, and/or fatigue, then eat the animal protein sparingly and limit it to one serving per day.

There is good news in all of this. You can recover your hydrochloric acid and strengthen your enzymes with a miraculous herb that's sold everywhere.

Rebuilding Hydrochloric Acid

The way to fix ammonia permeability (which, as we've just discussed, is often mislabeled as leaky gut syndrome or intestinal permeability)—and the first step in addressing virtually any other gut health issue—is to rebuild your stomach's supply of hydrochloric acid and strengthen your digestive system.

There's an amazingly simple and effective way to do this: daily, on an empty stomach, drink a 16-ounce glass of fresh *celery juice.*

This may not be the answer you were expecting. It may not seem like celery juice could be *that* beneficial. But take this very seriously. It is one of the most profound ways, if not *the* most profound way, to restore digestive health. It is that powerful. And keep in mind: while there are many juice blends out there nowadays that are fantastic for your health, you need to drink your celery juice straight if your goal is to restore proper digestive function.

Do not be derailed by the simplicity of this. Think of it like being assigned a ten-page paper on one specific aspect of daily life in a certain historical time period. If you hand in a paper that's an overview of the era, with only two lines about that one part of daily life, the teacher won't be impressed by all the extra facts. She'll wonder why you didn't go in-depth on the one topic she assigned.

That's how your stomach feels when it's trying to restore hydrochloric acid. A juice blend of 20 different ingredients, only one of which is celery, will be a distraction. Sometimes simplest is best. The stomach wants celery juice, and celery juice alone, so it can do its deep repair in this area. It's a secret method that can turn around the life of a person with a gut disorder.

Here's how to do it:

- Wash a fresh bunch of celery in the morning while you still have an empty stomach. (Or if you do this later in the day, wait at least two hours after your previous meal so your stomach is relatively empty again.) Anything else in your stomach will disrupt the effect of the celery.

- Juice the celery. Add *nothing* else, as any other ingredient will disrupt the effect of the celery.

- Drink the juice *immediately*—before it can oxidize, which reduces its power.

This works because celery contains unique sodium compositions, and these mineral salts are bonded with many bioactive trace minerals and nutrients. If you drink the celery juice first thing in the morning, it will strengthen your digestion of the foods you eat for the rest of the day. And over time, the mineral salts, minerals, and nutrients have the unique ability to completely restore your stomach's hydrochloric acid.

You should also know that it's common to have not just one gut issue, but several related gut issues at once. The rest of this chapter empowers you to deal with other gut problems.

REMOVING TOXIC HEAVY METALS FROM YOUR GUT

In our modern era, it's virtually impossible not to take in a certain amount of toxic heavy metals, such as mercury, aluminum, copper, cadmium, nickel, and lead. These heavy metals often accumulate in your liver, gallbladder, and/or intestines. Since heavy metals tend to be heavier than the water that's inside your digestive system and blood, they sink down and settle into the intestinal tract—just like gold settles at the bottom of a riverbed.

Toxic heavy metals are poisonous, and if they begin to oxidize, their chemical runoff will mutate and damage whatever cells are nearby. However, the biggest issue with heavy metals is that they're prime food for bad bacteria, viruses, fungi, parasites, and worms. That means these metals are likely to attract and serve as a feeding ground for *Streptococcus* A or B, *E. coli* and its many strains, *C. difficile*, *H. pylori*, and viruses. When these pathogens consume the toxic heavy metals, they release a neurotoxic gas that attaches itself to the ammonia gas and travels through the intestinal lining. In other words, the ammonia permeability takes on a friend, and that friend is heavy metal contamination. The ammonia permeability makes it possible for the toxic gas to get through the intestinal lining.

Do not confuse mycotoxins (fungal toxins) with permeability, however. It's currently unknown to practitioners that pathogens create neurotoxins when they consume heavy metals—and that these neurotoxins are very different from mycotoxins. Mycotoxins cannot create the many symptoms that neurotoxins do; mycotoxins tend to stay in the intestinal tract and get eliminated through defecation. Keep this in mind as you hear more and more about mycotoxins in the coming years. They are not the culprit in autoimmune disease. I don't want you to get swept up in a misguided trend—this is about you getting better and not distracted by the barrage of catchphrases out there.

Once the pathogens I mentioned above settle in, they'll start inflaming your gut—e.g., saturating the linings of your intestines or colon. They'll release poisons in your gut directly via neurotoxins they produce, and indirectly via their waste and toxic corpses. This is how most people develop illnesses and disorders such as IBS, Crohn's disease (an inflammation of the gastrointestinal tract), and colitis (an inflammation of the colon—which is typically a chronic infection of the shingles virus described in Chapter 11 coupled with *Streptococcus* bacteria).

Under a microscope, these by-products of dead viral matter and castoff viral casings often look like parasitical activity. This throws off many analyses of stool samples and results in numerous misdiagnoses, which means that it's often a mistake when someone is diagnosed with a parasite. This is a huge confusion in gut health today.

While heavy metals can lead to problems if not addressed, they're relatively easy to get rid of. So if you have any kind of gut illness, or even chronic digestive distress, it's best to play it safe by assuming heavy metals are at least part of the problem and taking the steps to remove them.

Here are some powerful options to remove toxic heavy metals from your intestinal tract:

- **Cilantro:** eat half a cup a day of this herb as-is, sprinkled on salads, or in a smoothie.

- **Parsley:** eat a quarter cup a day of this herb as-is, sprinkled on salads, or in a smoothie.

- **Zeolite:** buy this mineralized clay in liquid form.

- **Spirulina (preferably from Hawaii):** if it's in powder form (which is best for removal of metals from the gut), mix one teaspoon daily into water or a smoothie.

- **Garlic:** eat two fresh cloves a day.

- **Sage:** eat two tablespoons a day.

- **L-glutamine:** if it's in powder form (which is preferable for removal of metals from the gut), mix one teaspoon daily into water or a smoothie.

- **Plantain leaf:** brew this herb to make tea and drink a cup a day.

- **Red clover blossom:** brew two tablespoons of these flower blossoms to make two cups of tea a day.

THE GUT'S NATURAL PROTECTION

It's so far undiscovered in medical research that we're born with tiny, furry hairs that line the entire intestinal tract. This fur-like hair is microscopic, just a little bigger than bacteria itself. The hair helps protect your gut from invasion by viruses, bad bacteria, fungi, and worms. It's also there as a safe haven that harbors billions of good bacteria.

Until the 19th century, this hair normally lasted for a person's entire lifetime.

Since the industrial revolution, though, we've been assaulted by environmental toxins, prescription medications, and other chemicals that can scorch the gut; the heavy metals described in the previous section; and the stress of modern living and its accompanying scalding adrenaline. As a result, your gut's hair lining may be largely burned off by the time you reach age 20. This contributes to many of the gut health problems that people struggle with today.

The reason medical science hasn't discovered this hair is because most intestinal surgeries are performed on people age 30 and above. By this point, it's long gone. And in intestinal biopsies for babies, this microscopic, furry lining just isn't on the radar.

If you do have any of this protective hair left, you can help save and bolster it by eating foods that are especially healthy for your gut. These include quality lettuce (e.g., romaine, red leaf, and butter leaf); ancient herbs such as oregano, thyme, and peppermint; and fruit, with an emphasis on bananas, apples, figs, and dates.

Also take care to steer clear of foods that can harm your health. For a detailed list, see Chapter 19, "What Not to Eat."

RESTORING GUT FLORA AND MAXIMIZING B_{12} PRODUCTION

Good bacteria in your gut produce most of your body's supply of vitamin B_{12}. But this doesn't happen just anywhere in your gut. The *ileum,* the final section of your small intestine, is the main center of this B_{12} absorption and production. It's also where *methylation* occurs.

Whenever it's needed, vitamin B_{12} is absorbed through the walls of your ileum via microvessels that are capable of absorbing B_{12} and nothing else. It's the B_{12} produced in the ileum that's most recognized by the brain. Enzymes prohibit any other toxin or nutrient from being absorbed by these ileum blood vessels, and thus block them from entering your bloodstream.

Science has yet to discover this information.

Virtually everyone in the U.S. is dealing with a B_{12} deficiency and/or a methylation issue. These issues show up in a few different forms. First, when methylation goes wrong, it can prevent true bio-absorption of critical micronutrients and trace minerals. Second, a methylation issue can interrupt the conversion process of non-active, bulky vitamins and other nutrients into smaller, bioactive versions that can be absorbed by the body. Third, a heightened level of the amino acid homocysteine, caused by a toxic liver or an elevated pathogen load in the body that creates a lot of toxic by-product, can interfere with methylation, preventing proper conversion and absorption of nutrients.

You produce all the vitamin B_{12} you need when the ileum has abundant beneficial bacteria of a specific kind. Sufficient beneficial bacteria also make methylation strong, but everyone is short on these bacteria—that is, micro-probiotics that live naturally on certain foods, enter the gut when we consume them, and fill the ileum. You can't buy these bioactive microorganisms in probiotic supplement form at the store, or get them from fermented foods and drinks.

When you're suffering from low hydrochloric acid, heavy metal toxicity, and/or ammonia permeability, a lot of the good bacteria throughout your gut are likely to die. This inflames the ileum, which has a number of negative consequences, such as severely weakening your immune system. It also makes your gut's vitamin B_{12} production plummet or stop altogether.

You can't rely on B_{12} blood tests, because medical labs can't yet detect the levels of vitamin B_{12} in your gut, organs, and especially your central nervous system. While taking a B_{12} supplement can fill the bloodstream, so that your B_{12} levels will show up on blood tests as sufficient, that doesn't mean the B_{12} is entering the central nervous system, which critically needs B_{12}. So regardless of what blood tests exhibit, always take a high-quality B_{12} supplement. (Look for it as methylcobalamin—ideally, blended with adenosylcobalamin—rather than as cyanocobalamin. With methylcobalamin and adenosylcobalamin, your liver doesn't have to do any work to convert the B_{12} into a usable form.) Lack of B_{12} is a very real deficiency with very real health consequences. And as mentioned earlier, almost every person in the U.S. is B_{12} deficient in some way.

Also, take steps to restore your gut's normal levels of good bacteria. Cultured probiotics sitting on the shelves of the health food store or fermented foods that claim to have beneficial bacteria aren't the answers here. Most, if not all, of these microorganisms will die in your stomach before they descend and reach the small intestine. And factory-produced probiotics never reach that last part of the small intestine, the ileum—which is the region that needs them most.

There *are* probiotics that stay alive in the gut and are responsible for restoring the intestinal flora, including in the ileum. These are barely known, and we take them for granted. Yet they are remarkably powerful and can change your health and life in ways unimaginable. When people have good gut health, it's most often because they've accidentally and occasionally consumed these naturally occurring, life-giving probiotics and beneficial microorganisms.

Where can you find them? On fresh, living foods.

The special probiotics that live on fruits and vegetables are what I call *elevated microorganisms,* or sometimes *elevated biotics,* because they harbor energy from God and the sun. Elevated microorganisms are not to be confused with soil-borne organisms and probiotics derived from soil. Elevated microorganisms are the most gut-renewing option there is. They are the very microorganisms that the ileum harbors, and they create the B_{12} that the body, particularly the brain, most recognizes.

A top source of elevated microorganisms is sprouts. Alfalfa, broccoli, clover, fenugreek, lentil, mustard, sunflower, kale, and other seeds like them, when sprouted, are living micro-gardens. In this tiny, nascent form of life, they're teeming with beneficial bacteria that will help your gut thrive.

Again, these beneficial bacteria are different from soil-borne organisms and "prebiotics." Elevated microorganisms are always found aboveground, on the leaves and skins of fruit and vegetables.

If you have access to an organic farm, farmers' market, or your own garden, you can eat some of its vegetables and fruits to get elevated microorganisms into your diet. The key here is to eat the produce fresh, raw, and unwashed. (Although a gentle rinse without soap can be safe.) Millions of revitalizing probiotics and microorganisms exist on the surfaces of these foods. It's imperative to use your judgment, though, about when it's safe to eat unwashed fruits and vegetables. Only do it when you know the growing source and are sure that there are no toxins or other contaminants that could make you sick.

When you pluck a piece of kale from the ground, you can see a film in the pockets of the leaf. This isn't soil or dirt or soil-based organisms. This film is made up of elevated microorganisms—a naturally occurring probiotic that hasn't yet been washed off. (Not to be confused with a manure-caked piece of kale, which it's best if you gently rinse off.) When you eat the leaf of kale, the pockets of good bacteria get folded and trapped, so they often bypass the stomach. When they're released in the intestines, these millions of microorganisms have phenomenal effects on digestion and the immune system, as they find their way down to your ileum and replenish your B_{12} production and storage bank.

A raw, unwashed piece of kale straight from an organic garden—or a handful of sprouts from a countertop garden, or a fresh, pesticide-free apple plucked from the tree—outshines every single soil-based or lab-created probiotic and fermented food available. If you've eaten just one of these items that's coated with elevated microorganisms just one time in your life, it has protected you to some degree, without your awareness. And the more fresh, chemical-free, wax-free, unwashed produce you eat, the more benefits you get.

Note that *prebiotics* have recently become popular. What the term really translates to is eating certain fruits and vegetables that feed the productive bacteria in the gut. Truth is, every fruit and vegetable that you can eat raw feeds that good bacteria.

One other thing you can do is take quality store-bought probiotics or soil-borne probiotics. It's best that you additionally take in good bacteria from living produce, though, because nothing can compare. Ingesting the elevated microorganisms on a fresh vegetable leaf or fruit skin is like going for 9,000 horsepower, whereas store-bought probiotics have the power of one miniature donkey.

Rejuvenating gut flora with raw, organic, unwashed produce is how you truly restore gut health. It's also how you heal so-called MTHFR gene mutations and other methylation issues. Note that the medical communities' label "MTHFR gene mutation" is inaccurate, though. People with this condition do not actually have a gene defect; rather, their bodies are experiencing toxic overload that's preventing the conversion of nutrients to micronutrients. These powerful microorganisms can lower homocysteine levels and virtually reverse an MTHFR gene mutation diagnosis.

Once you've reestablished your stomach's hydrochloric acid, removed heavy metals from your gut and irritating foods from your diet, and revised your gut's ability to make vitamin B_{12} by restoring productive bacteria, any gut health problem you have is likely to heal.

MAKING SENSE OF FADS, TRENDS, AND MYTHS ABOUT THE GUT

There are a number of gut health trends, both in and out of mainstream medicine, that are really unproductive—and sometimes reckless. When we're unwell, we often become desperate, willing to try anything, which makes it easy to be persuaded by the variety of trendy treatments out there. Take caution, though. What follows are descriptions of the most popular fads, along with why you should steer clear of them.

Hydrochloric Acid Supplements

There are supplements that claim to provide your stomach's missing hydrochloric acid in pill form. While these are well-intentioned, there are two problems with them.

First, they aren't helping your stomach create hydrochloric acid on its own.

Second, and more important, the manufacturers of these supplements don't realize that your stomach's hydrochloric acid isn't composed of just one chemical. While science hasn't yet discovered this, your stomach houses a complex blend of *seven* different acids. (In approximately one decade, this truth will start to surface in sources other than this book.)

The supplements offer only *one* of the seven acids that make up your stomach's digestive hydrochloric acid, so they're a very incomplete solution.

Even worse, they can *hinder* your stomach's rebuilding of its digestive fluids by creating a chemical imbalance that overwhelmingly favors just one of the seven acids in the blend. Until this is properly researched and understood, hydrochloric acid supplements are not a good option.

These supplements are unlikely to do you any great harm. However, you're tremendously better off drinking a glass of celery juice daily. It's only with celery that you'll fully restore your stomach's store of hydrochloric acid and reclaim your gut health.

Sodium Bicarbonate and *Candida*

A lot of people are championing *sodium bicarbonate*—aka baking soda—as a treatment. They believe the culprit behind gut problems is *Candida*, based on the longtime trend of *Candida* diagnoses. They figure that sodium bicarbonate, which is heavily alkaline, will somehow stop *Candida* . . . which they believe thrives in an acidic environment.

Nearly every link in this chain of reasoning is wrong. The one exception is that, yes, many bugs do like an acidic environment. However, *Candida* is very seldom the cause of gut health issues. When your gut is dysfunctional as a result of heavy metals, you can develop infections from a number of sources, including *Candida*. But *Candida* is merely a side effect; and typically not a serious one.

In fact, the worst effects that are likely to result from a high level of *Candida* are irritated portions of your intestinal and/or colon linings forming calluses, which mildly hinder food absorption. In almost all cases, that's as bad as *Candida* gets. (See Chapter 9.)

Sodium bicarbonate is ineffective against *Candida* anyway. More broadly, sodium bicarbonate does *nothing* to help your gut. On the contrary, it's abrasive and will only create an imbalance. If you take a large dosage of sodium bicarbonate, any combination of the following is likely to happen:

- **Gastric spasms,** i.e., a twisting and tightening of your intestinal tract and colon.

- **A homeostasis crisis for your body,** which must strain mightily to reestablish balance after so much alkaline is abruptly dumped into it.

- **A toxic crisis for your body,** because while sodium bicarbonate is perfectly safe in small amounts, past a certain level it becomes an irritant to your stomach and intestinal tract. In some cases this causes diarrhea, vomiting, severe bloating, and/or other discomfort.

- A *worsening* of bacterial and fungal infections, because sodium bicarbonate disrupts your gut's good bacteria and so weakens your immune system.

- A *worsening* of your digestive issues, because sodium bicarbonate damages your hydrochloric acid and thus contributes to leaky gut syndrome. It also interferes with the absorption of food in your intestines.

There are many negatives to sodium bicarbonate as a "remedy." I've seen a lot of people struggle after using it.

Diatomaceous Earth

Another fad is trying to heal the gut by consuming *diatomaceous earth,* also called *diatomite.* This is a soft sedimentary rock that crumbles into a fine white powder. Some people believe diatomite has the ability to kill parasites and clear toxins from the gut.

However, it doesn't do a single useful thing for your gut. It can actually be quite dangerous for your health, if you're sensitive and have a health condition.

Diatomite clings tenaciously to the sides of your intestinal tract and colon, and severely interferes with their ability to absorb the nutrients from your food. On top of that, it damages your hydrochloric acid and kills good bacteria. In some cases it causes initial vomiting and diarrhea, followed by long-lasting gastric spasms and pain.

In other words, it has all the bad effects of sodium bicarbonate, only to an even worse degree. Plus it can take *months* to shake loose from your intestinal tract. So don't even think about taking diatomite or consuming food-based diatomaceous earth.

Gallbladder Flush

Yet another trend is trying to purge your gallbladder of gallstones and toxins by drinking various odd concoctions, such as a glass of pure olive oil, or olive oil mixed with herbs and/or lemon juice, cayenne, or maple syrup.

People believe these oil-based concoctions work because within a day after they drink one, they see what appear to be gallstones in their stool. What they don't realize is that they're seeing the *oil* they drank. When a large amount of oil is dumped into your body, your digestive system uses mucus to form it into little balls (sometimes in multiple colors, depending on what foods are in different parts of your intestinal tract) that can be easily expelled. This is to protect an overburdened liver.

I've run across people who have done gallbladder flushes for years, multiple times each year, and still report hundreds and hundreds of large gallstones. If gallbladder flushes really worked, this would have to mean there were thousands of stones in the gallbladder—a tiny organ that could fit in the palm of your hand. It's not humanly possible for someone to produce or harbor that many gallstones. If you *were* to flush out a gallstone, it would probably become caught in your gallbladder's duct. You'd then be headed to the hospital for emergency surgery.

Gallstones are made up of protein, bile, and cholesterol. You don't have to choke down a pint of olive oil—and potentially create a crisis—to purge them. The best way to get rid of gallstones is to lower your consumption of dense proteins and eat a diet that emphasizes sodium-rich vegetables and fruits that contain healthy bio-acids. By incorporating more spinach, kale, radishes, mustard greens, celery, lemons, oranges, grapefruit, and limes into your meals—and by drinking a glass of lemon water every morning and every evening—you can start the stone-dissolving process.

One safe and amazingly effective option for dissolving gallbladder stones and restoring the liver is to juice a handful of fresh, raw asparagus along with whatever other juice ingredients you like.

The best way to *prevent* new gallstones from forming is to follow the advice in this chapter for creating and maintaining a healthy gut.

Fermented Foods

Let's go back in time, before refrigeration was invented. For millennia in various parts of the globe, you would take your last crop of the season and, in order to survive another winter, throw the fruits and vegetables into pots. These harvests would then undergo a mysterious process that prevented total decomposition and instead preserved the foods. In Russia, for example, they threw cabbages into vats and let them dissolve until they were practically mush, creating what we know as sauerkraut.

This fermentation was critical—without it, people would have starved to death. No one had a supermarket to pop into on their way home from work, or a freezer or refrigerator to preserve their food supply.

In the present day, fermented foods have taken on a revered status—they're celebrated as a boon to health. That's not quite correct.

There's a misconception that because fermented foods helped humans along for thousands of years, they have health benefits. Truth is, fermented foods were about survival. A self-preserved food was the difference between life and death by starvation. It's better to view these edibles as an important historical stopgap, rather than as a health aid.

The so-called probiotics in fermented foods are not life-giving. The bacteria in them thrive off the decay process—in other words, they thrive off death, not life. When an animal dies in the woods, the bacteria that start to engulf its flesh are in the same category as the bacteria used to preserve fermented foods of all kinds.

They're in a different category of bacteria from the beneficial type we covered earlier in this chapter. The elevated microorganisms on living fruits and vegetables thrive on life, and are therefore restorative to your gut, because *we* are alive. They have a life force that the bacteria in fermented foods do not.

When we think of beneficial bacteria, we often think about yogurt. We've been conditioned to believe that the probiotics in yogurt support our gut health. If you're struggling with a health condition, though, yogurt is not a positive food to consume; dairy feeds all manner of ills. Plus, if it's pasteurized yogurt, the pasteurization process has killed the probiotics anyway. The beneficial bacteria that do thrive in raw, living yogurt cannot withstand hydrochloric acid and therefore die in the stomach, never reaching the intestinal tract.

The vast majority of fermented foods—kimchi, sauerkraut, salami, pepperoni, soy sauce, kombucha tea, and so on—breed bacteria from foods that are no longer alive. Such bacteria are useless for your gut.

For most people, these bacteria do no harm; they're simply passed through the digestive tract and quickly expelled by the body as unnecessary. I'm not opposed to consuming them.

Some people's bodies respond more harshly, however, perceiving the bacteria as foreign invaders and overreacting in efforts to banish them. This can result in bloating, stomach pain, gas, nausea, and/or diarrhea. Even if this occurs, though, it's a temporary situation that ends once the bacteria's flushed out.

So if you like fermented foods, it's fine to keep eating them for their unique flavor. And if fermented foods upset your stomach, or if you just don't like them, don't eat them. They don't provide a lot of health benefits to your gut.

And if you think they have major benefits, you're being misled. The hydrochloric acid in our guts is extremely sensitive to the bacteria on fermented foods, so it kills the unproductive bacteria even if it's harmless; it sees it as the enemy. This is in stark contrast to the life-giving bacteria from freshly picked living foods. The beneficial bacteria on a piece of kale straight from the garden is virtually indestructible by hydrochloric acid—so that's where you should turn your focus if you're looking for the true boon to gut health.

Apple Cider Vinegar

If you're concerned about a gut health condition of any kind and you're looking for cures, steer clear of the apple cider vinegar myth.

Don't get me wrong. Apple cider vinegar is by far the most beneficial, healthiest, and safest of all vinegars. It's better for you than cleaning vinegar, white and red wine vinegars, balsamic vinegar, rice vinegar . . . And apple cider vinegar is ideal for external use, such as addressing skin rashes, scalp issues, and even wounds. But any vinegar taken internally can act as an irritant to any gut health issue and will ultimately be detrimental.

If you can't resist vinegar, use high-quality apple cider vinegar, preferably with "mother" in it, which means it's unprocessed, living vinegar.

CASE HISTORY:
Able to Eat Again

Since she was a teenager, Jennifer's stomach had been sensitive. She would often get stomachaches, as well as occasional constipation and diarrhea. Jennifer could never foresee how her stomach would react to what she ate. As she was growing up, her unpredictable loss of appetite had been a frequent source of friction at the family dinner table.

She spent years visiting doctors. One told Jennifer that she must just be seeking attention. In reality, attention was the last thing she wanted. Her true desire was to be free of pain and discomfort so she could focus on things she loved, like volunteering at the local animal rescue.

Finally, when she was 25, a gastroenterologist diagnosed her issue as irritable bowel syndrome. Though the specialist didn't say so, all this label meant was that Jennifer was dealing with a mystery illness.

She found it comforting to have a name for her symptoms, but she still wasn't finding relief.

Jennifer turned to alternative medicine. She found a great practitioner who noticed she was allergic to wheat gluten and dairy products such as milk and cheese. He recommended she eliminate these foods from her diet and take plenty of probiotics. However, he also concluded that she must have *Candida* and warned her off all processed and natural sugars, including fruit.

For six months, Jennifer tried the doctor's diet regimen: chicken twice a day, lots of fresh vegetables, and salads with tuna or hardboiled eggs. Jennifer was strict about the food guidelines—though about once a month, the desire for something sweet would take over and she'd succumb to a piece of cake at her grandmother's house. She did notice some improvement— she no longer had diarrhea. Yet she still struggled with bouts of constipation, stomach cramping, bloating, and pain.

Frustrated, Jennifer decided to seek out a new alternative doctor. This one told her that not only did she have an allergy to wheat and dairy and an issue with *Candida,* but was positive she had leaky gut syndrome. He put her on a diet of only meat, chicken, eggs, fish, and leafy green vegetables—that is, almost all protein. She was to eat no grains or beans of any kind and no starchy vegetables, though she was allowed the occasional Granny Smith apple. To treat the *Candida* overgrowth and leaky gut syndrome, the doctor also prescribed an herbal intestinal cleansing product.

For eight months, Jennifer stayed the course—with no positive results. Instead, she was now becoming fatigued, beset by brain fog and more constipation, and her bloating was at the point that it was making her look what she called "preggers." She felt unattractive, and it was always a challenge to find a place where both she and her vegetarian best friend could eat. After a decade of struggling with her digestive system, Jennifer decided isolation and suffering were her lot in life.

Then one day Jennifer's mom mentioned her troubles to a friend, who referred Jennifer to me. Immediately in my initial reading, Spirit informed me that Jennifer had virtually no hydrochloric acid left, and this was causing ammonia permeability. The proteins putrefying in her gut were creating the ammonia gas—resulting in inflammation, pain, and the bloating that she thought made her look pregnant.

Jennifer also had heavy metals in her intestinal tract, and the microorganisms that are crucial to the health of the lower small intestine, including the ileum, were nonexistent. It was true that Jennifer was allergic to wheat and all other grains and gluten, as well as beans, corn, canola oil, and eggs, so she needed to avoid them. She'd also started to develop an allergy to animal proteins because they were not breaking down and digesting in her gut. Further, her liver was sluggish and struggling from an overburden of animal fat.

Right away, I advised Jennifer to start drinking two 16-ounce glasses of fresh, plain celery juice a day.

"My last doctor had me on a green juice blend," she said. "How is this any different?"

I explained that juice blends don't restore hydrochloric acid levels. Only straight celery juice taken on an empty stomach can do that.

To stop stressing the liver with too much fat, we lowered Jennifer's animal proteins to one serving every other day. In its place, we brought in all vegetables and fruits, most notably avocados, bananas, apples, all kinds of berries, papayas, mangoes, kiwis, lots of butter lettuce, and spinach, as well as a quarter cup of fresh cilantro in each of her salads to detox from heavy metals.

In contrast to the last diet Jennifer had been on, which was nearly all animal protein and virtually no fiber, the fruits in this new plan helped push food through her inflamed intestinal tract, which gave her some immediate relief from the constipation.

After one week, Jennifer's "preggers" bloating had decreased substantially.

After one month, she had no more constipation.

And after three months, the pain, cramping, brain fog, and fatigue were gone.

Her hydrochloric acid had restored itself, and the ammonia permeability had stopped. Jennifer's liver had also been freed up to process fats and store sugars properly, which had allowed her to lose the extra pounds she'd gained over the years.

She'd also spent the summer eating fresh, organic, unwashed kale and tomatoes from her grandmother's garden. The elevated microorganisms on the surfaces of these vegetables replenished the flora in Jennifer's gut, particularly the ileum, and allowed her body to start producing B_{12} again.

In the fall, Jennifer started working full-time at the animal shelter. She and her best friend renewed their bond and now spent Friday nights preparing plant-based meals for a growing group of pals from the shelter staff.

Jennifer's vitality is back. She can now eat the occasional "prohibited" food at a party or a friend's house, and her body won't pay the price. She never had leaky gut syndrome, nor an overgrowth of *Candida*—though they're two alternative diagnosis trends that lead countless people astray.

CHAPTER 18

Freeing Your Brain and Body of Toxins

Never before in our history have we been exposed to so many poisonous substances. These include the heavy metals mercury, aluminum, copper, lead, nickel, and cadmium; air pollution; pharmaceuticals; nanotechnology chemicals sprayed on almost everything manufactured; pesticides, herbicides, and fungicides; plastics; industrial cleaners; petroleum; dioxins in our oceans; and thousands of new chemicals introduced into our environment every year. These poisons saturate our water reservoirs and fall down from the sky.

The majority of these substances are so new that it'll take decades before science recognizes how dangerous they are to our health. And those risks will only be discovered if funding and common sense go in the right direction, which is unlikely. Most industries' MO is to put products on the market sooner rather than later—and deal with the consequences down the road.

Most of us are carrying around toxins that have been with us for almost our whole lives and have burrowed deep inside us. It's these old poisons that are the most dangerous. Toxic heavy metals, for example, can oxidize over time and kill the cells around them.

Toxins pose multiple threats. They directly poison your body, damaging your brain, your liver, your central nervous system, and other vital areas. They weaken your immune system, leaving you vulnerable to illness. And worst of all, they attract and feed cancers, viruses, bacteria, and other invaders that can instigate a serious health condition. In fact, these toxins are the primary triggers for our current epidemics of cancer and many other illnesses, such as Alzheimer's disease.

This chapter identifies major toxins and how you can avoid them, so you don't continually accumulate new ones. Living in this world, it's impossible to steer clear of everything harmful, so we'll focus on minimizing exposure to the extent possible. We'll also cover how to remove the toxins already in your body to protect you from potential illness and disease, making it easier for your immune system to recover and support you.

You always have the opportunity to turn things around. The pages that follow will empower you to take control over your well-being so that you can ensure many healthy years ahead.

MERCURY

For close to 2,500 years, man tried to claim that mercury was the fountain of youth. It was called the ultimate cure for all disease, the secret to living forever, and the source for eternal wisdom. In ancient Chinese medicine, mercury was so revered that countless emperors died from mercury elixirs that healers vowed would end all their problems—which I guess you could say they did, if you take a morbid view of things.

Mercury wasn't only a favored medicine in East Asia. All throughout England and the rest of Europe, mercury elixirs were celebrated. Mercury concoctions were all the rage as the New World developed, too. For a time in the 1800s, medical universities in the U.S. and England were turning out doctors fast, and the number-one protocol they taught students was to give a glass of mercury water to any patient who was ill—regardless of age, gender, or symptoms. This "treatment" was an especially common method to force a miscarriage and to treat what was labeled as "female hysteria," which translated to a woman speaking up for herself.

The 19th century wasn't exactly the Stone Age. It had been established that mercury was a dangerous toxin that destroyed the life of anyone who played with it, consumed it, or even touched it. For centuries already, people had borne witness to the millions who died from mercury exposure. So why was it still favored?

One factor was the great industrial demon that sat behind mercury. That alone was enough for it to be pushed as the top cure-all trend. Remember, health trends never catch on because they're effective.

The mercury movement finally hit a speed bump in the mid-1800s. Doctors had become more accessible than ever before in history to people from all walks of life—which seemed like a good thing. Yet as increasing numbers of people went to visit these new medical school grads, observers caught on that more and more of these patients were coming down with uncontrollable shaking, fevers, madness, rage, body tics, jerking, and gibberish talk. It became obvious that a visit to the doctor could result in poisoning.

For example, a wife and mother of five might have sent her husband to the doctor to help the husband with his gout. Upon arriving home, her husband would be delusional, yelling out children's rhymes as his eyes twitched. After just one experience like this, a family would have had enough.

Following this widespread realization, there was a 25-year ghost-town period for medical businesses. People preferred to risk the fate of whatever was ailing them; they knew that a visit to the doctor would give them a lower chance of survival. Medical universities hit an all-time funding low.

This was exactly the break natural practitioners and healers needed to gain some credibility. For this brief time, early forms of homeopathy, chiropractic treatment, and other varieties of alternative medicine exploded in popularity.

Finally traditional doctors' offices caught on and started advertising that they no longer offered quicksilver (liquid mercury) drinks, and traditional medicine gained back some credibility.

Yet the demon behind mercury still wanted the population to get plenty of exposure, so it worked on other hidden and inventive ways to get it into people's systems. Not only were industries dumping mercury into every river, lake, and waterway possible, but other forms of mercury-containing medicine were born by the turn of the 20th century. Plus, dentists were still using mercury amalgam fillings.

Hat production was one of the industries that relied on mercury—in the form of a solution used to speed the felting process. This is where the term "mad as a hatter" comes from; the average hat-maker survived only three to five years after starting work at a factory. And it wasn't just the workers who were exposed. Every man who wore a felt hat in the 1800s and the first half of the 1900s would get an infusion of mercury when his brow sweated. (Which reminds me: don't try on antique hats at the thrift store.)

Almost all mental illness of the time was from mercury poisoning. The asylums of the 19th and early 20th centuries were filled with people experiencing madness and convulsions. And what was the treatment protocol? Mercury concoctions to drink, or mercury pills to swallow. Abraham Lincoln's depression severely worsened from the use of mercury pills—a depression that had likely started from a few glasses of "medicinal" mercury elixirs.

The Dirty Secret

Why am I going on like this about mercury? Because it's the dirty secret we're not supposed to talk about. You're not supposed to know about what mercury has done to shape history, right up to this present moment. Mercury can be toxic even in tiny doses you can't see. And there's no hazard sign saying, "BEWARE—MERCURY."

If it were up to the mercury demon, we would think mercury was harmless, even good for us. Better yet, mercury would be entirely hidden, and we wouldn't even know it existed. Mercury never goes away—unless you take specific steps to detoxify it. It gets passed on from generation to generation, for centuries. It's practically guaranteed that your great-great grandparents and other ancestors tasted mercury elixirs. Your parents have mercury in them, and they got it from their parents. That same mercury got passed along to you at conception. Some of us have mercury in us that's a thousand or more years old.

Mercury casts an evil and soulless shadow that has engulfed so many. This toxic heavy metal becomes a part of us, and that reflects itself in our health.

Greed, carelessness, darkness, and ignorance are the major factors that have allowed mercury to prey on the population. A mercury mine owner of the past likely didn't care if workers only lived six months to three years after starting at the mine—because there was money to be made.

What good has mercury ever done? None. It's done *nothing* for us. *Nada*. It's an unnecessary neurotoxin. It could have been replaced in its medical and industrial uses with something safer.

Is mercury gone yet? Is the nightmare finally over? Have we come to our senses and learned to avoid it at all costs for the sake of humankind? For the sake of our health and well-being? For the sake of our children?

Nope. It's just that it's out of sight and out of mind. There's still plenty of mercury to be had. It's constantly at our fingertips, in ways that are extremely controversial.

Just as a result of modern living, over time your body will accumulate toxic heavy metals such as mercury. We're continually exposed to this toxin, because it slips through the cracks. Figuratively, it slips through the cracks of our health-care and industrial systems. Literally, mercury absorbs into the cracks of the brain. All of us have some level of mercury inside our bodies. It's unavoidable.

Why should we care?

Because mercury is a top fuel for cancers, viruses, and bacteria. Mercury exposure causes inflammation and can take people hostage with a vast number of symptoms and conditions, including depression, anxiety, ADHD, autism, bipolar disorder, neurological disorders, epilepsy, tingles, numbness, tics, twitches, spasms, hot flashes, heart palpitations, hair loss, memory loss, confusion, insomnia, loss of libido, fatigue, migraines, and thyroid disorders.

How often are people told they've brought a condition like depression upon themselves? It's all part of mercury's blame-the-victim game. Those depressive symptoms are the mercury speaking for the patient without her or his consent.

Sometimes mercury moves past the hostage phase and takes someone out, resulting in death by Alzheimer's, Parkinson's, dementia, or stroke. It's that serious. Mercury has injured or killed well over a billion people.

No one likes Alzheimer's; it's a frightening, terrible disease. Yet it's rapidly becoming common—and it's 100 percent mercury-caused. You heard that here first: Mercury is 100 percent responsible for Alzheimer's disease. You will never in your lifetime hear the truth about that anywhere else.

The medical industry will never blame mercury for that condition or any other—because then fingers would be pointed in the direction of the Mercury Man, whose true name is unknown. He's responsible for the original and very first good ol' boy industry.

And I've only covered the basics when it comes to the dirty secret of mercury.

If we can't stop the mercury demon from enticing people even today to expose us and our children to this toxic heavy metal, then we can take power into our own hands by becoming aware of situations that could bring us harm. To shield yourself and your family, you have to question *everything*.

We can also take full control over our health by ridding our bodies of the mercury we've accumulated from the generations before us and from present-day exposure. We can make simple detoxification programs part of our daily routine.

Your life is precious, sacred, and important. You deserve to know how to protect it.

Seafood

One of the many ways we take in mercury is through seafood. It's in all fish, but typically at higher levels in tuna, swordfish, shark, and any other large and oily fish. That's because our oceans are polluted with mercury, and eventually the mercury runoff from factory manufacturing (left over from the past and still accumulating today) finds its way into someone's tuna salad or tuna casserole.

You can mitigate the risk by eating small fish, such as sardines and mackerel. Wild salmon is also safe enough to eat in moderation.

Dental Amalgams

Dental amalgam fillings are another common source of exposure to mercury. So many of us have these silver fillings in our mouths, or have had them at one point.

It's becoming popular to get all mercury-based fillings removed at a holistic dentist's office. This may seem sensible, like the right thing to do, but you have to be very careful about the process. Getting all of your amalgam fillings removed at the same time can lead to an extremely high level of mercury exposure, regardless of the best techniques and protection available at the dentist's office. The exposure can put a heavy load on the immune system, becoming a trigger for any kind of health condition.

I know people who've had ten fillings dug out at once, and as a result, their blood platelets dropped so low that they almost died.

It's best to remove metal fillings only when an individual tooth requires it—such as if the filling becomes unstable, or the tooth is damaged. If your teeth and fillings are all in good order, and you're still anxious to have the amalgams removed, then get only one taken out at a time. Schedule at least a month between each removal.

If you've already had all your metal fillings removed, then it's time to do some cleanup to protect yourself.

And if you get new cavities, select the best ceramic filling option available—and know that anything is better than a mercury-based filling.

Heavy Metal Detox

The best way to remove heavy metals is to consume the following five items every day:

- **Barley grass juice extract powder:** draws out heavy metals from your spleen, intestinal tract, pancreas, and reproductive system. Barley grass juice extract powder prepares the mercury for complete absorption by the spirulina. Drink 1-2 teaspoons mixed into water or juice.

- **Spirulina (preferably from Hawaii):** draws out heavy metals from your brain, central nervous system, and liver and absorbs heavy metals extracted by your barley grass juice extract powder. Take 2 teaspoons mixed in water, coconut water, or juice.

- **Cilantro:** goes deep into hard-to-reach places, extracting metals from yesteryear. Blend one cup in a smoothie or juice, or add to salad or guacamole.

- **Wild blueberries (only from Maine):** draw heavy metals out from your brain. Also heal and repair any gaps created when the heavy metals are removed, which is especially important for your brain tissue. This is the most powerful food for reversing Alzheimer's. Eat at least a cup daily.

- **Atlantic dulse:** binds to mercury, lead, aluminum, copper, cadmium, and nickel, and crosses the blood-brain barrier. Unlike other seaweeds, Atlantic dulse is a powerful force for removing mercury on its own. Dulse goes into deep, hidden places of the body, seeking out mercury, binding to it, and never releasing it until it leaves the body. Eat 2 tablespoons of flakes daily, or an equal amount of strips if it's in whole-leaf form.

You should consume all five of these foods and supplements within 24 hours of one another for optimal effect. If you can't fit them all in, try to eat two to three daily. All five of these powerful heavy metal–removing foods leave behind critical nutrients for repairing heavy metal damage and restoring the body. If you want an extra boost, add burdock root to the protocol.

There is no more effective way on earth to remove heavy metals than this process. If you stick religiously to this heavy metal detox program over a long-term period, you can see a radical improvement. I've seen people make miraculous recoveries by removing generations of mercury from their systems. There's almost nothing better you can do for your health than to get heavy metals out of your body.

Note that there are other foods and herbs out there, such as chlorella, advertised as being beneficial for removing heavy metals. Beware. Although chlorella is trendy in the supplement world, its unpredictability makes it less effective than the items I listed above. Chlorella is irresponsible when it comes down to protecting you from the hazards of mercury.

WATER POLLUTION

In this modern era, even with everything we've learned about environmental damage, our water supply is continually being polluted.

There isn't much you can do to avoid air and earth pollution (other than move to an ecologically cleaner area). There *is* a whole lot you can do about your water.

You can entirely bypass local pollutants by buying bottled water. If you do this, make sure the plastic bottles storing the water are free of *bisphenol A* (BPA), an industrial chemical that's poisonous. Although plastics have their faults, bottled water is safer than tap water, which has a much higher elevation of plastic by-products.

You can also buy a high-quality filter to remove all toxins from your tap water. If you choose this option, buy a system that removes heavy metals, chlorine, and fluoride. (Many communities add fluoride to water in the mistaken belief that it's good for you. That's far from the truth. It's actually a by-product of aluminum—and a neurotoxin.)

There are water purification systems that use a reverse osmosis process, and yet others that produce distilled water. These processes are highly effective, but they remove minerals that are good for you along with the toxins. If you choose such a system, you'll need to also buy ionic trace mineral drops to add to your water to restore mineral solids that are removed by reverse osmosis or distillation.

A great thing to add to *any* processed water is a squeeze of juice from a freshly cut lemon or lime. Most water has lost its living factor due to filtering and processing. This tends to deaden water, while adding juice from a fresh lemon or lime reactivates and reawakens it, because the water that resides in the lemon or lime is alive. The water is then better able to latch onto toxins in your body and flush them out.

Anti-Chlorine/Anti-Fluoride Tea

For a powerful detox of chlorine and fluoride from your organs and the rest of your body, blend equal parts of blackberry leaf, raspberry leaf, hibiscus flower, and rose hips. Steep one tablespoon of this herb mixture per cup of hot water for tea.

PESTICIDES, HERBICIDES, AND FUNGICIDES

We're frequently at risk for exposure to pesticides, herbicides, and fungicides.

One avenue is conventional produce. Non-organic tomatoes, for example, are often sprayed at unregulated, off-the-chart levels. We can get a high dosage of herbicide in our systems just from ingesting conventional tomatoes, as well as other non-organic fruits and vegetables. At minimum, you should wash any conventionally farmed produce you buy to get rid of as much of its surface toxins as you can. (Don't get scared away from fruits and vegetables altogether—their nutrients are key to health.) Buy organic produce as often as possible.

If you eat animal products, they need to be at least organic, if not also grass-fed or free-range. Although these products will still have radiation from the fallout of Fukushima's nuclear power plant disaster in 2011, they will at least have lower concentrations of pesticides, herbicides, and fungicides, because non-organic animal products are extremely high in these chemicals, more so than any conventional sprayed fruit or vegetable. (More on radiation soon.)

Parks are also sprayed heavily with herbicides and pesticides. Take precautions, such as using a blanket (that you'll wash afterward) if you plan to sit in public green areas. Also avoid spraying toxic chemicals on your own lawn, and try to refrain from using insecticides inside your home.

Anti-Pesticide/Anti-Herbicide/Anti-Fungicide Tea

To remove pesticides, herbicides, and fungicides that are deeply stored in your body, blend equal parts of burdock root, red clover, lemon verbena, and ginger. Make a tea by steeping one tablespoon of the herb mixture per cup of hot water.

PLASTIC

We surround our world with plastic. If it were up to plastic manufacturers, we would come out of the womb wrapped in plastic.

We use plastic bags to hold the food and drink we buy until we get them home, plastic containers to organize and store our food and drink, plastic wraps to keep our food and drink covered, and more plastic bags to throw away the remains. Pharmaceuticals, too, are extremely high in plastics. As a result, plastic inevitably gets into our bodies one way or another.

Some types of plastic are relatively benign. However, others have properties that promote inflammation, disrupt your brain's neurons and neurotransmitters, confuse the body's hormones, and feed cancers, viruses, and bacteria. It's almost impossible to distinguish between harmless and harmful plastic.

It's therefore a good idea, for example, to use cloth bags to carry your food. Favor glass containers for your food over plastic ones. And when you can't avoid plastic—for example, when buying most bottled water, or a food processor—make sure the manufacturer is using BPA-free and human-friendly plastic.

Anti-Plastics Tea

To rid your body of plastic and plastic by-products, blend equal parts fenugreek, mullein leaf, olive leaf, and lemon balm. Steep one tablespoon of the herb mixture per cup of hot water for tea.

CLEANERS

Industrial cleaners are designed to destroy dirt and grime—without sufficient regard to the effect they have on the people breathing in their fumes. For example, traditional carpet cleaners use chemicals such as perchlorethylene, ammonium hydroxide, hydrofluoric acid, and nitrilotriacetate, which are hazardous to one's health, in cleaning agents and solvents. And many carpets have toxins in them, so the "cleaning" adds poisons on top of poisons. If you spend a lot of time indoors, you'll breathe these toxic fumes for most of each day, which can both weaken your immune system and possibly trigger a health condition.

One solution is to eliminate carpets in favor of hardwood floors and area rugs (although beware of hardwood stains and sealants, which also have the potential to give off toxic fumes when applied). Alternatively, you can buy a "green" carpet, and hire an environmentally intelligent carpet cleaning service—or maintain the carpet yourself using organic cleaners. Also try to avoid mainstream home cleaning products. There are numerous organic cleaners available to use instead.

Another source of toxins worth keeping in mind is clothing. Mainstream dry cleaners use chemicals that seep into your skin and your lungs as you wear your clothes day after day. To avoid this, seek out "green" dry cleaners.

Along the same lines, be aware that when you buy new clothes they're often covered with formaldehyde or other cancer-causing chemicals to keep them from wrinkling or becoming infested with mildew (i.e., fungi). Make sure to wash new clothes before wearing them.

Anti-Cleaning Solvents Tea

To minimize the effects of solvent exposure, and to cleanse your body of any of these stored chemicals, blend calendula, chamomile, bladderwrack, and borage in equal parts. For tea, steep one tablespoon of the herb mixture per cup of hot water.

RADIATION

When a nuclear power plant releases radiation into the air—as the Fukushima Daiichi power plant did following a 2011 earthquake and tsunami in Japan—that radiation lingers forever, mildly irradiating food, water, and air around the world.

There's nothing you can do to avoid this type of floating radiation. One way to *limit* exposure to radiation caused by the Fukushima Daiichi plant disaster is to eat lower on the food chain. At this point, all of our meat, dairy, and poultry supplies have high concentrations of radiation. These animals eat large amounts of feed or grass, all of which contain radiation from the nuclear fallout. It's a process called biomagnification that results in the toxic matter accumulating at greater concentrations in creatures higher up on the food chain.

I'm not trying to scare anyone with this. If you want to forget what you've read here, I understand.

You can also remove radiation from your body system and work to limit your exposure to all *other* radiation. For example, if you're getting X-rays at your dentist, insist that all areas of your body besides your mouth be covered with a lead apron or other protection. That includes your throat, which can develop thyroid cancer from radiation exposure. Try to minimize dental X-rays if possible, even if your dentist uses a digital process. Also, with any doctor, don't automatically say "yes" to X-rays. If you aren't sure whether an X-ray is necessary, don't hesitate to ask questions. Sometimes an X-ray isn't required, but rather optional for a particular medical concern.

Along the same lines, ask a whole lot of questions about any medical treatment that involves radiation. For example, if you're a woman receiving a chest X-ray, make sure you get a lead apron to cover your reproductive system. This isn't always offered, so you may have to ask.

Many times there are less aggressive treatment alternatives that hold lower risks. Women, for example, should consider a thermogram (which uses infrared imaging) for breast cancer screening, instead of feeling pushed into having another mammogram.

The human body is more sensitive to radiation than doctors realize. As with any other major toxin, strive to avoid it whenever possible.

Sea vegetables are a great way to protect your organs and glands from radiation. The fear that seaweed itself is saturated with radiation or heavy metals and can therefore harm your health is a misconception. Sea vegetables only take in toxins—they don't release them. So for example, if you eat a handful of dulse that *has* collected any pollutants from the ocean, they won't get discharged into your system. Instead, the dulse will hold onto the radiation and heavy metals—and collect even more of these toxins as it moves through your digestive tract, eventually expelling them from your body when you expel the dulse. Try to select seaweeds from the Atlantic Ocean, rather than the Pacific. They'll have greater capacity to absorb toxins from your system.

Anti-Radiation Tea

For an antidote to radiation exposure, blend Atlantic kelp, Atlantic dulse, dandelion leaf, and nettle leaf in equal parts. Make a tea from the mixture by steeping one tablespoon per cup of hot water.

MORE DETOX METHODS

Lemon Water

A highly effective way to detoxify the body is to drink two 16-ounce glasses of water on an empty stomach after you wake up, squeezing half of a freshly cut lemon into each glass. The lemon juice activates the water, making it better able to latch onto toxins in your body and flush them out.

This is especially effective for cleansing your liver, which works all night while you're asleep to gather and purge toxins from your body. When you wake up, it's primed to be hydrated and flushed clean with activated water. After you drink the water, give your liver half an hour to clean up. You can then eat breakfast. If you make this into a routine, your health will improve dramatically over time.

For an extra boost, add a teaspoon of raw honey and a teaspoon of freshly grated ginger to the lemon water. Your liver will draw in the honey to restore its glucose reserves, purging deep toxins at the same time to make room.

Aloe Vera Leaf Juice

A great way to detox your liver and intestinal tract is to eat the fresh gel of an aloe vera leaf once a day. To prepare it, cut off a four-inch section of the aloe leaf. (That's if it's large, as store-bought aloe often is. If you're using a homegrown aloe plant, it will likely have smaller, skinnier leaves, so cut off more.) Fillet the leaf as if it were a fish, trimming away the green skin and spikes. Scoop out the clear gel, taking care not to include any from the bitter base of the leaf. Blend it into a smoothie or eat as-is.

Juice Fasting

Another helpful component of your detox program is a practice of one-day "fasts" in which you consume nothing but juices.

Your juice should consist of celery, cucumbers, and apples.

If you want, add in a bit of spinach or cilantro for variety. The core ingredients must remain celery, cucumbers, and apples. This combination has the right balance of mineral salts, potassium, and sugar to stabilize your glucose levels as your body cleanses itself of toxins.

Make each juice 16 to 20 ounces, and drink one every two hours. Consume nothing in between except water—preferably a 16-ounce glass of it an hour after each juice. You should end up drinking six juices and six glasses of water for the whole day.

The first time you try this, do it on a weekend when you're at home. If you've never detoxed before, the poisons it brings out of your body may make you feel uncomfortable. If so, lie down and rest. After you've gone through this detox a few times and feel comfortable with it, you can optionally expand it to a two-day juice fast. Plan on being home for at least the second day, though, in case your energy dips. For many people, energy actually increases.

You can experiment with the juice and add other ingredients— say, kale instead of spinach, or an occasional pinch of ginger for taste, or some extra cilantro. Don't overdo it, though. The celery, cucumber, and apple all flush toxins out of you. If you put in too much of anything else, you're taking away space from these key ingredients.

If you do this juice fast every two weeks, you should achieve impressive detox results and really feel the difference.

Water Fasting

A more extreme version of juice fasting is water fasting.

For this detox, you consume water *exclusively*—specifically, a 16-ounce glass of water every hour, starting from when you wake up and continuing until you go to sleep.

Because you're not requiring your body to work at processing anything, you're giving your digestive system a one-day vacation. It will use this break to perform housecleaning, expelling toxins that it normally doesn't get a chance to deal with.

Perform this fast at home. You may find that you need to urinate frequently, which could be awkward at work. You may also experience dips in energy or strong emotions, in which case you shouldn't hesitate to lie down and rest or sleep.

If you like this fast and find it productive, do it once a month for at least three months. The results can be amazing.

Rebounding

Another way to detox is to use a mini-trampoline called a *rebounder,* which you gently jump up and down on. Doing this for ten minutes a day will forcefully promote circulation throughout your lymphatic system, and help detoxify your entire body, especially your liver.

Infrared Sauna

Another device that's surprisingly useful for detox is an *infrared sauna,* which emits infrared light on your skin for the purpose of healing. Its rays deeply penetrate your body, providing benefits such as increased blood flow and oxygenation of the blood, removal of toxins from the skin, elimination of aches and pains, and an immune system boost.

You can typically find an infrared sauna at local gyms, massage therapy centers, and/or sauna centers. Use it for 15- to 20-minute sessions twice a week. If you do it right, you should feel an immediate change for the better after each session.

Massage

Since the beginning of humankind, loved ones have put a hand on each other for support. Massage is our oldest form of therapy, and it remains to this day one of the most powerful methods of healing. A quality 45-minute full-body massage will promote circulation throughout your body and help draw out toxins, especially from your liver.

The massage is likely to boost your adrenal glands and kidneys, relax your heart, and ease tension.

Ideally, drink two 16-ounce glasses of fresh lemon or lime water directly following your massage. This will optimize the detoxing benefits of your session.

CASE HISTORY:
Alzheimer's Under Arrest

It had long been a family joke that Whitney was forgetful. Over the years, she'd lost her purse and keys countless times, blanked on her husband James's work number, and even forgotten her children's birthdays a few times. Each time they left for soccer practice, Whitney's daughter Kendra would ask, "Mom, did you forget anything?" before they walked out the door. The kids thought of it all as normal, and even funny.

That changed one Christmas, when Whitney was 53 years old. Everyone gathered early to open presents in the living room—everyone but Whitney.

"Where's Mom?" her daughter Miley finally asked. Whitney was usually the first one up for the holiday.

James found Whitney upstairs in the bathroom, applying makeup as though it were a normal workday. He told her the kids were waiting for her downstairs. Whitney looked at James with a furrowed brow but followed him to the living room. When she spotted the lit-up tree and the pile of wrapped gifts beneath, she was shocked. She'd already forgotten it was Christmas.

James accompanied Whitney to their family doctor, followed by a neurologist and several specialists. In the end, the diagnosis was Alzheimer's. The entire family was devastated at the prognosis: only three to five years ahead—at best—of quality living for Whitney. The unthinkable was before them. Whitney's doctors told James to get the family affairs in order while Whitney was still of sound mind.

Timothy, age 17, Miley, age 14, and Kendra, age 12, were old enough to understand the gravity of the situation. Miley started spending hours looking up Alzheimer's online, reading about the devastation it causes. Between panic attacks, Kendra began writing out lists of daily reminders for Whitney. Timothy dropped out of high school so he could help his mother out as much as she would allow.

Whitney's sister Sharon whisked her off to multiple alternative doctors, looking for an answer to reverse the disease. In one waiting room, Sharon stumbled across an article from the local newspaper that mentioned my name in connection with helping people heal from mystery illnesses.

During my first appointment with Whitney, Spirit directed my attention to two large pockets of mercury in the left hemisphere of her brain. They'd been there since her childhood. The mercury pockets were now oxidizing rapidly, causing runoff that was spreading fast, damaging brain tissue and accelerating the disease.

Spirit advised an immediate heavy metal detox regimen (as described in this chapter), coupled with a diet of little to no fat. That's because a high-fat diet raises blood fat, which makes mercury oxidize rapidly. A diet high in antioxidant-rich fruits and vegetables and low in fat slows down and even stops oxidation, and allows for complete detoxification of mercury.

Whitney removed all animal proteins from her diet because of the fat they contain and only used plant-based fats such as avocados, nuts, seeds, and oils sparingly. She switched her diet over to all types of fruit, especially wild blueberries, along with large servings of greens such as spinach, kale, and cilantro. Whitney was also allowed to consume potatoes, sweet potatoes, and other starchy vegetables.

Over time, Whitney's healthy, detoxifying, glucose-supporting, antioxidant-plentiful diet stopped the oxidation in its tracks. Her Alzheimer's symptoms started to reverse.

Timothy reenrolled in high school and got a weekend job at a local organic market so he could bring home discounted cases of produce. Miley redirected her Internet skills to looking up plant-based recipes. And Kendra started to breathe again and joined her sister in the kitchen to experiment with smoothie concoctions.

Six months into the program, Whitney's memory abilities were back to where they'd been before the Christmas tree nightmare.

One year into the program, Whitney's memory was better than it had been since before Timothy was born.

Today's trendy diets never would have allowed the level of fruit and starchy vegetables that Whitney needed for a true win. A fad diet would have been geared to higher levels of protein, which translates to higher levels of fat. It would have caused the disease to progress rapidly—not reverse.

With Whitney's Alzheimer's disease now arrested, the family is at ease again. It's an infrequent occurrence that Whitney forgets her keys anymore, but when she does, she, James, and the kids just laugh.

CHAPTER 19

What Not to Eat

We all want full control over our health. We want freedom of choice.

We like to decide what clothes to put on in the morning, and what shoes to wear. We want the ability to move away from someone holding a cigarette so we don't have to inhale the second-hand smoke. We like to choose the foods we eat.

We want to say what goes onto our bodies, around our bodies, and into our bodies.

Unless, that is, you don't mind any of that. You're allowed to wear the wrong size clothes, breathe in cigarette smoke, eat junk food, and not care—but you know you're doing it. That's your choice, one you make consciously, and that needs to be respected.

What if you were *unaware* that what you were doing could possibly be hindering you, or harmful to your health, though? That would take all choice out of it.

And that's exactly what's happening. People consume foods, supplements, and additives that can be instigating and irritating to their health, and limiting to the quality of their lives—and they have no idea. It's one thing to indulge in chocolate cake knowing it might be adding a few pounds to your waistline. It's something else entirely if that cake contains an ingredient that you don't know could harm your health, or could even take a year off your life.

Every day, people are tricked into consuming poisons, irritants, and other substances that deplete health. They have no say in it, because they don't know it's happening. It takes away choice, freedom, decision, and control.

Sure, you can have the attitude, "Well, it's just a little," or "What doesn't kill you makes you stronger," or "It'll put hair on your chest," or "Everyone else is doing it," or "It can't be *that* bad." If you're perfectly healthy and have zero complaints, if you're young and feel indestructible, maybe it's not so bad that certain toxic ingredients can enter your body without your knowledge.

But if you're at all concerned about your health—if you have any sensitivities or conditions, if you've struggled with illness, or if you're just concerned about prevention—then it's critical to avoid as many triggers and instigators as possible. Your body needs every possible level of support so it can heal and then maintain optimal health.

There's no such thing as "What doesn't kill you makes you stronger" when it comes to your health. This has been a popular misconception for ages. Truth is, ingesting poisons doesn't make you immune to them. Quite the opposite: the more poisons in your body, the weaker and more vulnerable you become.

By now, we've all heard of preservatives and artificial flavors—we know to avoid those, for very good reason. There are other problematic ingredients, though, which you should know to avoid. These ingredients can feed existing viral, bacterial, and fungal conditions, which can lead to inflammation—and can also wreak havoc with your digestive system, weaken and confuse your immune system, strain your glands and organs, hinder cells anywhere in your body, disrupt or destroy your brain's neurons and neurotransmitters, make you anxious and/or depressed, set you up for strokes or heart attacks, and more.

Health professionals are unlikely to warn you about most of these foods, additives, and supplements, because it's not common knowledge that they can substantially worsen already-existing illnesses, nor that they can trigger new health conditions.

You deserve to have full knowledge of what you consume, and what effects it all has on your body. By reading this chapter, you will start to protect yourself. You're *worth* protecting. It's time you had control and informed choice over what enters your body—it's a powerful step toward recovering your health.

CORN

Corn used to be one of the fundamental sources of nourishment on earth.

Unfortunately, the technology of *genetically modified organisms* (GMO) has destroyed it as a viable food.

Corn products and by-products create substantial inflammation. It's a food that can feed viruses, bacteria, mold, and fungus. Even if you see corn advertised as being non-GMO, the chances are high that it can still trigger any kind of health condition—and that it may still be GMO.

Try to avoid *all* corn and *all* products that have corn as an ingredient. These include foods such as corn chips, taco shells, popcorn, corn cereal, and anything that clearly incorporates corn syrup or corn oil. They also include less obvious products, such as soda, gum, high-fructose corn syrup (HFCS), toothpaste, gluten-free foods that use corn in place of wheat, and herbal tinctures that employ alcohol as a preservative. (It's most likely corn grain alcohol. Buy the alcohol-free versions of tinctures instead.)

Try to read ingredient labels carefully . . . and do the best you can.

Staying away from corn products and by-products can be a lot of work. For a treat in the summertime, it's okay to enjoy a fresh, organic corn on the cob. For the sake of your health, it's worth the effort of cutting out corn the rest of the time.

SOY

Soy has suffered a similar GMO fate as corn.

Soy used to be a healthy food. However, you can now assume that any soy product you encounter could have some GMO contamination or contain added MSG. Be cautious when eating soybeans, edamame, miso, soymilk, soy nuts, soy sauce, textured vegetable protein (TVP), soy protein powder, artificial meat products made from soy, and much more.

Try to stay away from soy the best you can. If you really enjoy soy and feel deprived without it, stick to the safest options: plain, organic tofu or tempeh, or the highest-quality nama shoyu.

CANOLA OIL

Canola oil is mostly GMO at this point in time. And regardless, canola oil creates a great deal of inflammation. It's especially damaging to your digestive system, potentially scarring the linings of both your small and large intestines, and is a major cause of irritable bowel syndrome. Canola oil can feed viruses, bacteria, fungus, and mold.

Beyond that, canola oil has an effect similar to battery acid on the inside of your arteries, creating significant vascular damage.

Canola oil is used in many restaurants and in thousands of products, often as a low-cost alternative to olive oil. Even reputable health food chains and restaurants use canola oil to keep prices down, sometimes advertising canola as a health food. Unfortunately, if canola oil is even a tiny part of an otherwise perfectly healthy dish of organic and all-natural ingredients, you should probably avoid that dish because of how destructive canola oil is.

If you're dealing with a mystery illness or a health condition, try to avoid canola oil at all costs.

PROCESSED BEET SUGAR

So far, GMO beets are mostly reserved for making processed beet sugar. You should therefore avoid products that contain processed beet sugar, which feeds cancers, viruses, and bacteria.

This is different from grating fresh, organic beets over your salad, or juicing fresh beets. If you stick to organic, most whole beets that you buy in the produce section at your local natural market or at the farmers' market are safe to consume.

EGGS

Humans have eaten eggs for thousands of years. They were once an amazing survival food for us to eat in areas of the planet where there were no other food options at certain times of year. That changed with the turn of the 20th century, though—when the autoimmune, viral, bacterial, and cancer epidemics began.

The average person eats over 350 eggs a year. That includes whole eggs and also all the foods with hidden egg ingredients.

If you're struggling with any illness, such as Lyme disease, lupus, chronic fatigue syndrome, migraines, or fibromyalgia, avoiding eggs can give your body the support it needs to get better.

The biggest issue with eggs is that they're a prime food for cancer and other cysts, fibroids, tumors, and nodules. Women with polycystic ovary syndrome (PCOS), breast cancer, or other cysts and tumors should avoid eggs altogether. Also, if you're trying to prevent cancer, fight an existing cancer, or avoid a cancer relapse, steer clear. Removing eggs from your diet completely will give you a powerful fighting chance to reverse disease and heal.

Eggs also cause inflammation and allergies; feed viruses, bacteria, yeast, mold, *Candida* and other fungus; and trigger edema in the lymphatic system.

People who are diagnosed with *Candida* or mycotoxins are often told that eggs are a good, safe protein that will starve the *Candida* and mycotoxins. Nothing could be further from the truth.

I know how popular eggs are. There's a growing trend that promotes them as a major health food. Plus they're delicious and fun to eat. If eggs were good for us in the current day and age, though, I'd be promoting them as such.

DAIRY

Milk, cheese, butter, cream, yogurt, and other such products contain a substantial amount of fat, which is a strain for your digestive system—and especially your liver—to process.

Dairy contains lactose, and the combination of fat and sugar has negative effects on health, especially if you're diabetic. Further, dairy fat in your bloodstream helps to breed viruses and bacteria.

Dairy is also mucus producing, and a major cause of inflammation and allergies.

Those are the issues that have *always* held true for dairy, even when it's organic and free-range. And now, conventional, mainstream practice has made a problematic food into a toxic one by creating farm industry pressure to give hormones, antibiotics, GMO corn and soy, and gluten to cows, goats, and sheep.

If you want a smooth healing process, it's best not to eat dairy at all.

PORK

Avoid all forms of pork, including ham, bacon, processed pork products, lard, and so on. It's difficult to heal any chronic illness while consuming any kind of pig product, due to these foods' high fat content.

FARMED FISH

Farmed fish are often raised in small, enclosed spaces. This breeds algae, parasites, and other diseases—so the breeders often give the fish antibiotics and treat the water with toxic chemicals. This makes consuming farmed fish risky.

The safest fish you can eat are wild ones, such as salmon, halibut, and haddock. No matter what type you select, beware of mercury— especially with larger fish such as swordfish and tuna.

GLUTEN

Gluten is a protein found in many grains. The forms of gluten to which people are especially sensitive are in wheat, barley, rye, and spelt (a type of wheat). (When it comes to oats, be aware that growing and processing sometimes cross-contaminates them with grains that contain gluten. Oats can be a very good food for people who are less sensitive, though. Look for those that are labeled gluten-free.) Grains that contain gluten also contain multiple allergens and proteins that can trigger any condition. They create disruption and inflammation, especially in your intestinal tract and bowels. They also confuse your immune system—which is your primary defense against disease— and often trigger celiac disease, Crohn's, and colitis.

Eating these grains makes it very difficult for your body to heal. If you'd like to recover from your illness as quickly as possible, minimize grains of any kind.

MSG

Monosodium glutamate (MSG) is a food additive that's used in tens of thousands of products and restaurant dishes. MSG is a salt that occurs naturally in glutamic acid (a non-essential amino acid). But there's nothing natural about the extreme damage it can do to you.

MSG typically builds up in your brain, going deep into your brain tissue. It can then cause inflammation and swelling, kill thousands of your brain cells, disrupt electrical impulses, weaken neurotransmitters, burn out neurons, make you feel confused and anxious, and even lead to micro-strokes. It also weakens and injures your central nervous system.

MSG is especially harmful if you have an illness that involves your brain or central nervous system. However, there are no circumstances under which it's good for you. As a result, this is an additive you should *always* avoid.

Because MSG is included in countless products, it's essential to read food labels carefully. It's also important to know what to look for. MSG is often "hidden" on labels because of its deservedly bad reputation. The following terms usually mean that MSG is an ingredient: *glutamate, hydrolyzed, autolyzed, protease, carrageenan, maltodextrin, sodium caseinate, balsamic vinegar, barley malt, malt extract, yeast extract, brewer's yeast, corn starch, wheat starch, modified food starch, gelatin, textured protein, whey protein, soy protein, soy sauce, broth, bouillon, stock,* and *seasoning.*

NATURAL FLAVORS

Any ingredient with a name like *natural flavoring* is hidden MSG. *Natural cherry flavor, natural orange flavor, natural lemon flavor, natural fruit flavor* . . . they're not just fruit extracts, and they're not your friends. The same goes for *smoke flavor, turkey flavor, beef flavor, natural peppermint flavor, natural maple flavor, natural chocolate flavor, natural vanilla flavor,* and all their "natural" and "flavor"-ful cousins. (Although pure vanilla extract is safe to use.)

Each type of natural flavor potentially contains multiple biohazards and chemical compounds. Natural flavoring has slipped under the radar and been allowed into thousands of health food store products that are advertised as good, safe, and healthy for you and your children.

Moms, take heed. Natural flavors are one of the newest and stealthiest now-you-see-it-now-you-don't tricks for hiding MSG. Take care reading labels so you and your family can avoid this hidden ingredient.

ARTIFICIAL FLAVORS

Artificial flavors can represent any of thousands of chemicals that were birthed in a lab. Don't take risks by consuming them. As much as possible, the best you can, stay away from chemical additives.

ARTIFICIAL SWEETENERS

Most artificial sweeteners act as neurotoxins because they contain aspartame. This can disrupt your neurons and your central nervous system. Long-term, artificial sweeteners can cause neurological breakdowns and strokes in your brain.

If you crave sweets, eat as much fruit as you like. Fruit fights disease and has powerful healing properties.

CITRIC ACID

Compared to the other additives in this chapter, citric acid isn't so bad.

That said, it's very irritating to the linings of the stomach and the intestinal tract, so it can create a lot of inflammation and discomfort if you're sensitive to it.

Citric acid (the additive) is not the same thing as naturally occurring acid in citrus. Try not to confuse the two. Citrus itself is a healing food. The isolated ingredient citric acid, however, is often corn derived.

Especially if you're experiencing any kind of stomach pain, keep an eye out for citric acid on ingredient labels and consider skipping foods that include it.

SUPPLEMENTS TO AVOID

Many over-the-counter supplements are wonderful. However, this section covers supplements that—depending on your condition—may not be appropriate for you.

L-Carnitine

If you have any form of the herpes virus, your doctor may have told you to go light on foods high in the amino acid *arginine.*

While that's accurate, the risk from arginine is minor compared to that of another amino acid called *carnitine,* which is a top fuel for all herpes viruses. The same goes for a variety of viruses beyond herpes. *L-carnitine* is not helpful with cancers, either.

You need to beware of L-carnitine. Always stay away from this amino acid in a concentrated supplement form.

Glandular Supplements

Glandular supplements made from animals are prime foods for viruses, bacteria, and cancers, which all thrive on concentrated hormones.

Be cautious when taking supplements containing concentrations, however small, of bovine or other animal organs or glands. These are low-grade steroid compounds, and they're often prescribed by doctors for adrenals and other endocrine glands and organs.

Whey Protein

Whey protein is a dairy by-product that does nothing notable for you except create inflammation. Plus it usually includes MSG.

However, you're generally safe with a high-quality organic hemp protein powder. Check the ingredients label before buying to ensure the powder contains nothing that's cautioned against in this chapter.

Fish Oil Supplements

The fish oil trend is unstoppable at this point. Yet it's important that people understand what they're putting in their bodies. While it's okay to eat wild fish sparingly, fish oil supplements are another matter. You would think it's all the same, but it's actually very different.

The primary issue is mercury and dioxins, which are present in most of the fish used to make these supplements. When you eat fish with mercury in its flesh, the mercury has a tendency to stay mostly in your intestinal tract, liver, and stomach area. It's another, more dangerous story when you consume fish oil supplements. Although manufacturers say that the physical mercury is removed from their supplements, it's an impossible and unrealistic claim.

In fish, mercury concentrates itself mostly in the volatile omega oils. So when millions of fish are processed for their oil, mercury levels are at an unparalleled level. The process that supplement manufacturers then use to try to lower the mercury content actually destabilizes the toxic heavy metal. It becomes a highly absorbable, homeopathic version of itself. (For those who are into homeopathy: the more the substance is diluted, the more its frequency increases, and the more power and influence it has over the body.)

This concentrated mercury that ends up in fish oil supplements has the ability to cross the blood-brain barrier and quite easily enter sensitive organs, bypassing and disrupting the body's systems. It can also strengthen and feed viruses and bacteria. Fish oil supplements put you on the fast track for Alzheimer's, dementia, and chronic inflammatory diseases of the brain.

Unfortunately, the fish oil trend train is barreling down the tracks, fueled by misinformation. It is powerful, popular—and harmful. Do your best to stay out of its way. Instead of fish oil supplements, look for fish-free, plant-based, algae-derived omega supplements.

Whenever you start to feel persuaded by the arguments in fish oil's favor, remember: fish oil is the snake oil of today! Treat it warily. It will not fulfill its promises.

I'm not trying to stir the pot with information that goes against the mainstream. I just can't bear to choose the path of least resistance and repeat the misinformation that's out there, as if popularity makes it accurate. This is about you getting better with the truth.

Iron Supplements

Even though iron in the right amounts is good for you, viruses love to feed on this metal. Almost all cases of anemia are caused by a low-grade viral infection. You should therefore avoid iron supplements that are not plant-based.

Increase your iron naturally by eating spinach, barley grass, Swiss chard, squash, pumpkin seeds, asparagus, sulfur-free dried apricots, and other vegetables and fruits with relatively high amounts of iron. Viruses are unlikely to consume iron from these sources because vegetables and fruits contain natural antiviral properties.

CHAPTER 20

Fruit Fear

Everyone is unique—that's well-established by now. I think we'd all agree that each person is different, and each person's soul is, too. No one would argue that Hitler's soul was the same as a saint's.

And think about rocks. There are sedimentary, metamorphic, and igneous—and so many types within each classification. There's a different story behind what went into forming each one. They look different, weather differently, and behave differently. You'd be cautious, for example, climbing up a rock face of shale, because of its tendency to splinter—you wouldn't want to lose your grip and fall to the ground.

And let's look at water: do all the bottled water companies think their offerings are the same? No; that's why high-end bottlers spend fortunes advertising their brands' singular benefits. And what if you compare a glass of drinking water to the water in the toilet bowl? Or to a puddle on the New Jersey turnpike. Or to a freshly melted snowcap on a pristine mountain. Or to the water in an aquarium or bathtub or swimming pool. They're all H_2O. But are they the same? Not a chance.

That's how it works with sugar. You can't lump together all the different types and say they're all bad. You can't say "sugar is sugar."

Yet that's what's happened in our culture. In recent years, certain important facts came to light about how the processed sugar that's added to so many foods—especially in the form of corn syrup—feeds obesity, viruses, fungi, cancer, and a myriad of other diseases. Suddenly a fire started in the collective health-care consciousness about *all* sugar. Natural and conventional doctors alike declared a well-intentioned war on it.

The innocent casualty was fruit.

Fruit has almost become a dirty word.

So much so that it's a little risky for me to even write this chapter. It sounds silly, but it's true. Because what I reveal about fruit in the pages to come goes against current thinking. It goes against the conditioning of fruit fear.

FRUIT IS NOT THE PROBLEM

There's a rapidly developing trend: millions of people who are struggling with their health all over the country visit doctors, practitioners, nutritionists, or healers and hear right off the bat, "Eliminate fruit from your diet."

Doctors who practice Eastern medicine will say fruit creates dampness in the body. Doctors who practice Western medicine will say fruit feeds *Candida* and cancer. Dietitians and nutritionists will say fruit contributes to diabetes. And physical trainers will say fruit will make you overweight, or even obese.

That's because health professionals and medical communities associate fruit sugar with high-fructose corn syrup (HFCS), processed cane sugar, sucrose, lactose, and other sweeteners and sugars. They're telling people that fruit is contributing to their problems with *Candida,* mold, weight, cancer, diabetes, cardiovascular systems, and even their teeth.

In truth, who eats that much fruit? In mainstream diets, it's become a novelty. While people may still have the occasional banana or lunchbox apple, more often fruit is an accompaniment to something else: the strawberries on strawberry shortcake, for instance, or a few glazed blueberries swimming in the butter, cane sugar, and lard of blueberry pie.

So are the millions of Americans who are sick with various illnesses unwell because of the occasional Granny Smith? Are millions of people with rotting teeth climbing into the dentist's chair for a root canal because of the clementine they ate at a holiday party? The reality is that even the average person who's concerned about sugar intake still consumes well over 100 pounds of *refined* sugar a year.

The sugar in fruit is not to blame for illness. It is not the same as HFCS or the sugar cubes at the diner.

Fruit is not making people sick.

I'm not saying that fructose that's been processed and separated from its fruit source is an ideal source of food. But fruit in its whole form, full of water and fiber-rich pulp, is the real deal for your health.

Fruit consumption in the U.S. has substantially declined in recent years. In 2000, each American consumed an average of 287 pounds of fruit per year, while by 2012 that had dropped to only 245 pounds a year,[4] a nearly 15 percent decrease.

For the record, 245 pounds of fruit isn't a lot. Let's put this in perspective: It's like eating only five cases of fruit in an entire year.

Do not get a pound of fruit confused with a pound of sugar. A pound of *sugar* is a pound of sugar. A pound of fruit is a unique blend of life-creating, life-saving, life-sustaining phytonutrients and other phytochemicals that stop disease and promote long life.

Fruit does not have that much sugar in it. Fruits are made up of living water, minerals, vitamins, protein, fat, other nutrients, pulp, fiber, antioxidants, pectin—and just a fraction of sugar. If we wanted to compare 100 pounds of refined sugar to the equivalent amount of sugar you'd consume in fruit, we'd be looking at thousands of pounds of fruit.

Since 2012, the fruit-hating trend has been in full swing. We're likely headed toward a 40 percent decrease from that 2000 figure in per capita fruit consumption.

That's not supposed to be the trend.

Before refined sugar production and trade became a major industry that turned products like table sugar and HFCS into dietary staples, we relied on a critical source of life. That source was fruit. Since humankind began, we've depended on fruit, in all its varieties, for our survival. The Tree of Life was an ancient symbol of interconnection, fertility, and eternal life—precisely because of this legendary tree's fruit. Fruit is part of our essence, a basic element of who we are. We cannot survive without fruit on this planet. It outweighs the nutrition of any other food.

Yet the current "health" movement toward low-carb diets has put fruit on the endangered species list, with the goal of making it extinct.

Is this denial? Ignorance? Foolishness? We're not talking about uneducated people who are driving the trend. We're talking about smart, highly intelligent professionals with advanced degrees in medicine and nutrition. If they're advising patients to shun fruit, it must be because of their training, the misinformation out there, or their own selective interests.

Have you heard of book burning? If the anti-sugar war keeps up its momentum, fruit trees will be next to go up in flames.

FRUIT AND FERTILITY

It's critical that medical communities start distinguishing between fruit sugars and all the rest. Otherwise, the war could be more dangerous than anyone realizes; it could result in other innocent casualties: womankind, and the future of humankind.

That's because without fruit, fertility is at risk. Women are already up against enough infertility issues, and well-meaning doctors have no idea that when they tell women patients to shun fruit, they're contributing to women's struggles to conceive. A woman's reproductive system is like a flowering tree that requires the proper nutrients to bear fruit. And those nutrients come from, well, fruit.

Fertility—and overall health—depends specifically on the fructose and glucose that occur naturally in fruit, as well as the phytochemicals bonded to those sugars. A woman's reproductive system also relies on the dozens of antitumor, anticancer antioxidants (and so many more components yet to be discovered by medical science) available only in fruit, as well as fruit's essential polyphenols, bioflavonoids, disease-stopping pectin, vitamins, and minerals. These elements help to stop polycystic ovary syndrome (PCOS), pelvic inflammatory disease (PID), and an overextended reproductive system— examples of conditions that cause mysterious infertility.

FRUITFUL LANGUAGE

It's for good reason that the Bible mentions fruit over 300 times: because fruit is vital to the essence of who we are. Humankind exists because of the fruit we picked off trees since our species' beginning. It is what has allowed us to thrive on this planet.

Fruit is the divine word of wisdom. For thousands of years, we have used fruit in our language to express powerful truths. To this day, we use phrases such as "fruits of our labors" and "a tree is known by its fruit."

We talk about fruit in terms of prosperity. In business, we talk about "fruitful" collaboration and projects coming to "fruition." Motivational gurus who teach about achieving financial freedom refer to "fruit-bearing" processes. We call children "fruit of the womb" and "fruit of the loins." We warn against the dangers of "forbidden fruit" and settling for the "low-hanging fruit."

All this fruit in our daily language shows that we connect on some level with fruit's significance. When we only connect to fruit's meaning, though, it's like extracting the sugar. It's like getting only the sweet buzz of a hit of processed fructose and none of the benefits of the fruit in its whole form.

For true mind-body-spirit-soul-heart wisdom, we need to incorporate real, unadulterated fruit into our diets. Only then do we start to walk the talk of all those phrases we throw around. When fruit literally becomes part of who we are, our lives become that much more fruitful.

Why avoid the food we were most meant to eat? Eating whole fruit can make *us* whole again.

FRUIT'S ANCIENT ROOTS

Humans have been cultivating fruit for thousands of years, all over the globe. In Asia, peaches and citrus had historical significance. In Russia, apples and pears were central. In England, it was berries and grapes. In the Middle East, figs, dates, and mangoes held (and still hold) an important place. And in South America, bananas and avocados have always had a vital role in health and culture.

Going all the way back to the Garden of Eden, fruit was a mainstay of the human diet. Once agriculture began and civilization and trade routes became established, it was the ones fortunate enough to have fruit delivered to them—emperors, kings, queens, dukes, earls, counts, barons, knights, and pharaohs—who lived the longest.

With access to fruit all year long, disease was not the problem for royalty that it was for the people of lower status. Peasants and other common people had to live off grains, porridge, scraps of dehydrated meats, and some vegetables. They went much of the year without a single piece of fruit. As a result, they were plagued by nutritional deficiencies.

Scurvy, a disease that research has pegged as a vitamin C deficiency but is also a deficiency in other critical nutrients found in fruit (as yet undiscovered by science), was rampant in these lower classes. Many people also died of rickets eating away at their muscles and bones. Simple infections were life threatening, too, and noncancerous tumors that thrived off protein, fat, and grain were responsible for a great many people's suffering at this time in history—all because they didn't have access to enough fruit.

Meanwhile, the fortunate kings of the planet led longer and healthier lives because of the sacrifices those below them made to bring fruit from all over the world. They'd order up oranges like we can call for pizza delivery, and lo, the oranges would appear.

(By the way, there's more sugar in pizza than you'll ever find in fruit.)

These rulers were constantly eating out of season, enjoying the best that other regions had to offer, and taking in hundreds of critical life-protecting nutrients.

SEASONAL EATING . . . AND EATING OUT OF SEASON

Which leads me to another topic: the seasonal eating trend.

It has its pluses. The popularity of seasonal eating has people visiting their farmers' markets for fresh fruits and vegetables—and of course that's wonderful. There's nothing like enjoying the local bounty that each season brings.

The downside is that out-of-season fruit (i.e., fruit transported from other parts of the country or globe) is getting a bad rap. Some people have started to walk past the grocery store offerings of blackberries in winter or oranges in summer because they don't line up with the growing season where they live. That's a crime for their health. This mentality robs people of disease-protecting nutrients, because they turn to other fillers in their diet instead. The truth is, those fruits *are* in season . . . in the places where they were grown.

If you took an autumn vacation from Michigan to southern Spain, wouldn't you eat the fresh mangoes there, even though they weren't available from the local vendors at home? Wouldn't you recognize that different parts of the world have different growing seasons and different varieties of produce, and let yourself enjoy the delicacy?

Just because you're not on vacation doesn't mean you're meant to ignore the fruits shipped in from out of town. It's how the ruling classes survived and thrived for thousands of years—and now their health secret is available to the masses.

Some people are less concerned about being out-of-tune with the seasons than they are about the environmental impact of transporting produce from other regions. That's understandable—though if the pollution from shipping is what's stopping you from buying Ecuadorian bananas, then you'll have to rethink using a car, a washing machine, a computer, a cell phone, or cloud storage, visiting the salon, wearing almost all modern-day clothes, ordering anything that's delivered to your door . . . the list goes on. You'd be much better off cutting back in one of those areas and letting yourself buy pears from New Zealand or honeydew from Mexico. The benefits that fruit will have for your health are worth it.

That said, if you prefer to eliminate all modern practices from your life and live as though it were 1850, I'm not here to stop you. Just know that limiting fruit in your diet will increase your chances of illness and shorten your expected lifespan.

THE TRUTH ABOUT RIPENING

Another popular misconception about fruit is that it's not worth eating if it was picked early and unripe, so it can withstand shipping and last on the grocery store shelf.

Truth is, if a fruit were truly picked too early to have nutritional value, it would never ripen at all, and you'd find it inedible.

Fruit trees and plants have a built-in database of information connected to the heavens. Once they log enough hours in the season and the growing conditions are right, the Higher Source delivers the signal, and the fruits enter their ripening phase. At this point, they can get picked at any time and still ripen and nourish your body.

It's true that it doesn't work to pick some fruits, such as berries, before they've ripened on the plant. With other fruits, though, such as mangoes, tomatoes, and bananas, they just have to cross that specific growing threshold, to which farmers are often well attuned.

HYBRIDIZATION

Don't get confused or concerned about hybridization or cross-breeding—not to be mistaken for genetic modification and the creation of GMOs. Grafting and hand-pollination are safe techniques that humans have used for thousands of years to create new varieties of fruit. It's a healthy adaptation and evolution of the cultivation process. While it's true that heirloom fruits can be more nutritious, don't shy away from their hybridized cousins. These fruits are still preventative wonders that fight cancer and other diseases.

MAKING FRUIT A HABIT

Fruit has properties that soothe your adrenal glands, strengthen your entire endocrine system, repair your vascular system, restore your liver, and revitalize your brain. There is no other food—and no pill—that enhances so many of your bodily functions as fruit.

Fruit keeps your body going in ways that science hasn't even begun to fully understand. It's an absolute necessity.

You can't function as a human being without glucose, the simple sugar into which your body breaks down foods. Glucose fuels your brain, your nervous system, and the cells throughout your body.

If you're an athlete—or a mom holding down multiple jobs between home and the office—then eating animal protein, nuts, and vegetables alone won't allow you to perform. You also need foods with sugar in them, and the highest-quality source of sugar is fruit. If you try to cut out all sugar from your diet, sooner or later your body will force you to "cheat"—because every muscle in your body functions on glucose—and eat something that provides the sugar you need. The chances are you'll binge on something that's not a nutritional plus for you, such as pastries or pasta or chocolate bars.

You'll be much better off if you make a habit of eating fruit every day. It will help curb sugar cravings—and make a huge difference in your health.

Fruit is best eaten by itself or paired with raw vegetables, especially leafy greens. That's because your stomach digests fruit and raw veggies quickly and easily. In contrast, protein, fat, complex carbohydrates, and cooked vegetables take a relatively long time to digest, so if you add fruit to the mix it'll be stuck in your stomach waiting its turn. While this does no serious harm, it can create gas and other discomfort that might discourage you from eating fruit—and *that* would be terrible. So consider consuming fruit on its own or with raw, leafy greens or other veggies, and any other type of food an hour or more after you've enjoyed your fruit.

FRUIT IS ANTI-DISEASE

Almost all health professionals and medical practitioners advise their patients to avoid processed sugar because cancer can potentially feed on it. That's excellent advice.

The trouble is, these health-care professionals often go on to point to fruit as a source of harm, too, because of the sugars it contains.

Fruit does not feed cancer. It's *anti*-cancerous. Fruit fights cancer *more effectively than any other food*. Any cancer patient removing fruit from her diet is giving up her most powerful natural weapon against the disease.

Vegetables combat cancer, too, but only about a quarter as well. If doctors insist you remove all fruit from your diet, you'd better quadruple your vegetable intake to compensate.

When doctors advise cancer patients against fruit, the irony is that cancer (and other disease) feeds on every food that is *not* a fruit or vegetable.

In the 1960s, there was a trend among cocaine addicts to double one's intake of vitamin C to protect the body from the damage done by the illegal stimulant. The more vitamin C they took, the more cocaine people thought they could ingest.

What I'm getting at is, the more chocolate cake, soda, animal protein, milk, cheese, fried, greasy, non-fruit, and non-vegetable foods you eat, the more you'd better counterbalance this fare with extra apples, berries, mangoes, papayas, grapes, melons, kiwis, oranges, vegetables, and leafy greens, and the like to protect yourself.

If you keep eating foods other than fruits and vegetables, there's no guarantee that you'll become disease-resistant. However, incorporating an abundance of fruit into your diet will be a positive, proactive step toward countering cancer's effects.

Cancer *cannot* feed off the sugar in fruit, which possesses critical components such as polyphenols, including resveratrol, and other antioxidants. These cancer killers cannot be separated from the sugar in fruit; they travel together as a team.

The research that's been done on the link between sugar and cancer has been on sucrose and high-fructose corn syrup. The appropriate studies have yet to be performed with an actual piece of fruit, or with most of the foods that truly do feed cancer. Yet the rumor mill is going strong, and fruit fear is in danger of stopping countless people from preventing cancers and other health issues.

Cancer is already climbing at an alarming rate. With fruit consumption taking a nosedive, I hate to imagine where this is headed. It's another blunder for which our children and our children's children will have to pay. Some things, like the nation's debt, are out of our control. It's in our control, though, to make sure that the generations to come know how to stay healthy and don't fall into the trend traps.

Not only does fruit fight cancer, it kills all types of viruses and bacteria. Certain fruits, such as bananas, wild blueberries, apples, and papayas, are the most powerful natural destroyers of viruses on earth.

Fruit is also vital to gut health—which is essential to a healthy immune system. For example, the pectin in apples, and the skin, pulp, and fiber in figs and dates, are exceptionally effective at killing and/or clearing out anything that doesn't belong in your intestinal tract, including fungi such as *Candida,* worms, and other parasites.

If you're worried that the sugar in fruit feeds *Candida,* turn to Chapter 9. You'll find that, first, the sugar in fruit is digested by your stomach so rapidly that within minutes, it travels straight into your bloodstream, meaning the sugar never even reaches your intestinal tract to feed *Candida.* And second, fruit *kills Candida* cells. (*Candida* is seldom a substantial problem of its own; it's often an indicator that something else in the body is amiss.)

Another misconception is that fruit sugar hinders the liver. That couldn't be more misunderstood. This trend only goes to show that something is amiss with our medical system.

Does the term "fatty liver" sound like a condition that comes from fruit sugar? No. The occasional piece of fruit that most Americans eat is *not* why liver disease and disorders of the liver are rampant and on the rise.

As the name implies, a fatty liver comes from consuming fat. Almost all liver diseases are protein and fat related, because viruses thrive on protein and fat. It's just that so many fatty foods are also high in bad sugars. And it's not always the obvious foods, like cupcakes and ice cream, but also whole milk (which combines butterfat and lactose), a hamburger in a bun (animal fat and carbohydrates), and French fries (drenched in oil) with ketchup (full of added sugar). So somewhere along the line, health professionals came under the misimpression that fruit hurts the liver because it has natural sugars.

The best way to get someone better from liver disease and/or hepatitis C is to feed them solely fruits and vegetables. It's the answer to their suffering.

Speaking of the liver, hypoglycemia often starts because of a dysfunctional liver that's lost its store of glucose due to a diet too high in fat and protein. Sugar isn't the bad guy here, especially sugar from apples, berries, oranges, melons, bananas, mangoes, papayas, kiwis, and other sweet and delicious fruits. Fruit *protects* the liver by providing the organ with the glucose reserve it needs in order to function and stave off illness, and to stabilize blood sugar.

Why am I championing fruit? Who cares if health-care professionals tell their patients to avoid it, and the practice of eating fruit vanishes altogether?

We *all* have to care and we *all* have to champion it, because it is critical to everyone's health.

It's imperative that women eat enough fruit so they can avoid fatigue, cancers, tumors, viruses, PID, PCOS, and other illnesses. It's important to the future of our children, who currently get the message not to eat fruit.

If you're in the business of wanting your liver, kidneys, and pancreas to break down, then go ahead and listen to practitioners' advice to eat a high-protein—and therefore high-fat—diet and shun fruit sugar. I don't side with any particular food program, diet, or nutritional belief system. I'm not against animal foods. It's just that if animal products take the place of fruit in your diet, you won't get enough nutrients to protect you for the long haul.

Fruit is a critical part of how you overcome illness. I have witnessed this in my clients for over 25 years.

Take comfort. Fruit is your friend. It does not cause sickness. Rather, no other food is as effective at preventing disease, killing pathogens, and repairing the body.

THE FRUIT FOUNTAIN OF YOUTH

Consider this: we're eating less fruit as a society than ever before, and more protein and fat. Life expectancy and fruit consumption are dropping at the same time. That's not a coincidence.

Longevity is a popular term right now. Everybody wants to know the secret to living longer. Yet so many people are blinded by an anti-sugar mentality that they can't see the truth. Out of all the limited foods we have left on the planet, there is only one food group that has the ability to grant us longer life. You've probably guessed what it is by now: fruit.

Alzheimer's disease, dementia, memory loss, and neurological diseases such as Parkinson's and ALS can all be prevented by fruit.

That's because not only does fruit prevent these diseases, it prevents *oxidation*—which is the process that ages us. It's the same process that makes the flesh of a pound of chopped meat turn brown after prolonged exposure to oxygen, just like our muscles break down from aging and oxidization. Essentially, we oxidize a little more every day—unless we take action against it. The best way to do that is to eat foods rich in *antioxidants,* which you'll find most plentiful, by a wide margin, in fruit. Antioxidants from fruit can even *reverse* aging.

The most powerful fruit on the planet is the wild blueberry. Science hasn't yet fully tapped into the healing, adaptogenic properties that wild blueberries possess. They're the most antioxidant-rich food available. They can prevent and reverse disease. They are the most powerful brain food in existence.

You can find wild blueberries in the frozen fruit case at your local grocery store. And don't confuse wild blueberries with their cultivated cousins. While cultivated (highbush) blueberries are a nutritious food, they're not the superfood that wild (lowbush) blueberries are. Every single wild blueberry contains thousands of years of survival information. Each one you consume allows this wisdom into your body, helping you adapt in today's changing times.

So if you want to look and feel younger and live longer, incorporate wild blueberries—as well as grapes, plums, oranges, and the like—into your diet.

We only have so many meals to eat in a lifetime. For the average person with an average lifespan (which is shorter than it used to be), that's roughly 80,000 meals. Since fruit is becoming less popular, it may account for about 10,000 of those meals—15,000 if you're lucky. Unless vegetables make up most of the difference, that's a lot of missed opportunity for nutrition.

If it's well-being and longevity you're after, you want every meal to count for something. One of the best ways to do that is to eat more fruit—and not to get sucked into the anti-sugar game.

Fruit is the true fountain of youth.

BEFRIEND FRUIT

If you were stranded on a desert island and the only foods available were chicken or eggs or beef, by the time you were rescued two years later, your health would be a disaster due to complete body system acidosis (not just one body system becoming acidic)—and that's if you were alive at all.

Yet if you were stranded on that same island with nothing but avocados or papayas or bananas, at the end of the two-year period, your health would not only be fine, you'd be thriving. If you don't believe me, commission someone to try this!

That old saying, "An apple a day keeps the doctor away," names a piece of fruit for a reason. It's not, "An egg a day keeps the doctor away," or "A cut of beef a day keeps the doctor away," or "A chicken breast a day keeps the doctor away."

Which is not to say that no one should eat chicken or beef. It's just that fruit is the foundation of health—and we've known this for a long time.

For some people, it's more like an apple a month that they incorporate into their diet—and that one apple is the underlying structure of any wellness they maintain.

Many of us live in a world now where fresh fruit is available year-round—fruit that has the power to heal disease, prevent it, sweeten our days, give us energy, and give us back our lives. As I've said before: Most health trends don't become popular because they work. The belief that all sugars are the same is one such powerful trend, and it's growing fast. It has turned so many health professionals against fruit.

If it keeps going at this rate, there will be some kind of fruit prohibition. We'll be camouflaging our raspberry bushes so they're not confiscated and hiding in closets to snack on plums.

When you hear from a friend or practitioner that you should avoid fruit, remember what you've just read. It's not their fault that they're spreading misinformation; they've just gotten on board the trend train. Keep your wits about you, and don't let the train take you away. You know the truth now.

CHAPTER 21

The 28-Day Healing Cleanse

Our bodies love us unconditionally. They do not judge or blame or hold onto resentment. Day in and day out, all of our body systems—ones like the lymphatic, endocrine, and central nervous systems—are working for us without complaint. The immune system is constantly ready for battle, patrolling every part of the body looking for invaders.

We take all this for granted. We eat things our systems don't appreciate, indulge in foods to comfort our emotions rather than feed our bodies and souls. As we seek out snacks, meals, beverages, and desserts that keep emotions at bay, our bodies become the victims of our soul damage. We get confused and cross the line between what we like to eat and what our bodies need.

Eventually, the physical body begins to show wear and tear. It starts with small breakdowns, then the larger breakdowns come. Imagine a car running low on oil. For a while you can get by on fumes, but at some point the oil will get too low. You'll turn on the car, the engine will heat up, cause friction, and *bang*—you'll blow a valve.

The human body is forever forgiving. Your body wants to heal. It *can* heal. Even after years of being ignored, mistreated, or misunderstood, your body will fight for you like nothing else and no one else can. When you tend to it in the right way, your body has the ability to rejuvenate and restore from the most extreme conditions and diseases.

You have to think of your body like an old friend in need. Imagine yourself reaching out a helping hand to this friend as she climbs out of a ravine. This is your commitment to use your free will and the power of your intention to give your body the support it's crying out for.

When we connect to our bodies, truly listen to them, and give them the nourishment they're yearning for, everything changes. True miracles happen.

Many of us grow up in this world with our pick of almost anything to eat. This can be a hard mind-set to change. Our food routines can feel like part of who we are. Hidden addictions and unproductive choices often go into them, though.

We all have cravings. It's important not to confuse these cravings with intuition. We may feel a strong desire to eat certain foods and mistake that desire for our bodies telling us we need that bacon cheeseburger, or that omelet.

Yet when people eat anything and everything under the sun, subjecting the liver, pancreas, gallbladder, heart, and more to greasy, dangerous, processed, fried-oil, gastronomic concoctions, it's because the soul and body are out of alignment. That happens because the hardships we encounter on this earth can damage our souls. We search for ways to literally fill the void with food, or to push down unpleasant emotions—except it doesn't work. Eating unproductive foods, we get sicker. Our souls suffer more.

If you are struggling with your health in any way, the game has to change. Eating restorative foods—and eliminating foods that cause problems—is the most critical aspect of healing any illness or health condition.

The healing food plan I present in this chapter can move health mountains. It's like a reset button for your body. Following these guidelines for four weeks will help reduce inflammation from illness—not just the conditions I cover in these chapters but also many more I didn't have room for in this book. It can make a huge difference in mental health. And the cleanse will help if you're healthy and just looking to lose weight, or if you want to maintain and maximize your potential.

I get that it's not just desire that confuses people about the right foods to eat. It's articles, fads, advertisements, peer pressure, and health-care industry advice. There's always a new superfood in the news, a new story about this or that diet, a new rumor about what seemingly healthy food secretly isn't good for you.

Now you get to tune out all that noise. Focusing your food choices for 28 days on the options listed here will let you stop wasting your energy on the information overload coming from the rest of the world. It's not about deprivation in any way; it's about abundance. This delicious, healing cleanse has brought profound results to countless clients. It has changed people's lives. It can change yours.

If you follow the advice here to the letter, you'll find that your body will respond in untold ways. It has been waiting patiently for you to discover this information. It's ready to work with you. It's ready to hit the reset button. It's ready to heal.

THE PLAN

Here's the deal: For four weeks, eat only raw fruits and vegetables.

For best results, follow the plan below for the whole 28 days. While that's the best length of time, even just a week is likely to bring you significant results. Another alternative is one cleanse day per week. And if this doesn't feel like the right time for you to try the cleanse for any length of time, turn your attention to the other healing techniques throughout the book and come back to this chapter when you feel ready. On the other hand, if your health is in dire straits, or if you have a lot of weight to lose, you're welcome to extend the cleanse beyond the first month.

One reason this plan is so effective is that it maximizes the nutrition you get in every meal. Fruits and vegetables in their raw state contain the highest level of nutrients of any foods, in the form most readily available to your body. When you consume these nutrients in such a high quantity, you'll flood your body with the building blocks it craves. The vitamins, minerals, microorganisms, and other nourishing components will help cleanse and strengthen every system in your body.

The digestive system is one of those beneficiaries. Digestive health has a major impact on immunity and overall health. Normally, digestion takes up an enormous amount of your body's energy.

It's almost like your body has a daily to-do list. There are the things it *has* to attend to every day, like keeping your heart pumping and your lungs inflating and food moving through your intestinal tract. Then there are all the things it *wishes* it could get to—taking out the toxin trash, repairing critical tissue, and so much more—if only it had the time and support.

Imagine a wobbly doorknob in your house. One of these days, it's going to fall off, and you're going to have a real problem. Every day, you mean to fix it, but paying the bills and making food for your family and shoveling fresh snow outside take precedence—plus your screwdriver's gone missing. Same with the body. When it's overloaded with tough-to-digest foods and it's missing critical nutrients, those wish list items just keep getting put off.

The body processes uncooked fruits and vegetables quickly and easily. These foods also have live enzymes, which makes digestion even smoother. When your body's not busy processing heavy fats and proteins, or additives and allergens, it frees up hours every day for your body to rebuild itself on a cellular level. It's as though someone appeared on the front step ready to snow-blow your driveway and sidewalks for free, and handed you a full toolkit at the same time. Suddenly, nothing would be holding you back from fixing the doorknob—or the nails poking out of the floor, or the dripping faucet.

Note that while meat, fish, grains, and starchy vegetables can have helpful nutrients, they can also be tough for the body to break down. When our bodies are overloaded by illness or toxicity or even just sluggishness, we lose the ability to process these foods in an optimal way. The plan below gives us the reboot we need to come back to these foods with digestive vigor.

It also helps cleanse and rebuild the soul. As your body remineralizes, alkalizes, detoxifies, and mends, your soul learns that powerhouse foods like fruit are the true sustenance that will bring it comfort. When you come out on the other side of the 28 days, foods that you know are detrimental to your health won't hold the same sway they once did.

Your soul, spirit, and body will also be operating on a new frequency. Each piece of fruit you eat, each raw spinach leaf, holds a living vibration. When you consume it, you assimilate that. The living food brings you back to life.

Are you ready to kick-start your healing process? Then for the next four weeks, eat the most healing foods on the planet—and nothing else.

In other words, consume raw (preferably organic) fruits and vegetables, with an emphasis on keeping fat intake low. Limit salt intake, too—only add a sprinkle of Himalayan salt to a dish as needed. Stay hydrated with plenty of water, coconut water, herbal tea, and/or fresh juice. (The hot water for tea doesn't destroy the nutrients in the herbs; it releases their medicinal properties.) If you're suffering from a condition for which this book lists a specific protocol of supplements and healing foods, then add those to the mix.

And that's it. Get ready for the healing to begin.

Early Morning

Start the day with a cleansing beverage. Celery juice, cucumber juice, lemon water, coconut water with Hawaiian spirulina, herbal tea, or barley grass juice extract powder reconstituted with water will do wonders to maximize the detox work your body performed overnight and hydrate you for the day ahead.

If your mornings are too rushed, it's fine to skip this step and start the morning with plain water instead.

Breakfast

Make a fruit smoothie for breakfast. A good baseline recipe is three bananas, two dates, and one cup of berries. If this doesn't fill you up, don't hesitate to add more bananas or berries. Don't deprive yourself—this isn't about going hungry. Papayas, pears, and mangoes also make delicious additions.

Other healthy smoothie add-ins include greens like a handful of kale, spinach, or cilantro; two stalks of celery; or a spoonful of barley grass juice extract powder. Just make sure that fruit remains the main ingredient.

Mid-morning

Make another fruit smoothie as described above (or make two servings first thing, and have your second serving now).

Lunch

At midday, make a salad with spinach, lettuce, and cucumbers as the base, then toss in the fruits of your choice. Examples include berries, sliced mangoes, papaya chunks, grapes, and orange or grapefruit segments. For dressing, blend half an avocado and a handful of cilantro with the juice from two oranges (plus garlic and/or fresh ginger to taste, if you'd like). This is meant to be a large salad, so make sure you eat enough to feel full.

Optional additions include chopped cabbage, celery, or cauliflower; arugula or baby kale; sprouts; and scallions.

Mid-afternoon

As you become hungry throughout the afternoon, snack on any fruits of your choice. Good examples include apple or pear slices, dates, oranges, and grapes. Munch on celery sticks alongside each serving of fruit. A spoonful of raw honey also makes a great pick-me-up.

Dinner

For a creamy suppertime spinach soup, combine two bunches of spinach, three medium-to-large tomatoes (or an equal quantity of cherry or grape tomatoes), the juice of one orange, one stalk of celery, a small handful of cilantro, and a clove of garlic (if desired) in a high-speed blender. You can adjust the recipe by using other herbs, such as basil, that appeal to you. For best results, blend the tomatoes and orange juice first, then add the other ingredients. If desired, garnish with sprouts, chopped scallions, chopped tomatoes, Atlantic dulse, and/or herbs.

It can also be a lot of fun to eat this dish served over cucumber noodles, which you can make with a kitchen gadget such as a julienne slicer or spiral slicer. These tools make it easy to turn vegetables into long, slim, crunchy strips. Keep in mind that while zucchini noodles have become popular (and are much healthier than wheat pasta), raw zucchini can be a bit uncomfortable to digest. If maximum healing and detoxification are your priorities, save the zucchini (and carrot and butternut squash) noodles for when you've completed this cleanse.

Evening

If you're still hungry after dinner, snack on an apple and a date.

MODIFICATIONS

You don't have to eat this exact menu every day. If you'd like, swap the lunch and dinner dishes. Or eat two salads. Or a smoothie for lunch or dinner. Cycle through different salad and soup greens if you'd like, too.

Pay no mind to the trend that says too much of a particular raw, leafy green such as spinach will cause you harm. That's misinformation. If you eat raw spinach soup every day for a month, it will be the best thing you've ever done for yourself. Don't be afraid to eat as many greens as you'd like.

It's also okay to eat an entire meal of just one fruit. For example, you can spend the morning eating only mangoes if they're calling your name. You can balance them with a few celery sticks, if that feels best. If you find yourself eating a lot of one food in particular, many grocery stores, co-ops, and farmers will sell you cases of produce at a discount.

Speaking of mangoes, one delicious alternative meal is mango salsa, which you can make by chopping mangoes, tomatoes, cucumbers, celery, cilantro, and garlic (if desired) in the food processor. Serve in cucumber boats, lettuce wraps, or over greens.

And in place of the avocado-orange juice salad dressing, try mashing up some guacamole, topping your salad with it, then sprinkling the whole thing with lime juice.

Another great detox dish is a food-processor grind-up of apples and cauliflower or apples and cabbage.

Point is, you have options. Just remember your mantra: raw fruits and vegetables.

Here are some more possibilities:

If your gut needs healing, start the day with a glass of fresh, plain celery juice on an empty stomach. (For more information, see Chapter 17, "Gut Health.")

If blood sugar or energy levels are of particular concern, employ the grazing technique I describe in Chapter 8, "Adrenal Fatigue."

For a really powerful cleanse, try a week or more with no avocados or other overt fats. Also try cutting out added salt entirely. You'll be getting plenty of natural sodium from the fruits and veggies.

And if, on the other hand, you're okay with a less rapid rate of healing, add a half-avocado at dinner. Further, you can use raw coconut butter, nuts, and seeds as add-ins to your salads, or as a creamy base for a dressing or dip.

You can also pull back the reins on this diet by swapping out the spinach soup dinner for a meal of simply cooked vegetables. Steam, roast (with a bit of coconut oil), or make a soup with veggies such as squash, potatoes, yams, broccoli, cauliflower, and/or asparagus. For maximum digestibility, eat them with some raw sprouts, greens, or celery. This can be part of a less intense cleanse, and it can also be an excellent way to transition into or out of an all-raw cleanse.

THE HEALING CLEANSE

	SAMPLE MENU 1	SAMPLE MENU 2	SAMPLE MENU 3
Early Morning	Celery juice	**Lemon-ginger water**	**Barley grass juice extract powder** mixed with water
Breakfast	**Smoothie** bananas dates frozen wild blueberries	**Smoothie** bananas dates frozen cherries barley grass juice extract powder	**Honeydew melon**
Mid-morning	**Smoothie** same recipe as above	**Smoothie** bananas papaya strawberries fresh aloe leaf gel cilantro	**Bananas with celery sticks**

Lunch	**Salad** baby spinach butter lettuce cucumbers sprouts orange segments **Blended dressing** fresh orange juice avocado garlic	**Chopped salad** spinach baby kale cucumbers tomatoes red onion **Blended dressing** lime juice avocado cilantro garlic	**Salad** baby spinach romaine hearts cucumbers tomatoes papaya cilantro **Blended dressing** tomatoes papaya scallions Atlantic dulse
Mid-afternoon	**Pear slices** **(plenty of them!)** **with celery sticks**	**Sliced peaches** **with strawberries** **and raspberries**	**Coconut water** **with spirulina;** **Grapes with** **celery sticks**
Dinner	**Spinach soup** spinach tomatoes celery cilantro fresh orange juice scallions *- Serve over* *cucumber noodles -*	**Mango salsa** mangoes tomatoes celery cucumbers cilantro garlic *- Serve over red leaf* *lettuce -*	**Cut-up mangoes** **(plenty of them!)** *- Serve with* *romaine leaves on* *the side -*
Evening	**Apple slices with** **date**	**Herbal tea**	**Apple slices with** **date**

TRANSITIONING

When you're adjusting to this way of eating, you may miss certain comfort foods. In their absence, one source of comfort is that this isn't forever. The cleanse is for a month. If you're 40, you've lived through 480 of those things. You've blinked before, and a month has gone by.

You may also experience unpleasant emotional and physical sensations as part of the detoxification. After the initial cleanse phase, in which your bloodstream will purify itself, your liver will then start to do its work, releasing toxins it's been storing for a long time—in some cases years, or even decades. It's natural to need extra rest during this period, and extra sensitivity and caring from loved ones. (For spiritual support, turn to Chapter 22, "Soul-Healing Meditations and Techniques," and Chapter 23, "Essential Angels.")

As your cells release toxins from unproductive foods you've eaten in the past, cravings and memories may burst to the surface of your consciousness. Consider each of these mental twinges a gift. It means a pocket of toxins is leaving you. If you give in to the craving, it may make you feel momentarily satisfied, but you'll cut off the detox process and seal remaining toxins in the liver.

This cleanse could also bliss you out. We don't just suppress negative emotions—we also suppress joy. Sometimes we feel overburdened by the world's worries, so we feel we don't deserve to be happy. This detox plan will help reset that thinking. As your body pushes out the toxic clutter, your brain will clear. You could find yourself experiencing realizations about who you truly are, and about the direction you want your life to go. Embrace that. Listen to it. Your happiness matters to the good of humanity.

As for transitioning on the other end: don't go out for a meat-lover's pizza to celebrate the day you finish the cleanse. Don't order a chocolate ice-cream cake. Your liver and digestive system will become overloaded if you reintroduce large amounts of fat right away. Be patient with the process. Bit by bit, here and there, start by adding in some cooked vegetables, legumes, lean protein, a little more fat, or some healthy grains such as quinoa or brown rice. If you want to enjoy your best health, then keep the foods listed in Chapter 19, "What Not to Eat," out of your diet for good.

And if you feel so great on the cleanse that you want to keep going, or keep going with minor modifications such as a bit more avocado, nuts, seeds, coconut, or cold-pressed olive oil, or a cooked meal here and there, then I'm not saying you should stop yourself from doing that. If you want to make low-fat, plant-based eating your way of life, go for it.

Everyone's different. Everyone has different nutritional requirements, different living and financial circumstances, different health histories, different bodies. Some people need animal protein in their non-cleanse lives to feel all is right with the world. Some feel that a bowl of brown rice with salmon at lunch is what keeps them going. Others don't.

Feel it out for yourself. Take it day by day. Do what's right for you.

CHAPTER 22

Soul-Healing Meditations and Techniques

Everybody is soul-searching. Even if they don't know it, even if they don't call it that, it's what they're doing.

We soul-search because part of us feels lost, or we don't feel whole, or because we feel like we're not living up to our soul's potential.

Often a negative experience, or a series of them, will prompt a person to feel broken or depleted and want to feel complete again. That's soul-searching. It can take the form of attending retreats, going to hear inspirational speakers, seeking advice from loved ones, enrolling in therapy, or any number of other activities. It's what we do when we're looking to heal and elevate our souls, to strengthen our purpose in life.

Sometimes the soul-searching will bring people closer to themselves. Many times it will leave them feeling more lost than ever. Under the guise of "help," you may have heard the false theory that illness is just a cry for attention. You may have heard that when bad things happen to us, we caused them by thinking the wrong thoughts.

I've said it before, and I'll say it again: If you are ill or going through a trial like a divorce or a loss, you did not manifest it. You did not attract it. It is not punishment or payback. You do not deserve to be sick or unhappy. It is not your fault.

You deserve to heal. You deserve to be happy. You deserve to feel whole.

This chapter will help you understand what happens to our souls when we encounter hardship, and it will teach you how to bring healing to your own soul. The exercises I describe are the true answers for soul-searchers. So get ready—you're about to learn the secrets to reviving your soul and spirit, finding peace, and feeling whole again.

EMOTIONAL DETOX

There's a significant emotional aspect to recovering from any injury or ailment—especially mystery illness. As your body cleanses itself of toxins or a viral load, you may find that emotional detox occurs, too.

For example, if you've suffered with chronic fatigue syndrome since college and have learned through this book that a virus was behind your condition, you might feel initial relief and even elation as you follow the chapters' guidelines and watch your body restore itself.

As your cells release those physical toxins, though, emotional toxins may bubble up. You may find yourself angry with the people who told you your illness was psychosomatic, and you may grieve for the years you lost to being unwell. You may feel intense cravings, as well, for foods that fed pathogens or contributed to inflammation in your body.

This emotional aspect is a perfectly natural part of healing. Take comfort in the knowledge that this is a temporary phase, and you don't have to engage with everything that comes up. You'll overwhelm yourself and risk dwelling in the past if you try to consciously process every tidbit that comes to the surface. That said, validation is essential to your recovery. Consider this whole book to be validation that your pain is real, that you didn't bring your illness or any hardships upon yourself, and that you deserve to live a healthy life.

During emotional detox, your goal is to release the negative emotions and painful memories (on a subconscious level when possible) and replace them with soothing, positive points of reference. The more at peace you are, the better an environment you're creating for the immune system to do its job. That's what this chapter will help you cultivate.

If you have an illness or health condition you haven't dealt with, this chapter is critical for you to strengthen yourself so you can face it and heal.

Using the meditations and techniques that follow, you can let go of the past and claim the life that God—the Higher Source, the Light, the Divine—wants for you.

FORMS OF MEDITATION

Meditation is a state of being that rewires your subconscious to be more at peace, which heals your soul.

Even if you've never tried it, you're probably familiar with more popular or traditional methods of meditation, which involve sitting in a quiet room, choosing a single thing to focus on—e.g., a mantra, a lit candle—and entering into a more peaceful state of consciousness.

Such meditation is wonderful, and recommended *if* it happens to work for you.

However, it's far from the only way to go. Any activity that you find relaxing, that reaffirms your sense of self and helps you recharge, can have a meditative quality. These activities include bike rides, swimming (especially in "living" water, such as an ocean or lake), exercising in other fun ways (e.g., dancing, jumping on a trampoline), listening to music, reading, praying, getting extra rest, caring for a pet, learning a new skill with new people, spending time with loved ones, getting a massage, and taking baths with Epsom salts and essential oils.

That's just a small selection. You may have a unique pastime—like cleaning the lint filter on the clothes dryer or doing longhand arithmetic—that calms you because it creates order in your universe. Whatever it is that brings you peace—that makes you feel positive and hopeful about the world—if you bring a meditative awareness to it, you'll promote healing for your body and soul. And when you feel grounded and optimistic, you're likely to encounter other wonderful people who love to be around you.

On top of developing your own special hobbies, you can try the following forms of meditation that Spirit has shown me to be extremely powerful. These are exercises that may seem simple on the surface—but if you understand their depths, they have the ability to help you reverse disease, reclaim your soul, and cleanse negative energy to make room for your best life.

Waves on the Beach

It's possible to attain a superior meditative state of healing by watching the waves on a beach—if you know how to tap into them. I have seen countless clients rid themselves of PTSD, pain, and suffering with this technique.

As you sit, stand, or walk on the beach, envision every wave as a surge of soul-cleansing energy. When a wave comes in, imagine it bathing any war wounds and scrubbing loose any damaging emotions or thoughts. As the wave recedes, watch it take away all those impurities. With each new wave, let yourself be cleansed of poisonous memories, injuries from past lives, and stains on the soul. See them all wash out to sea. When you feel purified, let each new wave bring strength and renewal to your spirit and soul.

For added benefit, call upon the Angel of the Ocean. She'll help put you in the best frame of mind for the meditation to have maximum effect. (You'll learn more about receiving the support of the angels in the next chapter.)

You can also benefit from wading. Understand that any natural water source—be it a lake, a river, a stream, the ocean—is alive. It has a breath to it, as well as a will and a spirit. When you step into living water, envision the things you want to come true in your life.

Surrounded by Trees

To get the most out of nature, it's not enough just to go for a hike. For the most healing effect, here's what you have to do: when you first enter a wooded area, whether a city park or your own property, call upon the Angel of Trees. Then take a moment to acknowledge the peaceful environment, especially all the trees that rise up around you.

Turn your mind to their root systems. Think about the minerals and water they're drawing from deep within the earth, up through their trunks, up through their branches. As you let yourself feel surrounded by this deep earth energy, envision roots growing out of your feet and into the Earthly Mother's soil.

When you intuitively feel it's time to end this glorious grounding experience, imagine that you're leaving roots protected and preserved in the earth as you break free and walk away. These roots remain a part of you. Wherever you are, transcending all time and space, you can draw healing energy from their spot in the ground.

This is the most powerful grounding treatment available. It will fortify every aspect of your being. It will reinforce your will to survive, invigorate your spirit to receive positivity and ward off negativity, and create a strengthening frequency for body and soul. It will prepare you to free yourself from fear and live life at its best.

Free as a Bird

Bird-watching is a healing activity simply because it takes you into nature. When you truly focus on seeing and hearing the birds, though, you elevate it to one of the most enlightening meditations you can perform.

Birdsong is the most sacred form of music; birds sing the songs of the angels and the heavens. Birdsong mends a fractured soul and can reverse disease. This is because the frequency of these melodies resonates deep within our DNA, which allows it to reconstruct the body on a cell level. If you listen to the birds with respect and appreciation and don't take them for granted, there's no doubt that your life will start to transform.

Observing birds is powerful, too. Here on earth, our souls can become caged up and our spirits suppressed. When we witness birds' freedom in flight, it ignites and unleashes the spirit and breaks the cage of the soul. Further, a bird lands only on an area it deems safe—and has the ability to flutter off if that spot doesn't work out. When we pay attention to the way a bird alights on a branch or the ground, it activates our own healing and promotes a sense of safety within our souls.

If it's healing you're seeking, enlightenment, connection to the Divine, spirituality, wisdom, compassion, knowledge, and understanding of your greater purpose, then seek not the owl. Seek the hummingbird. Admire the owl as a blessed and beautiful creature, yet take your cue from the hummingbird, which flies by day and feeds off the nectar of the earth's flowers, pollinating as it goes. This is the most spiritual form of eating and shows the greatest wisdom.

In order to heal, it's critical not to sleep by day as the owl does, and to instead follow the hummingbird's teaching and sleep by night (with short naps in the day as needed).

Hummingbirds are light-workers. Every time you spot one, recognize it as a true and sacred symbol of the Light. Witness it as a fairy spreading the holy light of the angels. Let it purify your thoughts and intentions, then send the hummingbird with a wish or a prayer. It will carry your message to the right recipient.

Bee Watching

Bee watching is a secretly miraculous meditation. As bees dance from flower to flower, absorbing the sun and distributing pollen along the way, they emit a healing frequency that reverses disease and promotes soul and emotional restoration. This is something we can't fully understand on a rational level, but our cells understand. When you make yourself aware of the bees and ask your body to tune its channels to their frequency, all of the cells in your body will start to resonate with this healing vibration.

Collecting Stones

When you want to cleanse yourself of negative emotions, take a walk in nature and keep your eye out for small stones that call to you. Over the course of your stroll, select three that feel good to hold in your hands. Name each stone by the label of whatever you're harboring that you'd like to leave you. For example, you might name the stones Guilt, Fear, and Anger.

Keep the stones on your bedside table. Develop a relationship with them; become friends. The healing frequency of the minerals will act as an antidote to whatever ails you, whether emotional, spiritual, or physical.

When the time naturally comes that you feel the stones have done their job and you're ready to let them go, carry them back to nature and release them into a body of water, such as a pond, ocean, lake, river, or stream. The living water will purify them of the venom they've drawn from you, and you'll walk away purified, too.

Sunbathing

It will be centuries before scientists discover all of the healing benefits the sun provides. Not only is it calming and warming, but the sun's rays contain mystery elements and promote biochemical reactions in our bodies that produce more than just vitamin D.

Just look at the way our pets love to find a warm, sunlit patch of the floor and bask in it. All animals love to sunbathe—they know it's a powerful healing tool.

To benefit from the sun, spend time each day letting your skin absorb it. Try to acclimate yourself to 15 minutes at a time (taking care not to get sunburned). If it's a cold time of year, find a peaceful spot inside where the sun comes through a window. To make the meditation most productive, call upon the Angel of the Sun to help the rays enter into your being to soothe your soul and heal your body.

Picking Fruit

Picking fruit is one of the most powerful meditations in existence. It is a sacred act of respect and gratitude to the Earthly Mother for the miracle of food. Even if you do it only once in your lifetime, it will be an experience you can reignite over and over, just by thought, to activate healing in the soul.

Each piece of fruit still on the tree is living food that's connected, via the plant's roots, to living water from deep within the earth. If you visit a pick-your-own apple orchard, for instance, then when you touch an apple on the tree, your cells will resonate with the apple's grounded nature, and peace will spread throughout your body.

On top of that, you'll naturally assume healing stretches and positions as you reach for apples and bend or crouch to collect them. These natural stretches supersede any human-created exercises. The joy in your heart and soul becomes one with each physical fruit-picking position, making it uniquely healing to you. While exercises such as yoga are beautiful, they are ultimately man-devised, so they won't create the same healing effect.

Picking berries, or even wildflowers, has the same effect. Since humans have existed on this planet, berry picking has been a celebration of abundance. When we follow in this millennia-old tradition, it ignites that ancient celebration of life within our souls and promotes healing.

As you gather strawberries or blackberries or raspberries or apples or peaches, meditate on all the months of development that led to this moment. First the plant started as a seed or root graft and grew to fruiting size. When it reached maturity, it didn't start bearing fruit every month of the year—rather, it developed with the seasons. Picture the tree or bush or vine in its dormant state, when it must have looked like nothing was happening. Next envision the leaves returning, the buds, the farmers tending to it all, the flowers blooming, and the pollinators paying visits. Our lives go through similar cycles. When we take the time to focus on nature's rhythms, we activate trust and faith within our souls that our efforts to live a good life will be fruitful.

Watching Your Garden Grow

Along similar lines, a wonderful form of meditation is tending your own garden. Getting your hands in the dirt for the sake of growing new life grounds your body, strengthens your spirit, and rejuvenates your soul. Further, the soil carries the soul of the Earthly Mother. Getting (literally) in touch with that puts you in sync with divine natural rhythms. If you grow vegetables or fruit, you get the added benefit of eating the toxin-free and super-fresh results of your labors. And if you grow flowers, you get to eventually arrange them in a vase or basket—which is itself a great way to meditate.

As you garden, you'll be absorbing the sounds of nature, which are very healing. Even if you can hear lawnmowers and cars at the same time, the effects of the nature sounds won't be lessened. The chirps of the birds, the buzzing of bees, the wind rustling through the trees—this is a sacred soundtrack that, if you attune your mind to it, will bring peace to your body and soul.

Weeding can have a profound effect on your life, too. If you envision each weed you pull from the soil as an ill thought, negative emotion, earthly war wound, instance of betrayal, or painful memory that you're simultaneously removing from your soul and mind, you'll make room for abundance in your life. Just as weeds crowd out your special plants—hog the water and nutrients in the soil, and overshadow seedlings below—these "weeds" of the consciousness keep the positives in your life from getting a chance to flourish. This exercise will make room for new opportunities to come into your life, seemingly from out of nowhere.

If you live in an apartment with no plot of land, then grow plants on your windowsill or balcony. Take frequent trips to the park and attune yourself to the cycles, beauty, and abundance of nature. And the city equivalent of pulling weeds is cleaning your apartment. If you turn it into a meditation, then as you straighten up clothing, vacuum up dust, and donate unused items, you'll be clearing detritus from your mind and soul.

Exercising Creativity

Art can be enormously beneficial for the meditative state, sense of agency, and cathartic effects that it promotes. There's a whole other aspect of creativity that you have to know about for maximum healing benefit, though: when you create art, you have an audience all around you on an angelic level.

When you paint, angels follow every stroke of the brush. When you write, they read every word. When you sing or play a musical instrument, the angels listen to every note. The angels witness every time you're being creative, in any way. Even if no human sees or hears what you make, your creative acts are never lost to the void. Creativity cannot die. It has a force all its own that lives beyond us and becomes written into the universe. When you become aware that the Angel of Creativity and other heavenly beings are watching you sculpt or dance or sew, it takes on new meaning.

The next time you sit down to make a sketch—or the next time you come up with an inventive way of packing your kids' lunches, or a creative incentive for your employees to track their billable hours—imagine the angels cheering you on. Making something beautiful or useful or therapeutic (or all three) is a divine act that becomes imprinted in the heavens.

RESTORING TRUST WITH SUNSETS

We all go through experiences that damage our ability to trust. Up to a point, that's helpful for survival. An abundance of innocence can lay the foundation for a major betrayal. And as this book has explained, unquestioning faith in even a well-intentioned doctor can be dangerous to your health.

However, if you endure a traumatic betrayal—for example, having a spouse cheat on you or a business partner steal from you—it can cripple your ability to trust *anyone*. And perhaps worse, it can endanger your belief in yourself and your judgment.

Along similar lines, if you've been told that you're sick because your immune system has gone haywire and is attacking you, you may on some level lose the ability to trust even your own body. Further, if you've been given incorrect information because—as is the case in many conditions in this book—the real culprit is a virus or bacteria, you may lose faith in your internal senses, too.

Such emotional blows create soul damage. They also hinder your ability to completely believe that you can overcome illness and recover your health.

A simple yet profoundly effective way to heal such damage is to become aware of the sunset. Toward the end of the day, take a few minutes to watch the sun go down (while never looking directly at the sun, which is damaging to the eyes). Or if you're in a building that blocks your view of the sky, be mindful of the sun during the time it's setting. If you're usually glued to your computer screen at this time of day, set a calendar reminder to shift your mental focus.

You may feel a sense of loss as the sun goes down, as if a friend has gone away . . . with the promise of returning tomorrow. That's what makes this technique resonate on such a deep level: you face the falling darkness with the absolute, irrefutable knowledge that the light will return. Performing this exercise at least three times a week will change how you experience life—in the best way. To get the most out of it, summon the Angel of Trust.

When the sun appears above the horizon the next morning, even if you're asleep when it happens, your body will be attuned to the earth's rhythms. You'll click with the fact that as promised, your friend has returned. The sun has risen every day of your life. It will continue to do so for the rest of your time on earth. Connecting with this truth that the sun will never let you down, the soul will relearn critical trust, which will activate healing energy.

GAZING BEYOND THE STARS

It's not uncommon for a person's soul to become damaged by adversity or stress, especially when that person has been dealing with mystery illness for years on end. That's why God created a built-in safety mechanism for our souls.

The majority of your soul is here, within you, on earth. Far up in the ether, though, beyond the stars, God has safeguarded the essence of your soul. The angels protect it there in the heavens so that no matter what happens down here, your soul will be secure. It's a little like keeping a second key to your house in a lockbox in the garage so that if your regular key goes missing, you can still get into the house. Or like securing your laptop with a password and keeping a backup encryption key in case you forget your login credentials. Along those same lines, God keeps the essences of our souls up beyond the stars in case we lose ourselves.

And there are so many ways for people to lose themselves here on earth. People's souls can fracture as they go through life, or pieces can even go missing. Injuries—whether physical or emotional, from past lives, work, or childhood—send people soul-searching. Addiction, too, comes in every shape and size—and can rob people of their souls. There's alcohol and drug addiction, but also food addiction, gambling addiction, addiction to seeing oneself in a negative way, and many more. Addictions are a poison that can take people so far away from themselves that they become almost soulless.

Yet you can never really lose yourself. You always have the ability to reunite with your soul because of God's safekeeping method, which Spirit has asked me to reveal here. You don't have to search for that sense of wholeness anymore.

To reclaim your soul, spend time each night gazing up at the sky. First get familiar with the stars; your soul has a direct telepathic connection to them. Let their light and the wonder of their existence resonate for a few moments.

Then shift your focus to the space *beyond* the stars. Envision that your true home lies way up there, in a place free from suffering. It's the place some call Heaven, God, the Light, or the Infinite. You may have uncomfortable associations with those words and prefer not to name the destination. Either way, remind yourself that part of you resides in this sanctuary, unharmed by earth's adversities. When you eventually pass from this earth, that's where you'll go. Tell yourself, *This is a home I belong to, and will someday warmly return to.*

Spend as much time on this exercise as you like. The goal is repetition and reinforcement. You can stargaze for just three minutes a night and find that your soul rejuvenates in dazzling ways.

WHO DO YOU WORK FOR?

Whatever kind of work you do—whether you're a nurse, a therapist, a bank teller, a truck driver, an attorney, a teacher, an artist, a volunteer, a stay-at-home mom, an executive, a postal worker, a waitress, an editor, or a landscape crewmember—there may be certain reasons you do it. You work for a paycheck, benefits, to support your family, to serve your clients, to please your boss. That's the part everyone knows.

If your job feels like a burden, though—if you have a demeaning supervisor or a grueling schedule, if you feel like your work has no meaning or no one appreciates you—then it's time to shift your mindset: no matter what you do, no matter where you do it, you work for God. Repeat this aloud—using whatever term feels most comfortable for you—each day, connect to it, and *everything* will change.

When you wake up in the morning, open the door to the day, and say it: "I work for God." (Or, "I work for the Higher Source," "I work for the Light," or "I work for the Divine.")

Maybe you're a cashier at a grocery store. You usually arrive for your shift to a harried manager and harried shoppers, and it's all you can do to get through until your break without crying because this isn't what you pictured for your life. You'd planned to change the world.

If you start the day by affirming that you work for God, you'll have a different perspective when you get to the store. Maybe your manager is still harried, yet it's not such a big deal—you know he's not your *real* boss. Then as the customers start to put their groceries on the conveyor belt, as you process food stamps and credit cards, you understand that you're making it possible for people to nourish themselves. Maybe someone in line will notice your glow and ask for advice—you could change a life without realizing it. By the end of the week, your manager may see you in a whole new way and ask you to join the store's community outreach team.

When you understand that you have a divine role in the world, you'll shine with the light of purpose. More opportunities that require your unique strengths will start to come your way. And if you feel overloaded with helping the world, then affirming that you work for God each day will help you find new ways of approaching the work, or connect you with others to help share the load. No matter what your challenge, if you remind yourself whose work you really do, your life will change in untold ways.

CHAPTER 23

Essential Angels

You were born with the God-given right to reach out to angels whenever you need them. If you've struggled with your physical or emotional health, they've been your witness. Angels want to help ease our minds, rebuild our spirits and souls, and heal our bodies.

They want to guide us in our most purposeful direction. Since humankind began, angels have existed to help us adapt and survive here on earth.

When you're searching for a partner, can't find work, or feel like new opportunities aren't coming your way, that's a *drought*. Angels are there to help us adapt to the circumstances and survive until they can bring the cool rains of the right partner, financial support, or exciting change.

When your cup is overflowing, and you have too much work, too many opportunities, or a relationship so abundant you can't keep up with it, you're in a *flood*. The angels are there to buoy you, to help you stay afloat and nurture your relationships as you balance out your commitments and turn down the spigot on projects.

A *heat wave* is when you have too much stress and too many demands upon your time, confrontations, responsibilities, or issues with loved ones. In this case, the angels are available to intervene in confrontations, help alleviate stress, lower demands, and strengthen you for any remaining responsibilities.

Finally, an *earthquake* is the name for when unexpected problems and disruptions arise—accidents, illness, getting laid off, losing loved ones. There are angels you can call upon to help loved ones pass onto the right place, to resolve loss, to recover from accidents (emotionally or physically), sustain a job, or heal from sickness.

Just like a weather map can display totally different conditions in different parts of the country, you can experience any combination of the categories above. You can even experience all four at once. For example, you could have a drought of support, a flood of work, a heat wave of responsibility, and then suffer an earthquake of loss.

You're not alone, though.

And your life and path are not set in stone. You can choose a new direction.

To say it another way: when our souls arrive here on earth, we can decide to play a certain role and not stray from that . . . or we can use our free will to write our own part. Everything is not already written. Everything hasn't all happened already.

We all have the option to break out of the mold. We have a say in our destiny.

The angels are here to help guide us in our decision-making, to make the most of our free will. They're here to intercept trouble and present opportunity. They're here to help us grow, change, and handle what life brings our way. They're here to help us see the light, guide us, and pull us out of darkness. However you need to envision or interpret the angels, whether as light beings or animals or another type of creature unique to your inner vision, they will take that form to help you. Angels don't exist to fulfill our every wish and desire. They're here to help us do God's work, whether that's healing ourselves from illness, reclaiming our souls, or helping others in need.

They've been doing it for millennia.

Here's the secret: you have to know the right angels to ask, *you have to know the right way to ask,* you have to have faith, you have to be open, and you have to work with them . . . and that's what I'll cover in this chapter.

THE TRUTH ABOUT ANGELS

Angels are sometimes best known by their individual names. Everybody loves Archangel Michael, for example, and Archangel Gabriel. They're powerful angels who have fought darkness for God for millennia.

Here's what you have to understand about these guys: they're so popular, they are cherry-picking their jobs at this point. Because they're so busy and revered, they like to choose gigs that really speak to them.

The three basic facts of angels are that they work for God, their powers are vast but finite, and they have free will.

Because of that last fact, they're susceptible to ego. (Any being with free will, whether human or angelic, is vulnerable to it. If you've ever heard of fallen angels, those are the ones whose egos got so big, they felt they were mightier than God and tried to overthrow Him—which caused a fall from grace.)

So since everyone knows about Archangels Michael and Gabriel, and they're flooded with requests for help from all over the globe, they may not be able to meet everyone's demands. I'm not trying to deter you from calling upon them. They are named and loved by God and hold extreme power. It's just that the need for God's angels is great right now—greater than ever before. Archangels Michael and Gabriel's phones are ringing off the hook.

There are other, more powerful angels we can call upon, ones who can be more useful in our lives and who will hear our prayers. These angels are female and rarely called upon. Each is best known by a word of power that represents her essence.

THE 21 ESSENTIAL ANGELS

Here is a list of the 21 essential angels who are critical for your times of need. The number 21 stands for rebirth, new beginnings, reclamation, rising out of the ashes, and fresh starts. Though there are many other known angels, these are the ones who are most powerful and beneficial in today's trying times.

Like essential oils, these angels are potent, and each has different properties. Just as you can use essential oils on their own or blended with one another, you can call upon these angels alone or as a team.

- **Angel of Mercy:** by far the most powerful angel to call upon in your darkest hour—more powerful even than the archangels. She is one of the strongest angels in

God's Angelic Realm. God has summoned her many times to battle darkness.

- **Angel of Faith:** call upon her in whatever way suits you. If you make this a daily practice, the rhythm will help you transition the habit into full-blown conviction. Tell the Angel of Faith you are finally ready.

- **Angel of Trust:** for help when you're struggling to recover from a betrayal.

- **Angel of Healing:** to provide temporary relief and/or to heal a loved one. (For long-term healing, you must call on other angels to help build you up to a point where you can heal yourself.)

- **Angel of Restitution:** she understands how the spirit and soul can be beaten down, and she can help you recover from emotional trauma. This angel will help you to resolve deep-seated issues.

- **Angel of Deliverance:** this angel provides relief to someone who's going through an earthly judgment— for example, one's spouse filing for divorce, or a school board unjustly firing a teacher. She can also help free your soul from the imprisonment of fear and anger, and from the injury of deception.

- **Angel of Sun:** call for her while you're in the sun to open up your body's cells so they fully take in the healing power of the rays.

- **Angel of Light:** name her in order to be bathed in restorative angelic light given to her by God. The Angel of Light is more powerful than any light on earth, and more powerful even than the light of the sun.

- **Angel of Water:** you can ask her to change the frequency of the water you bathe in to make it more cleansing, nourishing, and grounding. If you're soaking a wound, you can call upon her to quicken its healing.

- **Angel of Air:** right after a frustrating encounter such as an argument, ask for the Angel of Air to cleanse the negative vibration that person passed onto you. Her special, purifying energy will change the frequency of the air around you to promote harmony. This is a powerful technique to change your frame of mind.

- **Angel of Purity:** when you want to rid yourself of an addiction, this angel can help you break free from the poisonous chains of habit.

- **Angel of Fertility:** for aid in conception and carrying a baby to term.

- **Angel of Birth:** for health of mother and child during delivery.

- **Angel of Peace:** to help heal your mental distress and bring new seeds of hope and positivity.

- **Angel of Beauty:** if you feel closed off to the beauty of nature that surrounds you—the sun, the trees, the hills or rivers—summon the Angel of Beauty. She'll open you up to appreciate and absorb your surroundings in powerful ways you didn't think possible. This angel is also your ally when a romantic partner is obsessed with talking about people's physical appearance, when a co-worker's good looks have turned him vain, or when a sibling's physical beauty earns her all the attention and adoration. Ask the Angel of Beauty to shift people's mind-sets to recognize true beauty: the beauty of a shining soul.

- **Angel of Purpose:** call upon her if you're struggling with your purpose here on earth—if you're numb or confused or worried you're not useful to others or even yourself. If you've lost confidence in something or everything, the Angel of Purpose will be by your side.

- **Angel of Knowledge:** when a loved one needs advice and you're at a loss, or you want to give more than just a pat on the back, you'd be surprised at the healing, soothing words that come out of your mouth when you call upon this angel. You can also ask her for help when you need information or advice for yourself and don't know where or how to find it.

- **Angel of Wisdom:** for guidance when you're about to make an important decision.

- **Angel of Awareness:** people are always trying to be more present and mindful. It's critical to summon the Angel of Awareness to make this intention complete— only then will you be fully in the moment. Also, if you want the people around you to be less judgmental and better communicators, you can call upon this angel to help open their minds.

- **Angel of Relationships:** if you're having a problem with your spouse or someone you're dating, or if you're single and looking for a good match.

- **Angel of Dreams:** you can pray to her to enter your dreams and help you sort out and resolve emotional turmoil. So many have experienced the Angel of Dreams when they were younger—she was the one who could make them fly when they were asleep. Even if your waking life is troubled, you can call upon her to help you reexperience that soul freedom in your dreams.

UNKNOWN ANGELS

No one knows there's another category of angels. These *don't* have names; they're referred to as the *Unknown Angels*.

There are exactly 144,000 of these Unknown Angels in existence. This is a holy number that God reveres.

Because they are unnamed, they have no notoriety or acclaim, and therefore very little temptation to develop an ego. The Unknown Angels are some of the most powerful of all, and the least in demand. If you have faith in them, they can perform miracles. They do their work on you while you're asleep, restoring both your body and soul.

This group of angels can be so powerful because life instills a fear of the unknown in us. On earth, everyone and everything is named. It takes some rewiring for us to see the value of anything not known, and to tap into the deep reserves of faith required to believe in these angels. When we do get in touch with that utmost form of trust, though, it can have a radical effect on our lives.

While you might call upon, say, the Angel of Light to restore your soul while you're awake, when you go to bed, you can call upon the Unknown Angels to aid in your healing and rejuvenation as you slumber. And calling upon Unknown Angels while dealing with chronic illness can be life changing. You can ask for just one Unknown Angel, or you can ask for a group of them—say, three or four—together.

The Unknown Angels are eager for the chance to work on us. If you summon the Unknown Angels, you'll find yourself tapping into a resource of profound power for healing your body, mind, heart, spirit, and soul.

HOW TO ACCESS ANGELIC AID

Here's the most important thing I'll say about angels in this chapter: *You have to ask for their help aloud.* You can't just think it. (Unless you are unable to speak—in which case, see below.)

This is huge. Angels are dealing with so much negativity on the planet—violence, epidemics, corruption—that we need to be active (and proactive, whenever possible) in calling their attention. Our minds are spiderwebs of thought and emotion: obsessions, fear, anger, insecurities, guilt, worry, pain, TV jingles and other music, imaginary conversations with people we're mad at, and even happy thoughts . . . Angels don't want to get stuck in all of that; it's too difficult to disentangle the genuine requests for help.

Remember that angels have free will. It takes a little work on our end to show that we are sincere, honest, and committed. Angels don't like to be toyed with or tested; they want us to take them seriously.

In order to get a response from an angel, you must fully set your mind to her and say her name out loud. You don't have to scream or shout—even a whisper works. As long as it comes out of your mouth, that will separate it from everything else in your consciousness and signal it as a clean message, not one clinging to anything else.

And if you are deaf, have a speech impairment, or are too weak to speak, then use sign language or your thoughts to ask for the Angel of Deliverance. She will express your soul's wishes to the other angels.

This is the secret truth that will change your relationship with angels. People who have lost faith in angels, who haven't seen results from their prayers, who think the concept of angels is hogwash—this is what they have yet to learn.

The concept of how to contact the angels is similar to how you make a phone call. You don't just look at the phone and silently will it to arrange for a mulch delivery. No—you dial the number for the plant nursery, they answer the phone, you speak aloud and respectfully to the person on the other end (or if you're deaf, you use an interpreter relay service), and you ask for a truckload of mulch to be deposited in your driveway so you can keep the garden weeds down. When the delivery comes, you have to be willing to receive it, you have to move your car out of the driveway to make room for the mulch, and then you have to be ready with a shovel to dig in to the work of spreading it onto your plant beds. The process takes will and intention.

If you wanted to contact the Angel of Healing, you'd turn your attention to her and then humbly say, "Please, Angel of Healing, I need your help." If you do this with focused intention and you're willing to receive her, that will be enough. If she's not too busy helping others—an angel's powers are impressive, but finite—the Angel of Healing will arrive within anywhere from a few seconds to a few minutes to aid and comfort you. A miracle may not happen overnight. If you keep calling for her, though, she will sustain you until you get where you need to be.

You can access the Angelic Realm in this way anywhere, and at any time, as long as you're sufficiently focused on what you're calling for and truly open to receiving help and have faith that it will work. (And if you're short on faith, you may want to make the Angel of Faith your first call.)

You can talk to the angels about specific outcomes you think would be most helpful in your life, but be open. It's important to note that an angel's response may not be what you expect. If you're praying to the Angel of Relationships to give you space from your spouse, the angel might surprise you instead by changing your spouse's vibration and prompting her or him to apologize for the wrongdoing that made you want distance.

Another scenario is if you pray to the Angel of Fertility to give your daughter a little sibling—and yet you don't get pregnant. This doesn't mean the angel didn't hear your call. It just means that you may not have been destined for this exact outcome. Perhaps the angel knows that another baby would put too much strain on your finances, or she knows of an underlying health issue—but your sister will give birth to a boy who ends up being just like a brother to your daughter.

Don't be afraid to ask the angelic forces for help with your problems. Needing help doesn't mean you're weak. You don't have to frame your requests in only positive terms, or only use affirmations. You're not perpetuating the negative in your life by saying, "My body is weak. I can't even get out of bed to open the curtains and see the day. Please, Angel of Light, I'm desperate for help and hope." You're just stating the facts. And you're showing great strength and honesty by accepting the truth in your life and wanting to move forward.

You *get* to move forward with your life. You get to heal and have good things happen to you. If you start tapping into the angels' power in the ways I've outlined above, your life will change.

CASE HISTORY:
A Miracle from the Angel of Mercy

One evening when her husband was out of town, Edith was looking after their sick four-year-old daughter, Emma, when Emma's fever spiked to 105 degrees. Edith rushed to the emergency room, but before any doctors were available, Emma lost consciousness. The hospital admitted Edith's daughter into the intensive care unit, where she lay in a coma.

Doctors told Edith that a blood test had determined Emma had a vicious and rare form of meningitis. It was the worst case they'd seen in a long time. An MRI showed that brain damage had occurred, and the doctors said it would probably mean at least paralysis, if not death. They warned Edith that even if Emma came out of the coma and survived, she would need permanent care.

Edith dialed her sister, Valerie, who was my client. Valerie begged her to call me. My assistant reached me on my emergency line, and I got on the phone with Edith. Spirit told me this was a case for the Angel of Mercy, so I told Edith what she needed to do.

For the next hour, Edith sat by Emma's side in her hospital room, pleading aloud for the Angel of Mercy to come and save her daughter's life. Nurses tried to quiet her, but Edith just kept chanting: "Angel of Mercy, Angel of Mercy, please help, please help." Edith's husband arrived sometime in the middle of it all, but she didn't stop.

At one in the morning, Edith was slumped over her daughter's hospital bed, still calling to the angel. Out of nowhere, a light flashed. Even though Edith's hands were covering her eyes and her face was buried in Emma's blankets, it blinded her for a moment—that's the kind of light we're talking about here. Edith rushed to the window to see where the light had come from, yet saw nothing unusual in the dim parking lot. Reflected in the window, though, she also saw a figure standing over Emma's bed. Edith turned quickly—and instead of finding a nurse in the room, as she'd expected, saw another, smaller flash of light. The figure had vanished. Just then, Emma coughed. Edith shouted for a nurse and sent her husband racing down the hallway to bring someone back. When a nurse returned with him, they were both stunned to see Emma blinking back at them. She was out of the coma.

Two days later, Emma was released from the hospital. She made a full recovery—and the doctors still can't explain it.

That's the power of the Angel of Mercy.

CASE HISTORY:
A New Frame of Mind from the Angel of Faith

Jill was a single mom who'd long ago lost her faith in God. She'd believed as a child, but a college boyfriend had argued that faith in God was as naive as believing in Santa Claus. What gave her the right to believe in a benevolent, almighty force when so much suffering existed in the world? Didn't she watch the news?

Jill sat in her dorm room one day and tore up the book of prayers her Uncle Al had given her when she turned twelve.

When Jill came to me years later, her faith was at an all-time low. She'd been laid off from her job at a nonprofit, and after months of searching was now up for a position as the marketing director at a food bank—but she was one of 100 applicants. Her unemployment was about to run out. If she didn't get the job, she'd have to break the lease on her apartment, uproot her children from their school, and move in with her uncle, who was already supporting his grown son.

I brought up the need to believe that things could turn around, and Jill objected. That sounded too much like the type of thought process her ex-boyfriend had told her was narrow-minded, she said. If things could go so terribly in the world, what made her so special? As much as she wanted and needed the job, she didn't feel she deserved it. Maybe she should set her sights lower.

Spirit told me, first of all, that Jill *was* the best candidate for the position, and second of all, that the Angel of Faith was the only one who could help her see that. I coached Jill on speaking aloud to the angel. She was to ask the Angel of Faith to help her see that she works for God, that God does exist, that when we close ourselves off to Him, it's like drawing a shade against the sun. It doesn't mean the sun doesn't exist—it just means that we don't benefit from its light.

Later, Jill told me that after we got off the phone that day, she was ready to write off the whole conversation. But then she got to thinking about the good she could do for the food bank. She had a top degree in marketing and connections all over the city. She was probably better qualified than any of the other applicants to shape the charity's message and spread it far and wide, which would ultimately mean more hungry people fed. On top of that, Jill would be providing for her son and daughter and sparing Uncle Al the burden of looking after them.

That night she knelt by her bed like she had when she was a girl and asked, "Angel of Faith? If I get this job, I'll make the best of it. I will do God's work. Please help me believe that I can do this—that I *deserve* to do this."

Jill got called back for a second interview the next day. She whisper-prayed to the Angel of Faith just before she went into the meeting room—and proceeded to blow everyone away with her vision and conviction. Before she left, they told her she had the job.

When I talked to Jill that afternoon, she was elated—but feeling a little shaky, like she'd somehow asked for her needs to be put above others' and "messed with the order of the universe." I assured her this wasn't the case. If she hadn't been the best candidate, her prayers wouldn't have catapulted her above someone else. The Angel of Faith knew Jill would mastermind the re-branding that the food bank desperately needed to bring in the right donors. If this hadn't been the job for her, her prayers would have helped her keep the faith that some other plan would work out.

Jill absorbed this for a minute. "I guess it's time I pray to the Angel of Quit-Your-Whining-and-Say-Thank-You."

I assured her that no one, least of all the angels, thought she was a whiner. Faith is complex, and God loves it when we engage with these questions. I did tell Jill I was positive the Angel of Gratitude would love to hear from her.

CASE HISTORY:
A Renewed Connection from the Angel of Relationships

Ever since Nicole's parents divorced when she was in second grade, she'd had a difficult time keeping friends. Each time she made a new bond with someone, she was afraid she'd lose the person—just like she lost her dad to his new wife in another state. So rather than risk the pain of Jordan or Maya or Caroline blowing her off, Nicole would play it cool. If anyone asked her to hang out after school, Nicole would give a "maybe" and only show up half the time. The invitations trickled off before too long.

As Nicole got older and started dating, she noticed the same pattern with men. Even if she really liked a guy, she'd tell him his haircut was dorky or "forget" to call him when she got off work.

By the time she was 30, she'd been through a series of flings, each lasting only a few dates—if that. She was tired of holding potential relationships at bay with her noncommittal act.

When she met Ethan through a dating app, she decided she wanted this to be a real relationship—her first. It was time she tried to trust someone, she told herself. And for two years, things worked out. Then they didn't. Over brunch one Sunday, Ethan told Nicole that he felt she'd become co-dependent, and he wasn't the type to be tied down. "I think it's time for you to get your own life," he said.

Now Nicole was convinced she'd never feel safe in a relationship again—if she could even attract someone. She felt broken and unlovable. Over time, she did start to go out again here and there, but she couldn't find anyone who made her feel comfortable in her own skin. Whenever a guy asked her out a second time, even if she liked him, she declined. She was too afraid to get attached and end up with another broken heart.

At this point, Nicole came to me for help with her chronic stress stomachaches, which had started when her parents divorced and had gotten worse in the last year. The topic of relationships inevitably came up in our conversation. Nicole told me that commitment gave her the heebie-jeebies, and she didn't know how to feel safe taking that step with a new man.

Spirit said it was time for Nicole to learn about the Angel of Relationships. I coached her on how to ask aloud for assistance, and for the next few months off and on, Nicole practiced talking to the angel in the car. While running errands and during her commute, Nicole would speak to the Angel of Relationships about her fears and insecurities, as though the angel were a pal sitting in the passenger seat. "How am I ever going to find someone who gets me?" she'd always ask.

One day, Nicole stopped at the natural foods store to replenish her supply of aloe leaf and papaya, which Spirit had recommended for her stomachaches. As she parked the car, she changed her tune: "Angel of Relationships, what if there really is a guy out there for me? Please, please help me find him."

In the store, Nicole picked up her groceries and stood in line to pay. A magazine headline about couples who had met at yoga retreats grabbed her eye. Maybe, she thought, this was the Angel of Relationships trying to communicate with her. She flipped to the article and started to read. After a minute, though, someone tapped her on the shoulder. She turned to see a man she didn't know.

"Nicole!" he said.

The man introduced himself as Tyler, a former high school classmate, and asked if she'd like to meet for coffee sometime to catch up. Nicole hesitated. He didn't look familiar, and she wasn't sure if this was a scam. Then again, he looked genuinely happy to see her. She agreed to meet somewhere very public with a lot of exits—and somewhere with good herbal tea, since coffee made her stomach hurt.

At home, Nicole pulled out one of her yearbooks and found Tyler in a photo of the bird-watching club. She *did* remember him—as a scrawny boy the year below her who had always carried binoculars and barely hit puberty before she graduated. The Tyler she met at the store had really grown into himself, she realized. She texted him back to say so.

Two days later, as Nicole walked into the café they'd picked, she called to the Angel of Relationships under her breath. Maybe this could actually go well.

Before they'd even gotten to the counter to order tea, Tyler confessed he'd had a crush on Nicole back in high school. This gave her just the confidence boost she needed to be herself. Tyler shared about the fiancée who broke up with him a week before they were supposed to get married, and Nicole talked about her own relationship trials. She felt free as she spoke, not distracted like she usually was by insecurities. By the time they said good-bye that day, they had their next three dates planned.

The night before Tyler and Nicole got married, Nicole prayed aloud to the Angel of Relationships from the hotel room where she was spending her last single night. Nicole had checked in with the angel here and there over the last few years with Tyler, to ask for help with their occasional misunderstandings. This time, Nicole wanted to say thanks: "I just wanted you to know I don't feel spooked about this commitment. You changed everything for me."

AFTERWORD

Keep the Faith

Faith is tremendously lacking here on earth. Even if people believe in God, in a higher source, so many lose faith that they can heal from illness and other afflictions and go on to succeed in life.

It's understandable. Bad things happen in the world, from personal betrayals, to disease, to war. It's not easy to reconcile. Almost three and a half billion people on the planet don't have faith.

Yet part of the reason things go wrong is *because* of this lack of faith. When a person doesn't believe in the good of the world, it can cause her or him to behave recklessly—which can have extremely negative consequences for everybody else. One such action can cause countless people to question the good in humanity, to doubt their faith.

Sometimes this recklessness happens in the form of violence. Other times it's hidden—like the industries at the turn of the 19th century that started releasing toxic chemicals and heavy metals into our environment, causing people to get sick left and right with conditions such as goiters and cancers and mental illness. It didn't happen because the world is an inherently bad place. It happened because people in positions of power lost their faith and higher purpose somewhere along the way, and so they took a gamble and exposed factory workers and townspeople to untested chemical brews in the interest of profit.

So many people today struggle with their health. When you are ill, or your loved ones are, and you keep hearing more disheartening stories of people coming up against health issues, it's easy to get mad at life. It's easy to feel unsafe, unprotected, trapped in a world of disappointment and fear.

Always come back to this truth, though: You are allowed to live a good life. You *deserve* to live a good life. *A good life exists for you.* And the foundation of a good life is good health. You deserve to heal, to tap into your body's restorative mechanisms. You deserve to be happy and well.

It is not life itself fouling things up; it's people who lose touch with their essence and conviction, then make heedless choices as a result.

The most powerful thing you can do in the face of this is to have faith.

People without faith walk around with their eyes technically open, yet remain blind to the helping hands of God and the universe trying to reach out to them. They may make a compelling argument for the reasons they don't believe and convince others of the bleakness of the world—in which case, it's the blind leading the blind.

We can't let the news headlines or our physical trials make us stop believing. And we have to nurture our belief so that it becomes a part of our soul, building up to become faith that saturates our very being. It takes practice. It takes patience. It may take some help from the Angel of Faith.

If faith feels impossible to access, try this simple visualization: imagine faith as a golden rope—a lifeline—trailing down from the sky. Picture yourself grasping it, then pulling on it as though you were ringing a bell in the heavens above.

Over time, if you have faith that faith will come to you, it will enter your heart, soul, spirit, and body. When you finally experience an ignition of faith, and start to live in its glory and virtue, so much more becomes visible. Your conviction lights the way, and you can finally see how to leave the path of despair. You can restore yourself to health.

If you take the lessons in this book to heart, you will watch your life transform and understand that God, Spirit, and the Angelic Realm really want us to thrive. Then, just as one candle can pass its flame to thousands more, you'll be a light in the world that can ignite the faith of countless others.

Many blessings on your journey.

ENDNOTES

Chapter 3: Epstein-Barr Virus, Chronic Fatigue Syndrome, and Fibromyalgia

1. "U.S. and World Population Clock," United States Census Bureau, accessed March 17, 2015, http://www.census.gov/popclock.

Chapter 15: Premenstrual Syndrome and Menopause

2. Writing Group for the Women's Health Initiative Investigators, "Risks and Benefits of Estrogen Plus Progestin in Healthy Postmenopausal Women: Principal Results from the Women's Health Initiative Randomized Controlled Trial," *Journal of the American Medical Association* 288, no. 3 (2002):321–333. doi:10.1001/jama.288.3.321.

Chapter 16: Lyme Disease

3. "Circular Letter #12-32 to Director of Health," Connecticut Department of State, August 3, 1976, accessed January 8, 2015, http://www.ct.gov/dph/lib/ dph/infectious_diseases/lyme/1976_circular_letter.pdf.

Chapter 20: Fruit Fear

4. "Food Availability (Per Capita) Data System," United States Department of Agriculture Economic Research Service, December 4, 2014, accessed May 16, 2015, http://www.ers.usda.gov/datafiles/Food_Availabily_Per_Capita_Data_ System/Food_Availability/frtot.xls.

INDEX

Z

ACKNOWLEDGMENTS

Thank you to Patty Gift, Anne Barthel, Reid Tracy, Louise Hay, Christy Salinas, and the rest of the Hay House team for your incredible support and faith in this project. I am forever grateful for your enthusiasm and know-how.

For your kindness, generosity, and friendship, my thanks go out to Nanci Chambers and David James Elliott; Scott Cohn and Alayne Serle; Chelsea Field and Scott Bakula; Demi Moore; Naomi Campbell; Tanya Akim; David Somoroff; Kris Carr; Ann Louise Gittleman; Martin, Jean, Elizabeth, and Jacqueline Shafiroff; Carol and Scott Ritchie; Philip and Casey McCluskey; Dhru Purohit; Elise Loehnen; Ami Beach and Mark Shadle; and Caroline Leavitt. I deeply value your encouragement.

To the doctors and other healers of the world who help so many: you have my profound admiration. Dr. Alejandro Junger, Dr. Christiane Northrup, Dr. Richard Sollazzo, Dr. Deanna Minich, Dr. Ron Steriti, Dr. Nicole Galante, Dr. Diana Lopusny, Dr. Dick and Noel Shepard, Dr. Aleksandra Phillips, Dr. Chris Maloney, Drs. Tosca and Gregory Haag, Dr. Dave Klein, Dr. Darren and Suzanne Boles, Dr. Deirdre Williams and the late Dr. John McMahon, Dr. Jeff Feinman, and Dr. Robin Karlin—it's an honor to call you friends. Thank you for your dedication to the field of wellness.

Thanks to David Schmerler, Kimberly S. Grimsley, and Susan G. Etheridge for looking out for me.

Special thanks also to Stephanie Tisone, Megan Elizabeth McDonnell, Ally Ertel and Robby Barbaro, Victoria and Michael Arnstein, Muneeza Ahmed, Judy DeLorenzo, Nina Leatherer, Michelle Sutton,

Alexandra Laws, Peggy Rometo, Ester Horn, Linda and Robert Coykendall, Hy Bender, Sabrina Gaffney, Glenn Klausner, Carolyn DeVito, Michael Monteleone, Bobbi and Leslie Hall, Katherine Belzowski, Vibodha and Tila Clark, and Matt Houston.

Thank you to my countless clients over the years. I have cherished watching you transform your health.

Ruby Scattergood, this book would not be possible without your writing and editing. Thank you for your literary counsel. You saved me.

For your love and fortification, I thank my family: my luminous wife; Dad and Mom; my brothers, nieces, nephews, aunts, and uncles; my champions Indigo, Ruby, and Great Blue; Hope Pratt; Marjorie and her late, beloved Robert Stark; Laura Covone; Rhia Cataldo; Kelly Lombardo; Danielle Pickering; and all my loved ones who are on the other side.

Finally, thank you, Spirit, for being my constant companion, my patient teacher—and now for helping me deliver your message of health and well-being to the world.

ABOUT THE AUTHOR

 **Anthony William** was born with the unique ability to converse with a high-level spirit who provides him with extraordinarily accurate health information that's often far ahead of its time. Since age four, when he shocked his family by announcing that his symptom-free grandmother had lung cancer (which medical testing soon confirmed), Anthony has been using his gift to 'read' people's conditions and tell them how to recover their health. His unprecedented accuracy and success rate as the Medical Medium have earned him the trust and love of thousands worldwide, among them movie stars, rock stars, billionaires, professional athletes, bestselling authors and countless other people from all walks of life who couldn't find a way to heal until he provided them with insights from Spirit. Anthony has also become an invaluable resource to doctors who need help solving their most difficult cases.

www.medicalmedium.com

NOTES

NOTES